Illust

lishe
deplo
addec
unde
Ali
Le
be
Th
wi
to
men
ma
On
tig:
ne:
Wit
ness,
lives
auth
ther
ings
class
mor
succ
of t.
attit
vote

B:
peri
sci

SWIFT AND CARROLL

SWIFT AND CARROLL

A Psychoanalytic Study of Two Lives

BY PHYLLIS GREENACRE, M.D.

International Universities Press · *New York*

Manufactured in the United States of America

Contents

INTRODUCTION 9

Part I.   JONATHAN SWIFT 15
  1. Swift's Life Story 17
  2. Gulliver and Swift 60
  3. The Clinical Picture 83
  4. An Interpretation 88

Part II.   LEWIS CARROLL 117
  1. The Life of Charles L. Dodgson . 119
  2. The Character of Dodgson as re-
     vealed in the writings of Carroll . 165
  3. Reconstruction and Interpretation of
     the Development of Charles L.
     Dodgson and Lewis Carroll . . 207

Part III. CERTAIN COMPARISONS BETWEEN
           SWIFT AND CARROLL 247

Part IV.   NOTES ON NONSENSE 263
           REFERENCES AND NOTES 278
           BIBLIOGRAPHY 287
           ACKNOWLEDGMENTS 291
           INDEX 293

List of Illustrations

JONATHAN SWIFT   *Facing page 16*

Jonathan Swift at about 43 years of age.
From the portrait by Charles Jervas in the National Portrait Gallery, London.

STELLA AS A YOUNG GIRL   *Facing page 38*

By an unknown artist.
This portrait is frequently reproduced, but identity as Stella never has been absolutely proved.

LEWIS CARROLL AS A YOUNG MAN   *Facing page 118*

Portrait by O. G. Rejlander.
Reproduced from Helmut Gernsheim's *Lewis Carroll, Photographer.*

FRONTPIECE TO *The Rectory Umbrella*   *Page 130*

Drawing by Charles L. Dodgson, aged about 18.
From *The Lewis Carroll Picture Book.*

PHOTOGRAPH OF A YOUNG GIRL   *Facing page 144*

By Lewis Carroll.

THE LIDELL SISTERS, EDITH, LORINA,
AND ALICE   *Facing page 148*

Painted by Sir William Blake Richmond.

CARROLL'S SELF-CARICATURE, "WHAT I LOOK
LIKE WHEN I'M LECTURING"   *Page 167*

By Lewis Carroll of C. L. Dodgson.
From *The Life and Letters of Lewis Carroll.*

ILLUSTRATION FOR *Tale of a Tail*   *Facing page 232*

By Charles L. Dodgson, Age 13.
Reproduced from *Useful and Instructive Poetry.*

INTRODUCTION

The inclusion of Jonathan Swift and Lewis Carroll between the covers of one book may perplex many and offend some. These men seem so different, in many respects so nearly opposites. Inspection of their behavior and interests reveals such striking dissimilarities. Only deeper investigation shows the intrinsic likeness which exists in all opposites. To be sure, both were theologians, unmarried, and passionately disliked babies. Both were British Islanders, and island bound. Swift always planned to travel but did not accomplish it. Carroll made a vacation tour to the continent including Russia, but never repeated it. Both were secretive men and humorists, but their humor was of different textures. Swift's great strength was his hard-hitting satire, Carroll spoke more frequently the language of nonsense. Both wrote stories of adventurous travel in imaginary lands, stories which have become great English classics. Gulliver and Alice are immortals.

Swift was a man of the world, taking an active part in political controversies and affairs of state. For nearly half a century, Carroll lived at Oxford. Swift used his gift of satire to fight political and moral issues. Carroll developed his nonsensical fantasies to amuse little girls of whom he was fond. Swift was a man among men, attractive to women, but frequently distrustful of them and repelled by their bodies. A great eater and appreciative drinker among friends, he was a spasmodically convivial man whose sensitivity and irascibility sometimes alienated him from those for whom he cared most. His open revengefulness and his skatological ribaldry repelled many even among those who admired the richness of his fantasy and the robustness of his character. Carroll, by contrast, was temperate or abstemious in appetites and friendships, withdrew somewhat from men and especially from boys, preferring little girls of eight or so. He was fussily pedantic but was singularly lacking in ordinary shows of temper or direct aggressions. Both men were somewhat compulsive walkers, and fearful regarding their health. There is not the same cultist attitude of worship among the admirers of Swift that one encounters among the devotees of the author of *Alice,* who quiver in anticipatory anxiety at the very hint of a psychological study as though it were the ravishing of a temple. The enormous and lasting sacred popularity of Carroll and Alice (the two are linked almost in an interchangeability) is one of the most interesting aspects of any understanding of the nature of the shy mathematics lecturer whose fantasy tales for children have been translated into twenty-four languages and make the universal appeal of nonsense. It is interesting to note, however, that the use of *Alice's Adventures in Wonderland* as reading for school children was once banned, for in 1911 General Ho Chien, Governor-General of the Province of Hunan issued a statement forbidding its use on the ground that speaking animals were degrading (from D. Hudson's *Lewis Carroll,* p. 18).

This book attempts a psychoanalytic study of the two men. I came to this study through clinical psychoanalytic research. Working for some months on certain cases of fetishism which came continuously under my observation. I came to the conclusion that fetishism, and perhaps other perversions of emotional development, occurred in people who were constitutionally active and strong, but subject at certain critical periods in early life to external stresses of a nature which upset the integrity of the self-perception and the assimilation of the sensations of their own bodies. In other words, the body image becomes impaired; and the fetishistic perversion is an (unconsciously determined) attempt to stabilize this in such a way as to increase the capacity to utilize inherent aggressive and sexual drives rather than to be prematurely destroyed by them. One way in which this impairment of secure self-awareness of the body appeared was in disturbed subjective sensations of changing size of the total body or of certain body parts (1).[1] When it occurred to me that the two great classics, *Gulliver's Travels* and *Alice's Adventures in Wonderland*, presented through Gulliver and Alice exactly those sensations of which my patients complained, I determined to study the life stories of the two authors to see the relation of their lives and characters to the production of these remarkable fantasies. This led naturally to a study of their other writings as well, and especially to the scrutiny of the setting of events in the writers' lives at the time of the production of different pieces of work.

It seems obvious that an artist—as in contrast to a reporter—reveals, in one way or another, his own unconscious stresses and strivings. For no creatively driven man can ever get totally outside the web of his inner life, no matter how much his creativity may be mobilized by the impingement of external events. It is rather the exquisiteness of his truly economical expression which elicits some response in the audience (the full nature of which is generally not consciously appreciated) and stimulates there an inner, slow-working clarification that makes for the enormous power of artistic productions.

What seems so paradoxical to many is that such a movement in the recipient, stimulated from without, appears from inner depths and again works outward, emerging from the realm of inarticulate emotion into that of thought, ideas and

[1] Numbers in parentheses refer to the References and Notes at the end of the book.

action without the route being clearly marked in the individual's awareness.

This study springs then from clinical psychoanalytic interests and is intended primarily for psychoanalysts and readers already well-oriented in psychoanalytic theory and principles. It may be of interest to other students of literature and to that large group of people who as children or adults have enjoyed *Gulliver's Travels* and the *Alice* books. It is regrettable that it is impossible to make sufficiently full explanations of the technical psychoanalytic sections to satisfy the unoriented reader. Some effort has been made, however, to present the biographical chapters in as nontechnical language as possible, allowing the facts and the interesting time relationships between events of different orders to tell much of the story. The ordinary biography is generally quite lacking in details concerning events of the first years and the nature of the early family relationships, which are so important to the student of character development. Because of these lacks, I had always been averse to psychoanalyzing the dead or especially to psychoanalyzing fictional characters.

It was thus with caution and apprehension that I found myself well embarked upon the present study. It had seemed that either of these endeavors left too wide a range for the imposition of the interpreter's own subjective values. Indeed, this is a peril to all biographers. Official biography, like official history, is generally not very accurate, consisting too much of a series of individual or collective screen memories of accepted versions of events which partly represent and partly conceal what have been the true states of affairs, and are further filtered through the emotional attitudes of successive recorders. When a biographer writes of his subject's character or personality, "He *must* have felt thus and so," or "He *surely* knew these facts" without citing specifically the basis for the conclusion, one may question the objectivity of the interpretation at precisely these points. It is in regard to the understanding of just such equivocal areas that the pathographic method offers most help, if it is applied with tenderness, thoroughness, caution, real experience in fathoming the unconscious, and a willingness to state probability rather than to assert downright certainty.

It would be an undertaking of some merit, I believe, to present the technique of such a pathographic study and to show in an even more detailed way how the unconscious themes repeat themselves time and again in connection with the varying current stimuli of the artist's life and determine the form of the emotional reactions sometimes of a critical, though largely unconscious, force—reactions which are aroused repetitively. The study of the works of a prolific artist offers material as usable for psychoanalytic investigation as the dreams and free associations of the patient. In some respects, it may be more valuable and richer. With the two men, Swift and Carroll, the study is the more fascinating since both were directly uncommunicative regarding their personal lives, but inevitably revealed themselves anyway.

In the course of this study, an unplanned dividend appeared in the material which presented itself in regard to the relation of certain forms of humor (notably satire, parody, caricature and nonsense) to distortions of the self-image, based primarily on the disturbed body perceptions. It is a temptation to carry this further into a special study of those nonsense writers who, like Carroll, illustrated their own tales, or at least wrote with extraordinarily vivid pictorial effects. One thinks at once of the English Lear, the German Busch, and the American Thurber. Such a study would reach much beyond the boundaries of this book.

Some readers may complain that not enough attention has been paid to the cultural and social influences in the lives of the two men, and that I have confined myself too exclusively to the psychoanalytic approach. This I would freely admit if it had been my aim to present complete biographical pictures of the men in relation to their times. Much has been written regarding the impact of contemporary politics, world affairs, educational and scientific developments and social attitudes on the lives and writings of both men by others more competent in these fields than I. These biographical studies are important. But my own contribution must be in the area of my own interest and proficiency, an attempt to uncover and to understand the unconscious motivating drives arising from the early childhood, but operating incessantly throughout life, whether in amalgamation with or against the currents of the times. Further, it is what these tales record, not merely as a reflection of the time in veiled parody or outright attack, but of problems deep in the hearts of people of many lands and many centuries, that has given the characters and their authors everlasting fame.

PART ONE

JONATHAN SWIFT

IONATHAN SWIFT S.T.D.
Decanus Ecclesiæ Cathedralis Sancti
Patricij DUBLIN.

Geo. Vertue Londini Sculpsit

1.

THE LIFE OF
JONATHAN SWIFT

Swift's was an enigmatic character, full of apparent contradictions, opposing loyalties and attitudes. A man of highest ideals and tenderest sympathy, he was also touchy, power driven, inordinately active, callous in behavior, and daring; and frequently almost unbelievably afraid of gossip. He had many hiding places, but was generally in the public eye. He became in his day a power to be reckoned with politically, both in England and Ireland, a restless, energetic, ruthless man, always on the go except for brief periods of hiding out, seemingly in discouragement, depression or inertia. Much of his life was a pendulum swing between the two countries. He seems never to have ventured elsewhere. He disliked revealing facts directly about his own life, and when he wrote of himself, wrote frequently in the third person, sometimes metaphorically or playfully, but sometimes also in self-concealment. Yet he celebrated himself in poetry in a rather flagrant way. He wrote prolifically on many subjects: religion, politics, education, manners. He was famous for the satire of his prose and for the open obscenity of much of his poetry. In speech he was more often immaculate, charming and witty. It is reported that he never told an off-color story. This cannot be said of his letters.

Much of his writing was launched anonymously or under

a pseudonym, a practice not uncommon for the period; yet one gets the impression that he went beyond others in assuming disguises. Sometimes when he had set the country in an uproar by some particularly forceful, venomous or satirical pamphlet, he seemed to sit back and listen to the roar like the practical joker that he was. When his work was about to be attributed to someone else, he came angrily forth and revealed that he was the author, about to be robbed of recognition that was his due. Perhaps in no situation more than in this was the combination of his great timidity and his unparalleled courage revealed, together with his furious resentment at that which he had himself provoked.

When he was to be installed as Dean of St. Patrick's Cathedral (1713), the following verses were found nailed on the door of the church:

> Today this temple gets a Dean
> Of parts and fame uncommon;
> Used both to pray and to profane
> To serve both God and Mammon.
>
> This place he got by wit and rhyme
> And many ways most odd;
> And might a bishop be in time,
> Did he believe in God.
>
> Look down, St. Patrick, look, we pray
> On thine own church and steeple;
> Convert thy Dean on this great day,
> Or else, God help the people [1].

One might dismiss these as merely the spiteful work of a rival, did they not represent how Swift must have seemed to a number of the Irish when he returned to Ireland, discouraged and disappointed in political and ecclesiastical preferment in England, after a brilliantly successful few years there. But soon he was championing the rights of the

Irish people, and approximately a decade later he was being hailed as the greatest man in Ireland, the rescuer of the people from despoliation and poverty as the result of the English King's irresponsible granting of the right of money coinage for Ireland to a relative of the King's mistress. By the power of his satirical writing, Swift forced the abrogation of this privileged grant and saved the day for the Irish (The Drapier Letters). Of himself, Swift wrote: "A person of great honour in Ireland . . . used to say that my mind was like a conjured spirit that would do mischief if I would not give it employment" (2). The "person of great honour" has sometimes been identified as Lord Berkeley (3) but may have been Swift himself.

Swift came of a Yorkshire family. His written account of his own family was inclined to stress its aristocratic and English superiority over the Irish among whom he was born. He showed a considerable admiration for his grandfather Swift,[1] erected a tombstone in his memory, and worked over his memoirs, although he had never seen him. Neither did he see his father, who died seven months before his birth on November 30, 1667. There was certainly some bitterness in Swift about his birth: he repeatedly referred to himself as having been dropped rather than born on Irish soil, and mentioned several times that on his birthday he usually read the third chapter of the Book of Job:

> Job opened his mouth and cursed his day . . . and said, "Let the day perish wherein I was born, and the night in which was said, There is a man-child conceived; let the day be darkness; let not God regard it from above, neither let the light shine upon it. Let the darkness

---

[1] This grandfather, Thomas Swift, was a picturesque and vital man. He was married to Elizabeth Dryden, niece of the poet. There are many stories of his valor, courage and loyalty to his King, to whom he offered a purse of three hundred "broad pieces" (a considerable savings for a clergyman) in troubled times. He fathered fourteen children, ten sons and four daughters, of whom Godwin was the eldest.

and the shadow of death stain it; let a cloud dwell
upon it; let the blackness of the day terrify it . . .
Why died I not in the womb? Why did I not give up
the ghost when I came out of the belly?" etc. etc.

His parents had been married three years before he was born,
and one child, a sister Jane, was less than two years older
than the posthumous child Jonathan. A recent biographer
(4) believes that the marriage was a love match, but does
not cite evidence other than Swift's later attachment to his
mother, which is not really conclusive. Another (5) believes
it was a marriage arranged to cover and care for the ambiguous situation of a woman, mistress to an aging and
prominent man. It is true that the mother was several years
—perhaps as much as ten years—older than the father, and
perhaps of a lesser social standing. There have come down
two accounts of the birth of Jonathan Swift; one that he was
a premature seven-month baby, conceived out of marriage
and born after the death of his supposed father; the other
that he was born at term seven months after the father's
death, but that the father did not know of the pregnancy
at the time of his death, and therefore never knew at all of
his existence (6). Whatever the actual circumstances may
have been, these alternate explanations of the fatherless birth
would seem to offer the outline of Swift's own fantasies and
explanations years later, as well as the probable gossip at
the time. It was certainly not an easy way to begin life, and
his later emotional tension in regard to it was expressed, not
only in his insistence on the third chapter of Job, but in his
equally florid celebration of his own and others' birthdays
with poetry and festivity. He did not always regret having
been born, though certain attendant circumstances were inevitably sore spots with him.

His mother was an Englishwoman, some say the daughter
of a butcher. The father, also named Jonathan, had come to

Ireland from England with several brothers and had proved the least successful of them all. When he died, leaving many debts, the mother, Abigail Erick Swift, a woman without a dowry, probably turned to the Swift family, especially the older brother Godwin, who was the most prosperous one and head of the group of brothers.[2] The events of the first five years of Swift's life were dramatic in the extreme and may have contributed strongly to the pattern of his restless, driven, divided later life.

The records of the time indicate that the mother made great effort to collect certain money due her husband in order to clear his debts. Although he was admitted as a solicitor, he had continued as steward to the King's Inns, up to the time of his death, at the age of twenty-five. He had been appointed to this post through Sir John Temple (8),[3] father of Sir William Temple who was later to play so important a part in the younger Jonathan's life. In this setting of impoverishment one is surprised to learn that the family had a nurse for the two children, possibly furnished by Uncle Godwin, a successful barrister and a prolific husband and father. He had married successively four wealthy wives and had in all eighteen children. Possibly Abigail Swift with Jane and Jonathan lived at the Godwin Swifts' for a time after the death of the elder Jonathan.

Swift wrote of himself that he had been a frail baby; that when a year old, he had been kidnapped by his nurse "without the knowledge or consent" of his mother or his uncle, and had been taken by the nurse to the town of Whitehaven in England. When his mother discovered that he had been

---

[2] Godwin Swift, according to Sir Leslie Stephen's account, was not only a barrister, but a speculator and invester of money. For a time he was eminently successful attaining an annual income of £3,000., which he ultimately lost, however, and died in straightened circumstances (7).

[3] Denis Johnston has argued that Jonathan Swift was really the son of Sir John Temple. This argument is carefully reviewed at the beginning of Davis' *Stella* (9).

abducted, she sent word that he should not be returned until he was stronger and better able to stand the voyage. This did not occur until about three years later, i.e., when the child was approximately four. Accounts of later biographers give this absence as anywhere from two to five years. According to Swift's report, his nurse was so devotedly careful of him that before he returned he had learned to read and spell so well that he could read any chapter of the Bible. The situation or occasion of his return to Ireland is nowhere described. What is striking, however, is that rather soon after his return to his mother, she left him and herself crossed to England, returning to her native Leicester. Here she continued to live throughout her life, and seems not to have seen her son again for many years, i.e., until he sought her out when he was twenty-one.

The situation is the more baffling in that, while most of Swift's biographers mention the nurse's extraordinary love for the infant, probably taking their idea from Swift's own autobiographical fragment, there is no record that he himself ever again mentions her. In his original statement he had described her as an Englishwoman who returned home in order to see a sick relative from whom she expected a legacy, but included nothing about a husband or family. A later writer (10), not always considered reliable, and writing three years after Swift's death, gave the story of an Irish nurse who was married to an Englishman who had remained behind in Whitehaven and now besought his wife's return. There is a story of Swift's having once put himself out considerably to meet an old man from the village of Whitehaven, where he had spent the three years of his infancy, but other than this and the acknowledgment of his literacy, he seems to have consigned the nurse to anonymity, which was later his way with those who displeased him. (We will later rediscover the nurse in *Gulliver's Travels.*)

In contrast to this, the mother who had apparently deserted him twice, both actively and passively, before he was five years old, was described by Swift's second cousin, Deane Swift, grandson of his hated Uncle Godwin, as "a woman greatly beloved and esteemed by all the family of Swifts. Her conversation was so exactly polite, cheerful and agreeable, even to the young and sprightly." He further remarks on her generosity, her decorum, her industry, and that her chief amusements were needlework and reading (11). Whether this is a straightforward, sincere account or whether it was the face with which a difficult and uncertain relationship was covered for the world, is difficult to say.

When Swift came to know his mother later in life, he was fond of her and visited her whenever he went to England. On the other hand, he mentions her comparatively little in his letters and journal, and one gets the impression that there was something of a gulf between his relationship to her and the other important relationships of his life. According to some accounts, the mother maintained a playful attitude toward him, such that when she visited him unexpectedly in Dublin and found that he was out, she gained admission to his lodgings by persuading the landlady that he was her lover. (This is cited by one biographer as indicating that he acquired his tendency to practical joking from her; by another as evidence of the love relationship between her and the elder Jonathan!) She died when Swift was forty-three; and he then wrote that with her passing he had lost the barrier between himself and death. "If the way to Heaven be through piety, truth, justice, and charity, she is there." He put this memorandum away between the pages of an account book.

Swift's relationship to his sister Jane is obscure. She presumably stayed with her mother during her childhood; at least nothing else is said about it. The same second cousin, who wrote amiably of Abigail Swift, added that "She was equally fond of her children, notwithstanding some disagree-

23

ment that subsisted between them." We find to our surprise that Jane was for a time a member of the household of Sir William Temple, along with her brother who was about twenty-two when he entered this family life. It is further said that when she married a man of whom Swift disapproved, and soon after Swift had suffered in his first real love affair at twenty-nine, he gloomily declared that his sister's marriage would never succeed. The man was described as of fair family, decent but improvident, but he died unsuccessful in a few years, even as Swift's own father had died, leaving debts. Swift was distressed that his warning had not been heeded but had come true. While he contributed to her support thereafter, he saw her rarely and reluctantly. Later she became a kind of upper servant to Lady Giffard, sister of Sir William Temple, and made her home with the mother of Swift's friend Stella.

It is necessary, however, to understand more of the years between Swift's regaining and then almost immediate loss of his mother at the age of four to five, and his reunion with her at twenty-one. After his mother's return to England, Jonathan was placed under the care of his Uncle Godwin, who presently placed him in the boarding school at Kilkenny, sometimes referred to as the Eton of Ireland. At school, he was with two of his cousins, while vacations may have been spent among the eighteen children of Godwin Swift's household. Certainly from the age of five or six until he was twenty-one, young Jonathan lived an institutional existence which he hated. He spoke of the years at Kilkenny with bitterness, asserted that Uncle Godwin gave him the "education of a dog" and described himself as "discouraged and sunk in spirit." He was probably not entirely just, for there is nothing to indicate that he suffered more than the others from any mistreatment. Kilkenny was considered the best school in Ireland of the time. It is more likely that his homelessness and lack of any real parental tie at the time made him unhappy and resentful. He did not do well academically either at Kilkenny or during the years at Trinity. At eighteen he was finally given his Bachelor's degree by a special dispensation, *speciali grata*, which he was ever after to feel as a disgrace (12). There is no record of special trouble during these years; it is likely that he was compliant and blocked, not finding any outlet for his considerable abilities.[4]

It is from the early days at Kilkenny that he gives his first memory, undoubtedly a screen memory. This was included in a letter to Lord Bolingbroke and is described as follows:

> I remember when I was a little boy, I felt a fish at the end of my line, which I drew up almost on the ground but it dropped in, and the disappointment vexes me to this day, and I believe it was the type of all my future disappointments [14].

It is not the incident itself, but what it stood for and the attitude that was forming which he expressed through it which was important.[5] In school, the future Dean of St. Patrick's Cathedral received his worst marks in theology and rebelled actively against syllogistic reasoning.

Another incident during the Kilkenny days was subsequently told by Swift in a moralistic way to illustrate to im-

[4] According to the account of Sir Leslie Stephen, Swift's rebellious behavior after the dishonorable degree caused him to be under censure for seventy weeks in less than two years, i.e., for at least three quarters of the time. The offenses were "town-haunting," "notorious neglect of duties and frequenting the town." On his twenty-first birthday he was punished for exciting domestic dissensions, despising warnings of the junior dean, and insulting the latter with contemptuous words. He was once sentenced to ask pardon of the dean on his knees, publicly in the college hall. His behavior at this time was probably more defiant than licentious (13).

[5] The episode of the fish is repeated with variations in Gulliver's voyage to the Lilliputians, but the object lost is a hat on a string rather than a fish. Gulliver loses the hat when the string breaks. The hat is later retrieved, and attached by hooks on cords, is dragged in by five horses. Gulliver found it not quite so hurt as he had feared. The further significance of this will be discussed later. The second version appears as a restitutive correction of the first, and interestingly appears at a time when Gulliver is enormously big and powerful.

pecunious young people the folly of undertaking the responsibilities of marriage without adequate money. He told of how he so much wanted a horse that he invested his entire capital in a worn-out nag which was the only horse he could afford, only to find that he had no money with which to buy feed for the poor nag. The problem was finally solved by the horse's lying down and dying. His connecting this story with marriage is probably significant. It is my impression that the nag somehow represented Swift's own sick and impoverished father, for whom he was longing, but who had also lain down in death. (The emphasis on the symbol of the horse as a substitute for the parent is seen again in the chapter on the Yahoos in *Gulliver's Travels.*)

During these school years young Swift is described as outwardly obedient, though frozen. Only after the attainment of the dishonorable degree did he become openly rebellious and with his rebellion begin to liberate some of his intellectual powers. To be sure, his Uncle Godwin had then begun to fail, and he was possibly not so much burdened by the load of gratitude which may have hemmed him in and increased his silent resentment. While studying for his Master's degree at Trinity, he attained some notice as a rebel and writer of scurrilous harangue of such a nature that one of his biographers described it as showing "The will and capacity to wound, and above all a directness in insolence, a mercilessness in savage laughter" (15). During this period he seems to have been admired by his cousins, Thomas and Willoughby Swift, who were generous with him. He left Trinity without his higher degree, ostensibly because of Uncle Godwin's decline in health and fortunes. This uncle went into some kind of gradual dementia, which seemed to impress Jonathan greatly, probably because he had envied, hated, and reviled him, and feared becoming like him.

Swift, then at the age of twenty-one or twenty-two, turned

to England and his mother,[6] and embarked on the first flirtation with a rather undistinguished young woman named Betty Jones, who subsequently married an innkeeper. Whatever this affair amounted to, it provoked some self-examination, for he wrote afterward to a friend that "his own cold temper and unconfined humor were the greatest hindrance to any kind of folly" (16). He seemed also to turn to youthful thoughts of power and pride, for again he wrote, "I hope my carriage will be so as my friends need not be ashamed of the name," and added that he did not care a fig "for the obloquy of a parcel of wretched fools," and above all else "valued his own entertainment." This reaction—certainly not uncommon in youth—was to deepen rather than lessen in his life. It is important because it shows some distrust of his own ability to love or win the love which he certainly craved. He was always morbidly sensitive to any hurt or hint of rebuff in his affectional life, and tried time and again to heal his wounded pride, by finding recognition in the world rather than by looking for some other woman whom he might love. This flirtation meant enough to him, however, to make him keep the girl's letters for ten years and then ask someone else to burn them. It was after all the first venture in the direction of love, by a young man who had been singularly robbed of childhood attachments which form the substratum of the adult ones.

At the age of twenty-two, Swift entered the employment and household of Sir William Temple, who had been for many years a friend of the Swift family. There seems little doubt that the contact was made through his mother; but it will also be remembered that Sir William's father had been

[6] Swift's departure from Dublin coincided with the time when James II had been driven from the throne and was being displaced by William. In the accompanying social and political upheaval in Ireland, many English people in Ireland fled back to England. At this time Swift certainly felt himself to be English, and may have been influenced by this. It is a time when an outer revolution coincided with a personal inner one.

responsible for getting the elder Jonathan a berth when he was just the age the younger Jonathan was now. According to some, Lady Temple was distantly related to Abigail Swift. With him were his sister Jane and his cousin Thomas, with whom he had spent his school days. The Temple household was large and complex, the extensive establishment of a man of wealth and culture, previously ambassador to Holland, a man who had had his hand in many affairs and was planning now to sort out his papers and put them in order. Even more important are the facts that both Sir William and Lady Dorothy Temple were extraordinarily fine and able people of learning and integrity, and that they had an uncommonly good relationship to each other. They had had much personal sorrow and only two months before had lost, through suicide, their youngest and at that time only surviving child of a family of nine. John Temple had thrown himself in the Thames soon after his appointment as Secretary of the State for War.[7] It seems he was in a depression, and believed he had been betrayed by a confidential agent whom he had recommended to the King. In the household also was Lady Giffard, Sir William's sister, who had made her home with the Temples for many years since being widowed within the first year of her marriage. Swift was supposed to serve as secretary to the aging man in his literary work and in the editing and arrangement of his letters and documents.

It was a situation which might seem peculiarly suitable for the homeless and talented young Jonathan, and to promise him enrichment in many ways. Swift seemed to admire and then to envy the older man. He could not feel as readily at home in this expansive way of life as he would have liked.

[7] Irvin Ehrenpreis has made an extremely careful study of the evidence available concerning the nature of the relationship between Sir William Temple and Swift at this time and shows very well how complex it was on both sides, with mutual ambivalence *and* admiration (17).

When he was envious he was likely to develop grievances, and he was soon unhappy and discontented. Much has been written concerning Temple's treatment of Swift, but there seems little evidence of real basis for the latter's frequent complaints. In a sensitively perceptive study of this period in a recently published critical biography of Swift, John Middleton Murry has also advanced the theory that young Jonathan Swift craved a father and worshipped Sir William Temple more intensely and imperatively than the older man, not yet through the mourning for his own son, could respond to or perhaps even fully comprehend. Consequently the younger man, with his exaggerated needs and inordinate touchiness, was hurt and took himself off. This seems not only plausible, but probably true, and the understanding of it brings into perspective the inner and outer events of Swift's life at this time (18).

Even before the first year at the Temples was up, he returned to Ireland supposedly because he had developed an indisposition, attributed to eating stone fruit in the Temple garden. This may have been the first attack of a chronic and increasing periodic ailment, probably Ménière's disease. The onset of these symptoms seemed to precipitate Swift's hypochondriacal fears which had already been given special coloring by the prolonged and rather frightening dementia of his Uncle Godwin (19). Throughout his life he was pursued by anxieties for his physical and mental health, and was constantly exercising to show and to improve his strength. That these attempts at self-cure had a ritualistic quality during the time he was at Moor Park, the second Temple estate, is suggested by Swift's own account that he would interrupt his studies every two hours to run up and down a nearby hill. He kept track of the speed of his performance with care. Throughout his later life he recommended vigorous walking or riding as the cure for distemper of all sorts.[8] He stayed away only a few months and then returned to the Temple household, where he remained for a second stretch of time, until he was twenty-seven (1694). This seems to have been the special period of his growing worship of Sir William Temple. It is possible that the first flight was due to an unconscious fear of his feelings for Sir William.[9] Now, however, there was a period of expansion in his life. He began again to write, and especially poetry. He retired often to Mother Ludwell's cave, a place on the Temple estate where he found inspiration and calm. It was a pathetic and almost successful attempt to form at last the emotional family ties which his disrupted early life had been unable to produce. He was profoundly hurt by the sharp criticism of his poetry by his distant cousin, Dryden, who told him he would never be a poet, and should turn his pen to other pursuits. It came at a time when he was raw anyway and he felt it as a merciless attack. He began also to write serious satirical prose and dated the inception of the *Battle of the Books* and *A Tale of the Tub* from this time, although they were not published until some years later.

He became more sophisticated too: he made the acquaintance of King William, who was a visitor at Moor Park and fancied young Jonathan sufficiently to offer him an appointment in the cavalry and to instruct him in the proper method of eating asparagus. There were still recurrent periods of resentment and restlessness; and at twenty-seven, having obtained his Master's degree at Oxford at twenty-five, he decided to leave Temple and enter the Church. Murry presents the hypothesis already mentioned that the more or less bitter break with Temple at this time, almost surely exaggerated

---

8 See *Swift's Journal to Stella* (20) and *Vanessa and Jonathan Swift* (21). He even offered advice for robust exercise of this kind to Mollkin, younger sister of Vanessa, when she was dying of tuberculosis.

9 Swift wrote of Temple:
　　Shall I believe a spirit so divine
　　Was cast in the same mould as mine [22].

in Swift's presentation of it, was due to the fact that Swift felt the loss of inspiration and the failure of his poetic creativeness as due to Temple's inability to respond to him, and further reacted to this as though he had been betrayed by Temple. He felt as one who has offered devoted love and been met with almost blankness. He was angry as though he had been deceived. This emotionally hungry young man may have placed an inner overvaluation on Temple's early kindnesses and really made unspoken demands for more than could be given. This sense of betrayal and of deception is what turned him, says Murry, to satire and especially to the satire of *A Tale of the Tub*. Seen from this angle, *A Tale of the Tub* has elements of bitter attack on Sir William, with his interest in education, church, and government, his idealism and his goodness. The great insult was his failure to father the young man who had been sent to him and needed him so much. Sir William was in so many respects cut out to be the good father where none had been known before. It may be, too, that Swift was pushed from within by his own genius without realizing it. He had been partly uncorked, but the pressure was not yet relieved and it made him uncomfortable and arrogant. The vitriolic character of his satire may be an indication of the extent and intensity of his frustrated longing and admiration.

During those years in the Temple household he had become acquainted with a young widow, a Mrs. Johnson, who was a lady-in-waiting, with an eight-year-old daughter Hester, or Esther. He took an interest in this little girl, who seems to have been the favorite of the household and of Sir William Temple. He taught her to read and write, the latter so effectively that later he was chaffed that her round even letters might be mistaken for his own. There is indication of some gossip concerning this child's relationship to Sir William Temple, who is reported to have tutored her also and indulged her generally. Was Swift jealous? Did he overcome this in his peculiar devotion to the little one? She was a girl of fifteen, on the brink of womanhood, when Swift left Temple for the second time. She was to play a strangely important part in all his later life. Did he have any intimation of this then? What were his relations with his own sister at that time, this sister of whom he probably cherished a fantasy image during his own childhood? The silence about her later is conspicuous.

What it meant to Swift to become a clergyman can only be surmised. His most respected forebear had been a clergyman, and it may in a sense have meant "good family" to him. But he had already attacked religion and the church like an atheist. He was unhappy and felt unappreciated and insufficiently advanced by Temple. He was chronically anxious, and at times frantic. The church may well have seemed security to him, a less personal kind of father, and also a retreat. He was later to use being a man of the cloth as the strongest rationalization for all his neurotic fears of gossip and exposure. At any rate, he was granted the small prebend of Kilroot, a dreary country place on the shores of Belfast Lough. Here the parsonage was called the Egg because of its odd shape; the parson soon became known as the Mad Parson who skipped stones in the water for his amusement and became angry if watched. One can imagine the loneliness after the stimulating though unsatisfying life at Moor Park. It would be a wonder if he had no regrets at having made the change.

It was at Kilroot that his second and greater infatuation for a young woman occurred. The girl, Jane Waring, is generally reported to have been the sister of a college friend, though later accounts state she was a cousin and was the daughter of the Archdeacon of Dromore.[10] She was the first

---

[10] According to the account of J. E. Ball (23), Jane Waring was the daughter of Rev. Roger Waring (Archdeacon of Dromore), who had died in 1692. Her mother later married Robert Greene. She was the cousin rather

of the three women who played the most important roles in his adult life. He gave them all pseudoclassical names suggesting goddesses. She became Varina (a Latinized version of her last name); the little girl at Moor Park, Hester Johnson, rose later to ascendancy as Stella; while the third, also Hester, with the family name Van Homrigh, he called Vanessa. All three were the daughters of widows.

There can be no doubt that he really wanted to marry Varina; he was emphatic and fervid in his statement of this, though he sometimes had an odd way of expressing it—that "he could not be blamed for working for a cure for his violent desire" which he likened to distemper. Much was written between them of her ill-health, and from Swift's side, of her dependence on her family. He wanted to get her out of this "sink." He was by turns peremptory and suspicious that he would lose all he valued in marriage. One gets the impression that he was passionately assertive rather than tender, and that her attitude was one of frightened uncertainty but continued attraction. How much this was neurotically fore-

than sister of Swift's roommate, who might have been William Waring who matriculated in 1681, or Richard, who matriculated in 1684. Her brother Westenra was at Trinity also but did not matriculate until three years after Swift had left. She seems to have been the oldest of eight children. She died unmarried in 1720.

An Ulster Parish by Edward D. Atkinson (24), the Rector of Donaghcloney at Warington in 1898, deals also with the Waring family. According to this account they came originally from Lancashire, the founder of the Irish branch of the family being John Waring, who settling in Dorriaghy, near Lisburn, married the rector's daughter and had three sons. They became influential members of the community, two became prosperous farmers, and a grandson introduced linen making in Belfast. This account is not clear about Jane Waring's place in the family and quotes the Sheridan biography of Swift that she was the sister of his roommate. It also gives her name as Elizabeth, probably mistaking an incident of Swift's directing the burning of some old letters "to Eliza" written in his youth, for letters to Varina. It is more likely that they were letters to the flirtatious Betty Jones in Leicester.

Swanzy's *Biographical Succession Lists of Dromore Diocese* indicates that Jane Waring was born on the 8th of October, 1674, and was the oldest of eight children. This account perpetuates the story that she was the sister of Swift's roommate, but has probably taken this over from others, as it is contrary to the very facts otherwise recorded by Swanzy (25).

cast and how much genuinely in reaction to his extreme intensity is impossible to see. In a letter of April, 1696, he wrote philosophically of love urging that "to resist the violence of our inclinations in the beginning, is a strain of self-denial that may have some pretences to set up as a virtue . . . but 'tis possible to err in excess of piety as of love." This, for Swift, was going very far and saying a great deal in a personal setting. Whether from nervous squeamishness or good sense, she did not agree to marry him at once and after two weeks he left. Had she capitulated, it is possible this would have scared him, and he would have fled as quickly. On the whole, one's sympathy is with Swift, and it may be that he was saved from a disastrous entanglement. But the effect was unfortunate: he turned from her and from hope of marriage itself, even steeling himself against it. He again returned to the work with Sir William Temple.

When he next visited Ireland at thirty-two (1699), after Sir William Temple's death, he and Varina were again in contact and the girl seemed more willing to consider marriage, perhaps because he was more settled and seemed a better prospect in a worldly way; perhaps she was bound to him in some fascination. Then he became righteously abusive and insulting, offering to marry her under conditions which no self-respecting woman could accept. He probably did not expect to be accepted, and he was not. In his letter offering marriage he especially emphasized his demands for cleanliness in a woman, which was certainly the strongest neurotic obsession with him. He was repeatedly warning young women to be clean; and characteristically he used the term "slut" as a term of endearment. Later in life, paradoxically too, he addressed his cook as "sweetheart" when she especially displeased him. In his last letter to Varina he no longer addressed her by the goddess-like name. She was subsequently to disappear in the mire of the cast-off and unspoken. It was just at this time that Jane Swift married the undesirable Fenton.

Swift had always the fear of a woman as filthy; and this was written so often and so large in all his works that it appears as one of the dominant themes of his life. This will be discussed further in the later clinical interpretation. He was himself more than scrupulously clean, and that in an era and location where rigid cleanliness was a luxury and a labor. In his repeated attacks on whatever he felt as evil, noisome, dirty and corrupt, whether it was a woman's body or some matter of state, his writing was so vindictive, so foul in language, so violent, that presently the stench seemed to come from him rather than from the subject or object which he was treating. On the other hand he was generally immaculate in speech. Just before his final rupture with Varina and his consignment of her to the dust of oblivion, he wrote a series of resolutions for himself, the *Resolutions when I Come to be Old*. There were seventeen of them, and they seemed to represent resolutions to overcome areas of vulnerability in his character: one was not to marry a young woman, another not to harken to flatterers or conceive "that I can be loved by a young woman," and another "not to be fond of children, or let them come near me hardly."[11] From his terrible hurt, his bitterness was making him an armor of renunciation.

This was one of the critical times in his life. That he was passionately aroused toward Varina and wanted marriage with her seems certain. But his preparation for marriage was

---

[11] This resolution not to allow himself to come near a child is hard to understand. Leslie Stephen thought it was a warding off of his attraction to Stella (26). But Stella was nineteen at the time he wrote it, and he would under ordinary circumstances not have thought of her as a child then but, as he actually said, as "the brightest virgin on the green." It is possible that he had already become sensitive to his earlier attraction to her and was fearful of this; or it may be that the resolution was without clear conscious motivation and represented some mixture of unconscious defenses against children, at a time when he was attempting to renounce marriage and the possibility of fatherhood.

lacking, for he had no experience of sustained parental love himself, and scant evidence of good marriage relationships in those around him. He had neither emotional rootedness himself, nor the good vision and ideal of marriage to bring to such a union. To be sure, he may have been inspired not only by the character of Sir William Temple, but by the relationship between Sir William and Lady Dorothy. But he felt excluded when he most wanted full acceptance; and so he left. His violent satirical genius came to the fore and in *A Tale of the Tub* he would deny these ideals and attempt to show that they were illusions only. It was partly the outcome of his affectional disappointment and his sexual frustration. "It is a prolonged whoop of laughter over a dead self" (27).

The relationship to Varina has been given but little understanding. Yet it was an important turning point. The first serious love affair is an inner landmark in any life, even when unsuccessful; however, it generally leads on to another, such is the intrinsic expansiveness of growth. But Swift was too hurt, and, attempting to call a halt, actually regressed in his emotional interest. *A Tale of the Tub* and the *Digressions* are replete with backside fun. From then on the skatological jokes and excremental metaphors became more numerous and more open in his writing. The question whether Swift was physically able to marry—i.e., whether he was sexually potent—has been often implied or directly raised. It is a question which cannot really be answered, as it generally has been, by a categorically positive or negative assertion. That he was definitely potent or that he was almost certainly impotent—these are the statements which are generally made, dressed to be sure in more delicate and ambiguous language. Yet potency is not a fixed and unchanging function, as anyone must recognize who thinks of the matter clearly. The very tendency to be so emphatic and decisive about it may be an indication of the diffusely anxious state which is aroused by the need to consider it. The fact that Swift wanted so passionately to marry Varina and in his letters gave no hint of doubt about his physical adequacy in the marital relationship, is no proof of his later security in this or of his continued healthy functioning. Indeed, in a man of Swift's temperament it would not be unusual if the failure of this first love venture had produced physical-emotional repercussions, affecting the balance of his sexual functioning. He had turned quickly from his exaggerated sense of rebuff from Sir William to the actual collapse of his suit for Varina; and then back to Sir William. A calmer period of work with him (1696-1699) was terminated by Sir William's death. It was not long after this that he wrote his *Meditations Upon a Broomstick* which he palmed off on Lady Berkely as a practical joke when she napped during his reading to her. Certainly the *Meditations* show a strong preoccupation with sexual inversion.

Before Varina, there had already been the little girl, Hester Johnson, "Stella" in whose education Swift had interested himself. Eight years old when he first saw her, she was fifteen at the time of his last sojourn with the Temples. She was nineteen and Swift was thirty-two when Sir William Temple died. This seems to have been the closing of an emotional era with Swift. Temple was dead, and Varina was gone. He became more cautious, more aggressively touchy, and opened his heart to others less rather than more. His negativism, always conspicuous, seemed to become stronger. He seemed like one who can only feel himself a person through opposing, the more so as he must thus save himself from the counter demand of his nature, to lose himself completely in another. Swift decided that he would not let himself love again: it may be rather that he *could* not in a sufficiently mature way for any happiness, as he craved rather the unconditional love of infancy and was doomed to be angry at eternal disappointments against which he threw up ramparts of defense.

After Temple's death, the relationship with the family fell apart and then became poisoned with acrimony. The break came supposedly, when Swift published without specific approval a certain lot of Sir William's papers involving matters which Lady Giffard, Sir William's sister, thought should not then be given to the public. Swift's handling of this seems arrogant and then revengeful. It was disproportionate to the situation and may have been the arena in which he played out his long disappointment at not being really one of the Temples. With Temple dead, he threw himself into political activity and writing, among the Whig group of the time. At the same time he was again seeking a home and a living in the Church. Disappointed in the preferment he sought and seeing that even ecclesiastical appointments were influenced by cash payments, Swift wrote two of his bitterest and foulest poems, *The Discovery* and *The Problem*, described by a recent biographer (28) as writings in which he "acts like an animal who relieves itself upon the carcass of a despised adversary." It is improbable that he was actually so inexperienced as to be stunned by this discovery of ecclesiastical maneuvering and bargaining, but that this was again a symbol to him of his exclusion and his homelessness and he was furious. He obtained a holding, however, at Laracor, a small country church twenty miles or so from Dublin. The congregation was estimated at fifteen people. It is said that the garden there which he created with prideful care reflected in miniature some garden of the Temple estate.

Swift had tutored Stella since the age of eight or ten. He later said six, but that is definitely inaccurate and it can be noted that he frequently gave the ages of both Stella and Vanessa as two or three years younger than they actually were. He had a theory, often expressed, that young women should cultivate their minds to be as much like men's minds

STELLA AS A YOUNG GIRL

as possible, only in this way could they hope for a secure marriage. He warned against interest in dress, frivolous talk or similar light pursuits. A woman should, he thought, be a kind of second version of a man. He carried out these beliefs in his teaching of Stella and the shaping of her attitudes.

After Sir William's death, Stella lived in lodgings with an older woman companion, Rebecca Dingley, who earlier had been part of the Temple household. Two years later (almost exactly the same period of time as that which elapsed after his own father's death before he was transplanted to England by a nurse who sought a legacy there), Swift persuaded Stella and her nurse companion to leave London and come to live near him in Ireland.[12] The great rationalization was that they would have more money as living was cheaper in Ireland and their money would last longer. The life in Ireland proved unusual. Stella, always accompanied by the faithful Dingley, lived with or near Swift at Laracor, or when he was Dean of St. Patrick's Cathedral in Dublin, transferred her residence to be near him there. When Swift left for England for months together, Stella and Dingley remained behind in Ireland, moving, however, into Swift's own quarters where Stella carried on his routine business for him, like a junior version of himself. He schooled her to be discreet to the point of secrecy and only much later is it certain that she confided in anyone but Dingley. Swift rarely if ever saw her except in Dingley's presence. The latter is supposed not to have been in the least infatuated with Swift nor he with her. For twenty-seven years this strange triangle continued with Swift complaining openly of Dingley's stupidity but keeping her like a protective guardian always at hand. It seemed that Stella must represent a woman in Swift's life and yet not quite be one. She must be a protection against

---

[12] The similarity of this to his own kidnapping has been tacitly recognized by an earlier biographer who referred to it as the *Abduction of Stella*.

other women too. The whole constellation appears as a defense against sexuality.

The nature of Stella's inner relationship to Swift is not clear. We know little of her father except that he had been a steward in the Temple household, though perhaps not at Moor Park. He was probably not many years dead at the time of the first meeting of Swift and little Hester. But Stella's relationship to her father, real or fantasied, is a blank. By some it was said that she was not his child. She was sickly until fifteen, then blossomed out, but later developed tuberculosis. Until her death in middle age she lived on in this synthetic family, with the brilliant Jonathan Swift as her (platonic lover) "father" and Dingley as a kind of nurse-mother. Her own mother remained in England until her death. After the death of Jane Swift's husband, Jonathan helped to support her and arranged for her to live with Stella's mother. A curious exchange! It seems amply clear, however, that the Swift-Stella-Dingley menage was a condensed repetition of Swift's own early life, with Mrs. Johnson playing the part of Abigail Swift with the daughter, Jane. The real Abigail continued to live in Leicester until her death.

There was nothing to indicate a sexual relationship between Swift and Stella, and much to suggest that for Swift the idea was loathsome and perhaps impossible. He addressed Stella as "Young Sir," wrote to her: "Why are you not a young fellow, and then I might prefer you?" and again declared that Stella and Dingley were not women. She never complained. Swift portrayed her as a stern and exacting idealist who, when necessary, chided others in such a way that they would be ashamed to complain and yet could not resent (29). She was a prudent economist like himself, generous with the poor and frugal in the selection of clothing. Swift himself tithed regularly. When another clergyman sought Stella in marriage, Swift was pushed to a declaration "in conscience and in honour" in which he told "the naked truth," but proceeded to such an appraisal of Stella's fortune and intellect while seemingly supporting the suit of his rival and hinting that the gentleman might presently be obligated to marry her in order to satisfy the gossip, that the poor man retreated. Swift's letter at this time is extraordinarily cold. It may be that he was really in conflict at keeping her bound to him so and really wanted to be fair. She was probably an essential part of his balance.

At the time of Swift's mother's death, when he was forty-three (1710), he was at the height of political influence in England. He savored this often with arrogance, sometimes with revenge. He was often generous, surrounded by friends, and very active. There seemed a peculiar stamp to many of his relationships. If he was interested at all, he ran the risk of a kind of possessive identification which demanded that the other person should be a reflection of himself. When this could not be tolerated or when his great sensitivity caused him to be hurt, he became either openly bitter and vengeful, or saved himself by a kind of annihilation of the other by an utter disregard or a sweeping aversion. Stella was his most steadfast shadow; she would certainly have had too much strength for that had she not been so persistently shaped by him in his own image. It is likely, too, that she believed profoundly in his genius, and so could consecrate her life to it.

In 1710, too, Swift began his famous *Journal to Stella,* a series of letters always frequent and sometimes daily, which continued for three years. This *Journal* is fascinating, for side by side with his account of his political and literary achievements are chronicles of his complaints and illnesses, together with barely decipherable personal communications written in a kind of baby-talk pig Latin with many abbreviations, known to Swift and Stella as the "little language" (30).

It was in 1710 also that the third goddess and the second Hester emerged clearly on the scene; the woman who was to be known as Vanessa. Swift developed a friendship in England with the Van Homrigh family, a widow with four children, the oldest of whom was Hester. Her husband had been Lord Mayor of Dublin, and Swift had met the widow and her children on the boat between Ireland and England two years before. Now he was living close to them in London and a considerable intimacy developed. Mrs. Van Homrigh was a hospitable woman used to entertaining, and Swift was soon at home in the household. As in the case of Mrs. Johnson and her daughter Hester, he corresponded with mother and daughter alike at first. The new Hester was about seven years younger than Stella. It is interesting that Swift frequently carelessly misstated the ages of the two Hesters, making them two to three years younger than they were. (This corresponds to the age difference between himself and his sister Jane.) While Hester Van Homrigh was older than Stella had been when Swift first met her and was more worldly, she was as direct and as intolerant of deception as he had trained Stella to be—and as little concerned with the conventional feminine interests of the day. Swift jotted notes of his frequent meetings with the Van Homrighs in his *Journal to Stella,* and the mother's name appeared more than a hundred times to the three times that he mentioned the daughter. Swift once wrote to Hester Van Homrigh's (Vanessa's) cousin, Mrs. Anne Long, about her in such terms that it provoked the protest that he sounded as though he were describing a hermaphrodite. Vanessa was said actually to resemble Swift in features. She was not as docile a woman as Stella, and a more developed one. Further, Vanessa was older at the time of the loss of her father than Stella had been under comparable conditions. Swift, nonetheless, found it necessary to instruct her in letter writing and to select her reading for her. It would seem he was again playing the nurse tutor as he had with Stella, and as he had himself been taught in his early childhood. Stella sensed his interest and became mildly jealous.

But the situation could not be stopped there. Stella's protection of Swift had failed, through a period of absence. It is probable that there was a craving for something personally more exciting in connection with his stirring political life—now among the Tories—than could be satisfied through the "little language" letters to Stella, no matter how endearing they were. Stella was definitely more reliable; Vanessa more animated, witty, and not always compliant. While Vanessa showed reverence for Swift's genius, she also fell in love with him, not in baby talk alone, but as a woman falls in love with a man; a state which became increasingly distressing to them both, and infuriating to Swift to an extent that must have turned him to coldness and to destroy her. He kept up visits and correspondence with the two young women, one in Ireland and the other in England, sometimes apparently with amazingly similar expressions. He besought them both to behave as young men, and often treated them like children. To Vanessa he wrote endearingly as "brat" and to Stella as "agreeable bitch." He kept the brat and the bitch apart as long as possible. In what is left of the correspondence between Swift and Vanessa, a pitiable proportion of her letters is devoted to her urgency to see and hear from him, and her disappointment at his frequently broken promises. His infrequent statements of feeling for her, other than placations, were obviously treasured by her. Toward the end, they were followed by seeming coldness and flight in him. It was Vanessa who elicited from him some kind of a passionate response, which he felt the need to describe in a way half-revealing and almost concealing in his famous poem *Cadenus and Vanessa*.

The exact nature of the relationship between Swift and Vanessa will probably always be obscure, shaped by the subjective interpretative slant of each new student of the situation. It is clear, however, that there was an exciting quality to his contact with Vanessa, quite lacking in the protectiveness of Stella. Vanessa had spilled coffee in the fireplace on an early occasion of their acquaintance. As they knew each other better, they frequently drank coffee together, and this became some symbol and secret language between them. There are frequent references to coffee drinking in their letters in a way which has the appearance of a lover's joke, indicating probably some special intimacy, if not a full consummation. The greatest doubts that such occurred arise from the failure of such an experience to be reflected in Swift's writings and other behavior. Ten years after they had first met and eleven months before Vanessa's death, at a time when she was distraught and needed comforting, Swift wrote her, urging her to get herself a horse and travel among her neighbors, exacting reverence by her natural superiority. This was his cure, like walking for low spirits and other lesser ailments. He added then: "The best maxim I know in life is to drink your coffee when you can, and when you cannot, to be easy without it . . . . This much I sympathize with you, that I am not cheerful enough to write, for, I believe, coffee once a week is necessary for that . . . . I have shifted scenes oftener than I ever did in my life and I believe, have lain in thirty beds since I left the town; and always drew up the clothes with my left hand, which is a superstition which I learnt these ten years." Ten years was the period of his friendship with her. It would seem again that there was some harking back to an early playfulness between them, something private and intimate, which he would revive in thought to solace her. But Vanessa seemed at this time to be beyond the reach of such dubious comfort and her next letter was sadder than ever.[13]

13 "I have worn out my days in sighing, and my nights with watching and thinking of --, --, --, --, --- --- --, who thinks not of me." Vanessa's letter from Celbridge, 1728 (31).

But in the early years of their relationship Swift had been active in political affairs—Tory—in London, and engaged in the writing of political pamphlets, one of which, *The Conduct of the Allies,* was so successful that it was credited with ending the war between France and England. He was not uniformly popular, however, for he offended many, and sometimes fell into disfavor. He might then retire in temporary discouragement or inertia and go away for a time. Stella had been able to tolerate these withdrawals without open complaint, but Vanessa time and again annoyed him with her solicitude and he punished her by turning away. In June, 1713 he became Dean of St. Patrick's Cathedral in Dublin, but characteristically remained there only three months before his first return to England. And so the eternal oscillation continued. Now Vanessa committed the folly of visiting him unexpectedly in his retreat. He scolded her sadly and instructed her further in discretion and secrecy.[14] Poor Swift! He tried so hard to escape from love, but could not quite succeed.

Swift suffered greatly at this time from the decline of the Tory power and his own consequent unpopularity. But even among the Tories his prestige and power had waned, and

[14] A poem to Love in Swift's handwriting was found in Vanessa's desk after her death.

> In all I wish, how happy I should be
> Thou great deluder, were it not for thee!
> So weak art thou, that fools thy power despise
> And yet so strong, thou triumph'st o'er the wise
> Thy traps are laid with such peculiar art,
> They catch the cautious, let the rash depart,
> But too much thinking brings us to thy snare
> Where, held by thee, in slavery we stay,
> And throw the pleasing part of life away.
> But, what does most imagination move,
> Discretion! thou wer't ne'er a friend to love.
>
> But the poor nymph, who feels her vitals burn
> And from her shepherd can find no return
> Laments, and rages at the power divine
> When, curst Discretion, all the fault was thine [32]

there was no opportunity to rebuild it. He could not well bear this atmosphere of disapproval and began to be personally grouchy as well. He began to complain of being old, and to consider epitaphs. The appointment as Dean of St. Patrick's, not originally to his liking, offered a new field to his energies, however, and he began to ally himself with Ireland and the Irish people more than he had ever done before. At this point, unfortunately, Vanessa came to Dublin: the two women of his life whom he had affectionately called his brat and his bitch, were now but a short distance apart. Vanessa had come with her younger sister Mary, ostensibly to retire to the Irish estate left by her father, and doubtless to be closer to Swift. The relationship between them began to have a desperate tantalizing quality. He behaved sometimes in a placating way, often dwelling on the past with sentimental tenderness, and treated her with what Scott (33) was to call "cruelty under the mask of mercy." She complained that he "kept her in a languishing death." His feeling for her had not died, but his loyalty and obligation were to Stella, and the division of feelings between the two women must have produced an incessant struggle within him, which was reflected in his attitude toward Vanessa. She was to suffer so extremely because he had long schooled himself to suppress and deny passionate love. Now he could no longer do so, and was attempting fiercely to re-establish his defenses. When she was in trouble, she appealed to him and he replied with compassionate words, but delayed seeing her. He even twitted her with behaving as though she were in love. He was not a man who could bear it to see illness or suffering, or hear first-hand complaints. From such an appeal he had a terrible need to escape. Finally overcome with her own urgency, she wrote a tragically appealing letter which threw him into rage and panic, seemingly because it was delivered indiscreetly on an evening when he had guests and when it might compromise him by increasing the "nasty tattle" of the town. So he wrote her admonishingly.

There is a gap in the correspondence between Swift and Vanessa in the years between 1713 to 1718. He seems to have destroyed most of the letters from both women after 1713; and in Vanessa's neatly numbered packet of letters from him, there was only one to represent this period. The famous *Journal to Stella* had comprised the years 1710 to 1713. It is possible that being caught in this personal fix, this great man who was not courageous in personal relationships and had an almost morbid fear of gossip, began to destroy the evidence; or more likely that he devoted himself largely to Stella and attempted to dissolve the affair with Vanessa through starving it.

At any rate, during this interval some event occurred which gave rise to later stories, never clearly established, but perpetuated by word of mouth and then incorporated as official biography, that Swift had married Stella. There is no direct documentary evidence to indicate that a marriage actually occurred. It was said that there was a proviso that they should continue to live as before. Stella's demand for such a marriage, and Swift's willingness to acquiesce, are understandable enough as part of the growing tension of the triangular relationship. The interpretation of the situation has varied according to the attitude of the biographers, among whom Sir Leslie Stephen is probably the most impartial in considering that the fact (of marriage) was never either proved or disproved. The rumor concerning its occurrence was apparently commonly reported throughout Swift's life and was believed by his intimate friends Delaney and the elder Sheridan, as well as by Mrs. Whiteway, who cared for him as he began to decline. On the other hand, it was denied by Dr. Lyon, who was one of his guardians when he became incompetent, and was repeatedly denied by Mrs. Dingley, Mrs. Brent (his housekeeper), and by the executors of Stella's will (34).[15] Our present concern must be, however, primarily with the significance of this story and all the doubts and reaffirmations in regard to it, rather than focusing only on the question of whether a formal marriage ceremony was accomplished.

The marriage is reported to have occurred in 1716, in the Deanery garden in Dublin. Stella was ill and jealous, having learned of her rival's presence in Ireland. Accounts of the event reputedly come from two clergymen, friends of Swift, and of the Bishop of Clogher who was supposed to have been the officiating churchman. It was later said that when the marriage ceremony was to have been performed, someone revealed that Swift and Stella were actually brother and sister, both being the natural children of Sir William Temple. The occurrence of any near marriage even was denied by those close to Swift and Stella, namely Swift's housekeeper, Stella's nurse Dingley and Stella's executor. But this in itself is no proof. The actual facts of the situation can never be unequivocally known. That the rumors represent some sort of fantasy—with what grains of truth?—is obvious, but again like the stories of Swift's birth, it is not clear from whom they originated. One may well conclude that in either situation there were at least the hazy and implied doubts due to a thoroughly ambiguous and contradictory set of conditions, springing from Swift's own conflicting attitudes. One may further ask whether it is conceivable that these fantasies sprang in some way from Swift himself, representing an older

[15] Stella signed her will "Esther Johnson, Spinster." It is argued by some, e.g., Craik (35), that this was not significant and was only part of the pact of secrecy; by others, e.g., the recent psychologically minded biographer, Evelyn Hardy, that Esther Johnson was very unlikely to compromise in this way. Quintana puts the matter succinctly from the angle of ordinary reason: "Despite all that has been brought forward in proof of the marriage, it is significant that none has ever suggested a really plausible motive for it. Both Swift and Stella lived with superb pride by the code of rational conduct. If they broke this code to participate in a secret ceremony that had no significance, the explanation must be sought not in the realm of reason but of nonsense" (36).

longing of his own, and were advanced or hinted at by him in a way to block the marriage and attempt to keep the situation in a state of permanent compromise. It is not out of harmony with the peculiar facts of Swift's life and temperament.[16]

Eleven years after the "marriage," Swift was again writing to a young woman to prepare her for marriage, part of his ecclesiastic duty probably, and stressing the need for a rational love and an intellectual companionship. The girl, like several predecessors, was named Elizabeth. Always there was the emphasis on cleanliness, discretion (by which he meant secrecy), and avoidance of gossip; and, importantly, he warned the girl not to be sentimental, or rapturous, or to taunt a man about his physical deformity, or his lack of family fortunes. Of love itself or spirituality, Swift said nothing; all should be purely reasonable.

In 1718, when Stella was thirty-eight, Swift addressed his annual birthday poem to her as though she were thirty-four, as follows:

[16] This question of the marriage seems to have a very wide appeal, and much of the interest in the provocative mystery and contradictions of Swift's nature becomes condensed on this never solved riddle. It is probably this, rather than merely malicious love of gossip, which incites people to take sides overly strongly as to whether the marriage did or did not occur. Mr. Denis Johnston, who has written a play concerning the subject, offers another version: that Swift was the son of Sir John Temple, father of Sir William. It can be definitely proved that it was impossible for Sir William to have fathered Jonathan, as he was in another part of the world at the time. Johnston cites the facts that investigation of the transcriptions of the elder Jonathan showed that they had become increasingly unsteady to the point of practical illegibility for some months before his death. He was a considerable drinker, and was ill as well. It is unlikely, says Johnston, that he was in a state to beget a child. On the other hand, it can be shown that Sir John Temple was often in Dublin during the infancies of Jane and Jonathan Swift. Sir John was sixty-seven at the time that the younger Jonathan Swift was born, certainly a marginal though not impossible age for fatherhood. Objectively there does not seem much biological choice between the aging Sir John and the alcoholic Jonathan Swift Sr. This explanation of Johnston's is not impossible, but it only puts the external facts in a different arrangement and does not appreciably alter the inner constellation.

Stella this day is thirty-four,
(We don't dispute a year or more)
However, Stella, be not troubled
Although thy size and years are doubled
Since first I saw thee at sixteen
The brightest virgin on the green,
So little is thy form declined
Made up so largely in thy Mind.
Oh, would it please the Gods to split
Thy Beauty, Size and Years and Wit
No Age could furnish out a Pair
Of Nymphs so graceful, wise and fair
With half the Lustre of your Eyes
With half thy Art, thy Years and Size;
And then before it grew too late,
How should I beg of gentle Fate
(That either Nymph might have her Swain),
To split my worship too in twain [37].

It is not a poem that would please many women. It is curious and noteworthy that Swift, already in a dilemma between two women, now fantasies compounding his dilemma by figuratively splitting the first woman in two. Two months later he is writing in a comparable vein, but in French, to Vanessa. He did seem indeed to be troubled with an emotional diplopia.

Though Swift destroyed most of Vanessa's letters, she made some rough drafts which she kept. From these one can read her growing disillusionment with Swift, who continually besought her to be sincere and was himself so indirect. At first masked in humor, her increasing resentment gradually showed through; and Swift developed a disinclination to open letters. Stella wrote a poem on *Jealousy* and Swift reproved her for hot-headedness and reproached her for quarreling. His own self-concealment increased. He wrote Vanessa under another name or less frequently, and sometimes reprovingly like an immaculate priest. Her struggle with her tumultuous passions and his varying averseness are movingly apparent in her letters. She too had an idolatry of Swift, but there was more fire at her shrine than at Stella's. She was a keen observer, showed some talent in her writing, and while she struggled with her increasing hatred, she was not generally vindictive nor malicious toward Swift, or toward Stella. When she wrote Swift of the approaching death of her sister Mary or Mollkin, of whom the Dean had seemed to be fond, he advised her not unkindly to get her friends about her, adding "I want comfort in this case and can give little"; and so he stayed away. Yet he was not really so completely callous. One feels rather that he could rarely be called upon for personal help, though he gave it often when there was no personal claim involved; nor could he stand it to be confronted with suffering. Then he too often felt worse himself and stayed away, plagued by anxiety, concern, and perhaps guilt which he could not admit, preferring to consider the suffering of the others as largely "unhappy imagination." He was definitely more considerate of Stella and concerned for her health throughout the greater part of their friendship than was true with anyone else. Stella was more truly a part of himself.

Vanessa died in 1723 at thirty-six. One story was that some time earlier she had heard of Swift's supposed marriage to Stella and had written Stella to ask the truth. Some say that Stella gave the cryptic answer "Yes" and then turned the letter over to Swift, who went in a rage to Vanessa's home, threw down the letter and withdrew, without a word. This cannot be verified. One can only say it is somehow a "valid" rumor, representing a Swiftian sort of annihilation. At any rate, the last months of her life were filled with the anguish of lonely bitterness and increasing illness, probably from tuberculosis. Some indication of her resentfulness is evidenced in her changing her will and revoking one in which

51

she had left what she had to Swift; and probably with a final mixture of vindictiveness and self-justification, she directed her executors to publish Swift's letters to her and the famous poem, *Cadenus and Vanessa* (38), which he had written to her early in their friendship. Thus she refused to be swept away unnoticed. The executors were friends of Swift's, closer to him than to Vanessa, and surprised at being called to officiate for her. On hearing of her death, Swift found it necessary to hasten a southern trip which he had planned for some years. Now he left on the following day. He stayed away for four months, traveling on horseback and among strangers, seeking "companionship among those of least consequence and most compliance," and sleeping, according to his own account, eighteen out of twenty-four hours. Here again it would seem he did not feel consciousness of grief or guilt, but a strangely strong counteraction of it in impersonal "compliances" and anger at the poor conditions of the countryside. Such a sleep is frequently the sleep which promotes deep repression to the point of denial. He rode five hundred miles on horseback, probably too a way of avoiding the feeling which he feared so much, even as earlier he had spent his tension first in physical exercise, in walking, then in crossing back and forth between Ireland and England. He could not go to England now because of his prohibitive unpopularity there. No wonder, then, that he developed "vapors and vertigo" and could not spend himself in his habitual letter writing.

True to the pattern of his earlier life, Swift climbed out of this silent despondency by becoming again politically active in a noble cause. Perhaps he restored his self-esteem in this way. What he could not do for Vanessa, who had been closer to him in an emotional way than anyone else, even including Stella—whose closeness was tempered by great rationality, reflective of his ideal of himself—he did for the suffering people of Ireland. During 1724 he wrote a series of letters, under the name of M. B. Drapier, befriending the Irish because of the coinage of half-pence, the right to which the King had unjustly granted as a favor to a relative of his mistress, even though this irresponsible act might ruin the Irish trade. The force of his satire caused the abrogation of this act. His popularity in Ireland then rose to new heights. He recovered his self-esteem, and presently was testing his personal power by a practical joke, which incidentally belittled the people who admired him, and so in a peculiarly hidden way hit back at himself. When a crowd gathered to watch an eclipse, Swift sent out word that the eclipse had been postponed. The crowd instantly dispersed.

Two years later, he completed *Gulliver's Travels* which he had begun before Vanessa's death. From then on, as long as he was able, he remained the protector of Irish interests. It seems probable that Swift thought much about *Gulliver's Travels* but especially of the Fourth (last) Voyage, while he was on the journey of masked mourning. He had had the main ideas for the *Travels* for a long time, and had already accomplished much of the writing, but the Fourth Voyage is only scantily mentioned in the earlier drafts. The significance of this Voyage will be presently discussed.

On the whole, Swift seems to have been both esteemed and feared by men contemporaries. His great wit and his keen intellect won him social recognition, and his periodic forays into politics brought admiration. Often his friendships did not remain unbroken, not only because they were intertwined with his political activities and shifting allegiances, but perhaps also because of his possessiveness, and the effect of the interplay of his personal charm and the fierceness of his pursuit of a cause, once he had espoused it. He was also tenaciously revengeful of personal slights, and did not take criticism easily. In 1705, Addison wrote of Swift as "the most agreeable companion, the truest friend, and the greatest genius of his age." These remarks were written on the flyleaf of a presentation copy of one of Addison's own books, to be sure, but represent nonetheless a considerable enthusiasm. There was one man, Charles Ford, however, with whom Swift maintained a relationship of confidence and friendship, unequaled by anyone else, through many years. The full extent of this friendship was probably not recognized by the earlier biographers, who scarcely mention Ford. Much of the correspondence between the two men did not come to light until 1896.[17] Rarely can a person endure emotional stresses such as Swift experienced without some trusted confidante. Stella served in this way for some time until the feminine side of her nature involved her inevitably in the tragic struggle with Vanessa. Ford became the constant, reliable and not too demanding friend, and was surely an emotional bulwark.

Charles Ford was born in 1681 and was thus fourteen years younger than Swift, or almost exactly the same age as Stella. The family lived in Dublin until the father in 1698 bought an estate not very distant from Laracor. Swift probably came to know him in 1707, about the time that Ford obtained his Master's degree, and was about to marry a young woman, Dorothy Maper, and the marriage agreement was drawn up. For what reason the marriage failed to take place is nowhere indicated. Their correspondence began in 1708 when Swift was forty-one and Ford was twenty-six. The latter seems to have been gay and intelligent, and had recently succeeded to the country estate which he occupied while his mother remained in the Dublin house. The relationship between the two men developed in confidence and always remained cordial. Ford began to spend time in London, sometimes overlapping with the times Swift was there. Swift obviously found he could relax with the younger man, and in his *Journal to Stella* wrote of Ford as an "easy companion always ready for what I please, when I am weary of Ministers" (40). Ford

[17] See Introduction to *Letters of Jonathan Swift to Charles Ford* (39).

had no regular profession or occupation, was a good scholar, and described as joyous, but was never profound. One sees between the lines of the letters to Stella and to Ford that Swift tended to absorb him as he did Stella, one or the other copying Swift's pamphlets for him and doing various errands and chores.[18] Stella and Dingley stayed at Ford's country estate, Wood Park, for some months after Vanessa's death, while Swift was away on his southern journey. Swift, on the other hand, introduced Ford to the prominent political and social lights of the day and in due time had Ford made official Gazetteer, a post which may not have been entirely suited to Ford or appreciated by him. Swift was also rather didactic about Ford's letters, telling him when they had approached that degree of near-perfection to make them worthy of becoming memoirs. From about 1714 to 1718 Ford was much on the continent; and later, somewhat patronizing toward Dublin, he established his residence in London except for brief summer holidays in Ireland. Ford later practically abandoned Wood Park, which he finally sold, and in the way of neglected Irish houses, it subsequently fell apart and has now disappeared. Although Ford lived less and less in Ireland, and Swift came to feel exiled there, the two men remained friends. Ford never married, and his ambitions were not such as to make him in any sense a rival.

No matter how difficult Swift's balance had been between the two Hesters, as soon as one was gone, he began to decline. He was about sixty, terribly afraid of aging, and he became increasingly frugal and parsimonious. He spent time with Ford, and then with Sheridan (grandfather of the playwright), a charmingly improvident man, whose crazy house-

18 Swift went to such lengths to preserve the anonymity of his writings until after their publication, that he had his manuscripts copied by someone else, lest his handwriting might be recognized. He then had the manuscript deposited at the publisher's at night, by someone else. Charles Ford sometimes performed this service of dropping the manuscript (41). (This too has the suggestion of a symbolic meaning, repetitive of the unusual conditions of Swift's birth.)

hold lent itself to a kind of friendly raillery from Swift. It might seem extraordinary that the overly cleanly man could visit his dilapidated but gentle friend so long, for the place was described as ill-kept, dirty, and almost in shambles. This letdown did seem, indeed, to mark the beginning of Swift's deterioration, which continued with slow progression. Here in 1725, he revised *Gulliver's Travels,* and likened his friend's place to the abominable country of the Yahoos. Twice more he went to England, now definitely seeking reforms for Ireland, and was again disappointed and raging.

Gulliver's Travels, published in 1726, won Swift a renewal and increase in fame. Soon his poem, *Cadenus and Vanessa,* was also published, probably by Vanessa's directions to the executors of her will. Swift's reaction is variously described. Some accounts say that, consulted about this in advance, he was inclined to deny his feeling for Vanessa in the statement that the poem had resulted only from frolic and merriment among ladies; and that printing could not make it more common than it was. If this is true, he again cast off something, once seemingly precious to him, as though it were waste material. The poem itself, well worth reading, was written early in their friendship and revised seemingly after a passionately declared expectation from Vanessa, which Swift felt the need to record, leaving the full nature of his response in doubt. Other accounts are that Swift seemed really unaware that the poem cast any discredit upon him (42), and was also blind to what its publication might do to Stella.

He inveighed further about the need for secrecy and discretion. Yet there was in his tacit permission to publish the poem a complete obtuseness to what this would do to Stella. He could have stopped it and made no definite effort to do so. Even so did he betray how bound in himself he was, and unable to give a man's love to a woman. The situation was the more poignant in that the poem was more nearly a love poem, and was at least the narrating of a passion, hinting at sexual intimacy, more than had been the case with Stella. Since the poem became the subject of interest and speculation generally, Stella was fated to overhear some discussion of it, by people who did not know her identity. When the unwary ones remarked that Vanessa must have been an unusual woman to have inspired Swift to this extent, Stella replied that the Dean could write finely concerning a broomstick! (43)

Stella began to fail in health, and Swift, when away from her, began to speak of her in the past almost as though she were already dead, and to bemoan that he had invested any affection in anyone. He was quite aware of his distaste for seeing Stella ill, as he wrote quite clearly to Sheridan, and characteristically, too, was glad that he himself felt ill "for it would have been a reproach to me to be in perfect health when such a friend was desperate" (44). He did gather up some initiative and return to Ireland, stay for a while, and then was off again to England. The terrible meanness of his neurotic fear became apparent in his almost obsessional caution that Stella might die in the Deanery. This is somehow related to his anger at Vanessa for sending the troubled letter which arrived inopportunely when he had guests. It was part of his absorption in himself and his strong system of self-defense by denial of feeling. But this time he did not entirely walk out of the situation, only dallied long enough to increase his frenzy when he finally did set out for Ireland. Stella was forty-seven when she died, on January 28, 1727. He was with her almost till she died; yet the end came while he was entertaining guests at dinner. He could not bear to attend the funeral, but sat in the next room in the church, writing his account of her while the service went on.

His touchiness increased and his resentment, if he was not shown the honor that he merited. But he wrote a sermon *On the Difficulty of Knowing One's Self*. He incessantly reviled the body, especially the body of a woman, as disgusting, resented children as dirty nuisances who cluttered up the world, and again, under the strange guise of a savage attack upon the conditions of poverty in Ireland, wrote one of the fiercest satirical essays known, entitled *A Modest Proposal for Preventing Children of Poor People being a Burden to their Parents,* in which he suggested that infants of impoverished parents be roasted and served at the tables of the wealthy. He wrote both fair and filthy verse, became pugnacious in espousing the causes of the suffering, paid a pension to Dingley and to his own sister, whom he did not wish to see, devoted himself to the foolish and improvident Sheridan, and took on the minor problems of many people who had little or no claim upon him.

By 1730, both Stella and Vanessa were dead. Ford was definitely settled in London, and by 1732 had put up his Dublin property for sale. But Swift remained in Ireland. It is said that he never saw Ford after 1730, although they continued to correspond for three more years, during which the Dean was repeatedly concerned for Ford's health. At various times, Swift uttered again a phrase with which he seemed to delude himself throughout the years: that life is not worth holding on to, but that health is, and he sermonized to Ford about earning one's health the way laborers work for bread, again enjoining Ford to take walks regularly. Another decade found the two friends communicating seldom, but still on good terms. Ford was the greatest exemption from Swift's talent for quarreling. Both were failing, Ford having taken to regular drinking and a succession of mistresses; and Swift suffering from outbursts of rage and a progressive failure of memory. By 1742, Swift's decline was such that it was necessary to examine his mental competency. It is reported that before his capacity to think had become quite clouded, he would look at himself in a pier glass and mutter, "Poor old man, poor old man," and again, as though childishly philosophizing to himself, repeated "I am what I am; I am what I am" (45). At one period he was silent for as much as a year. He died at seventy-eight in Dublin, on October 19, 1745. He left his fortune of £12,000 to found a hospital for fools and madmen.[19] Vanessa's fortune, by contrast, had been left to George Berkeley, to whom she was unknown, to be of aid in establishing a college in the Bermudas (46).

[19] Swift had forecast the reactions to his own death in a poem written before arteriosclerotic senility had rendered him helpless: From

The Death of Dr. Swift
He gave the little wealth he had
To build a house for fools and mad
And showed by one satiric touch
No nation needed it so much.
That Kingdom he hath left his debtor
I wish it soon may have a better.

St. Patrick's Hospital, still called "Swift's Hospital," was opened in 1757.

2.

GULLIVER AND SWIFT

Gulliver's Travels is generally considered Swift's masterpiece. It is said to have been written largely in a period of four years, 1721-1725, and was published in 1726. These were years of paramount importance in Swift's personal life. Vanessa had died in 1723; and he had reacted with wandering and sleeping excessively, such a sleep as indicates a need for denial and deep repression. Just how much of the *Travels* had been written or thought out at this time is unclear. The narrative had certainly been forecast much earlier. It is to be expected under any circumstances that some imprint of Swift's own emotional struggle will be found in this, his greatest literary creation. But with his capacity to turn away from his conflicts and to recover balance through particularly strong inner defensive maneuvers, it was inevitable that Swift's tale of himself should appear in a thoroughly disguised and symbolic form. How much he wrote of himself was hidden probably even from his own awareness. It is likely that the latter part of the *Travels*, the Fourth and most terrifying Voyage, was elaborated after Vanessa's death, in June, 1723.

A fairly definite idea of the period of Swift's writing the *Travels* is contained in his letters to Charles Ford, none of which were published until 1896. Apparently he wrote consistently and intimately to Ford. A letter of April 1721 announced that he had begun the *Travels* and planned to pub-

lish them in a larger volume—a statement which certainly
suggests that he had had them well in mind before this (1).
In January, 1724 he wrote accusingly to Ford, who was in
France, and who had told Bolingbroke of Swift's essay on the
Brobdingnags and on the Yahoos (or at least Swift thought
that Ford had done so). He wrote:

> Else how should he [Bolingbroke] know anything of
> Stella and the Horses? 'T is hard that folks in France
> will not let us in Ireland be quiet. I would have him
> and you know that I hate Yahoos of both sexes, and
> that Stella and Madame de Villette are only tolerable
> at best, for want of Houyhnhnms. My greatest want
> here is of somebody qualified to censure and correct
> what I write . . . I have left the country of Horses,
> and am in the Flying Island where I shall not stay
> long, and my two last Journyes will soon be over [2].

The date of this, early in 1724, certainly suggests that Swift
may have been preoccupied with the *Travels* during or immediately after his return from his horseback journey following Vanessa's death, a period at least part of which
Stella spent with Dingley at Ford's estate. Successive letters
to Ford in 1724 repeated the charge that Ford had betrayed
him to Bolingbroke. In April, 1724, he wrote that he would
soon finish the *Travels;* in August, 1725, he reported that he
had finished them and described them as "admirable things,
and will wonderfully mend the world" (3). From the sequence of letters, it seems that their writing also helped to
mend Jonathan Swift.

The book is manifestly an adventure story, burlesquing the
reports of world explorations at a time when new areas of
this strange world were being opened up, and the explorer
was a romantic storyteller, a conqueror and a chronicler of
anthropological mysteries. It was also an era in which other
writers, e.g., Defoe, used this form as an allegorical medium.

Perhaps in these particular aspects *Gulliver's Travels* might be compared to the better comic science fiction of today. But the *Travels* have endured as a fairy-tale classic as well, and obviously their universal appeal must be based on their closeness to profound and unconscious problems of mankind. In addition, they contain bold satirical attacks upon political and governmental policies of the day, and students of history point out sly darts of ridicule directed at certain individuals whom Swift honored with a particular contempt. It is clearly not their specific historical political significance, however, which has made an appeal to children.

The *Travels consist* of Four Voyages: the First to Lilliput, the land of the little people; the Second to Brobdingnag, the land of the giants; the Third to five places, Laputa, Balnibarbi, Glubbdubdrib, Luggnagg, and Japan; and the Fourth, final Journey to the strangest land of all, that of the Houyhnhnms. Lemuel Gulliver, the traveler, was a young man of Nottinghamshire, the third among five sons and recently apprenticed to a surgeon, Mr. James Bates. But he had always an interest in travel and prepared himself, in addition to his medical training, by studying navigation, mathematics, and two years of physics at Leyden. His master, Bates, then recommended him as a ship's surgeon on the Swallow,[1] where he served for three years on voyages to the Levant. Later, again under the influence of Bates, he undertook to settle in London and practice his profession. Accordingly he married Mrs. Mary Burton, second daughter of a hosier, who brought him a modest dowry. But his good master, Bates, dying within two years, left Lemuel with few friends, a fast failing business, and a strong conscience which did not permit him to imitate the bad practice of others of his profession. He went back to sea and started his maritime career which was to last for more than fifteen years. He sailed on

[1] Swift liked to pun on the names Swift, Martin, and Swallow, all being birds.

the Antelope, leaving Bristol in May, 1699 and returned from his Fourth and last Voyage arriving at his home on December 5, 1715.

It is interesting and fitting to compare the lives of Lemuel Gulliver and Jonathan Swift, his creator, both as to sequences of events and the occurrences at specific dates in the two lives. Gulliver was a few years older than Swift. Unlike Gulliver, Swift never traveled far, though he several times planned to; but he was a constant voyager between Ireland and England, sometimes dividing the year between the two countries. Swift was a clergyman, preoccupied with the ills of his own body and the political ills of the state, but could hardly bear to consider the bodies of others. Gulliver was a surgeon's apprentice, who went on to explore the topography of foreign lands and peoples. Gulliver went to Cambridge at fourteen, the age at which Swift entered Trinity. While Gulliver was being apprenticed to his master Bates, Swift at a corresponding time was working for his Master's degree. Both left their native soil at the age of twenty-one, Gulliver going to Leyden to prepare for travel, and Swift to England to find his mother. At twenty-seven, Gulliver married and attempted to settle down in London. At the same age, Swift was wishing to marry Jane Waring and settle into the life of a clergyman. Both men lost their benefactors, Mr. Bates and Sir William Temple respectively, at the age of thirty-two. Gulliver then returned to the sea, and Swift to the Church. The year 1699, in which Gulliver set out on his first recorded voyage, was a landmark in the life of Swift, being the time of Sir William Temple's death, of Swift's final rupture with Jane Waring, and of the marriage of Jane Swift. The date, December, 1715, of Gulliver's return from his last voyage in a state in which he abhorred his wife, was only a few months before Swift's supposed marriage to Stella.[2]

[2] There are certainly four sets of time comparisons which may be condensed in the *Travels*. (a) The ages at which similar or contrasting events

If one may summarize the qualities and contents in the Voyages very briefly, it can be pointed out that the first two are much concerned with relative body size. In the First, Gulliver is the giant in the land of tiny folk; in the Second, he is comparatively tiny in the land of the giants. In the Third Voyage, changes of size, but especially the movement of inanimate objects in a land of abstract geometric fantasies not subject to reality testing, are striking elements. The land of the Fourth Voyage is inhabited by ideal creatures and foul creatures, and the interrelations between these and their relation to the *Travels* comprise the climax of the tales.

The Voyage to the Lilliputians, the best known of the *Travels*, extended from May, 1699 to April, 1702. Heading for the East Indies, the ship was wrecked by storms in November, 1699, and Gulliver alone was saved. He dragged himself ashore on a strange island and fell asleep. On awakening, he found himself pinioned by a lacing of ropes fastened to pegs driven into the ground. He soon found he was in a land of tiny people, who thus sought to restrain him and hold him down. They first attacked him, then brought him to a temple which had been profaned by the murder of a man.[3] Here he was placed in full view of the populace, tethered by a chain to make escape impossible. Thus he found it difficult to achieve excretory relief inoffensively. In panic he defecated once indoors within the temple, but later went into the open air for this purpose.[4] He explains all this

---

occurred in the lives of the two men. (b) A similar comparison as to specific dates, e.g., 1699, 1702, 1715, etc. (c) The conditions of Swift's life at the time of his writing different parts of his fantasy travels. (d) The correlation of the sequence and quality of events in the *Travels*, with certain events in the infant years of Jonathan Swift. In understanding the unconscious revelations of the *Travels*, one must utilize these and other principles of understanding dreams.

[3] The association of involuntary guilt and unknown murder is striking.

[4] The meticulous accounts of the toilet facilities and unavoidable emergencies during the *Travels* remind us strongly of the dilemmas of a child who is straining to be good by performing his toilet functions in the right

in detail, and remarks with a Swiftian preoccupation with cleanliness: "I would not have dwelt so long upon a circumstance that perhaps, at first sight, may appear not very momentous, if I had not thought it necessary to justify my character in point of cleanliness to the world, which I am told some of my maligners have been pleased upon this and other occasions to call into question." (Involuntary moral guilt and unavoidable physical dirtiness are clearly associated.)

There are several general motifs in the tale of Gulliver's life among the Lilliputians. The most pervasive one is the problem of disparity in size between Gulliver and the Lilliputians. The latter are afraid that Gulliver, now called the Man Mountain, will impoverish them with his need for food and the expense of his clothing.[5] He in turn pretends that he may eat up some of the little folk himself. Finally accepting the burden and responsibility of his care, they set out to train him in their language and ways. Thus they tentatively adopt him. Most conspicuous of all, however, is the effect of awe or offensiveness to the Lilliputians, of Gulliver's mountainous body. He sneezes and creates a tornado; his urination produces a torrent of "noise and violence"; his defecation causes a national health problem. He brandishes his sword, and the sunlight on the blade causes them to kneel down in blinded awe. When he shoots his pistol in the air, a hundred men fall down as though struck dead.

---

place and at the right time, but at the same time getting a secret satisfaction through irregularities of performance.

[5] It may be recalled that at the time of his birth, Swift's family was greatly impoverished, and the problem of how to feed and clothe the new infant was a drastic one. The question of the dire distress caused by the needs of growing children in poor families is violently portrayed in Swift's satire entitled *A Modest Proposal for Preventing the Children of Poor People being a Burden to their Parents.* In this he suggests that the expense of caring for a child up to the age of one year (the age at which Swift was kidnapped) might not be prohibitive, especially as the child might eat at the mother's body during this period, being nursed; but that at this age children might then be sold and roasted, to be served at the tables of the rich.

The mutual sport between Gulliver and the Lilliputians is interesting. Threads, ropes, and cords are important in their games. Not only is there the opening incident of Gulliver finding himself bound, but he is later to find that feats of tightrope walking and exhibitions of rope dancing are required for great employments and high favors at court. In other games, colored cords or threads are the prizes given for skill in jumping over hurdles held by the Emperor. The ropes were of different color, and were worn around the waists of the recipients, indicating different degrees of distinction, like colored ribbons of merit in an exhibition or race. Gulliver, in his turn, staked out a small parade ground or arena for the exercise of the King's cavalry, and played with the horsemen much like a child playing with toy soldiers.[6]

The interest in, awe at, and revulsion from the human body is played actively and passively between Gulliver and his tiny hosts. While Gulliver watched the games, antics and movements of the Lilliputians, they in turn were repeatedly impressed with his body structure and primitive functions. So with a reversal of the toy cavalry game situation, the Emperor directed Gulliver to stand like a Colossus with his legs apart, while the soldiers paraded through the arch thus formed. To the soldiers, the Emperor issued orders to "observe the strictest decency" with regard to Gulliver's person, but this did not prevent the younger ones from looking heavenward as they passed under him, and the state of his breeches was such that the sight "afforded opportunities for

---

[6] Horses obviously had a special significance to Swift, as well as to Gulliver. There is the story of the nag purchased by Swift at too great expense during his Dublin student days. Further, King William, who came to know Swift at Sir William Temple's, was impressed with the young man's horsemanship and offered him a post in the cavalry. Swift rode horseback when troubled. It should be remembered that he probably wrote the last of the *Travels,* in which the horse is the noble or idealized creature, while he was on a prolonged horseback journey begun on the day following Vanessa's death, or soon thereafter.

laughter and admiration." Further, in a kind of treaty between the Emperor and Gulliver, it was agreed among other
things that Gulliver should survey the Island of the Lilliputians by means of a computation of his paces around its
border. They in turn guaranteed him food equal to that con-
sumed by 1728 Lilliputians, this figure being arrived at by
their computations of his body size. Under the terms of the
treaty, Gulliver was permitted to visit the capital city. This,
too, was a mutual sight-seeing expedition in which the populace gathered to view the Man Mountain and he showed
ingenuity in getting his oversized eye to the window of the
Emperor's private apartment. Since this was an authorized
peeping, the Empress threw him a kiss.

Presently the problem of relative size appears in other
guises, as Gulliver learns that the country has for a long time
tended to split into factions. Currently a struggle was going
on between the conservative High-Heels and the progressive
Low-Heels. While the Emperor appointed only Low-Heels
in his administration, it was observed that the Emperor himself had heels of uneven height which caused him to hobble
and brought disturbance into his cabinet. As a background
to such struggles, there was a low-grade chronic warfare
between Lilliput and the neighboring country of Blefuscu,
concerning whether an egg should be opened at the large
or the small end in preparation for eating. This had assumed
the quality of a religious war. The Big Endians, having suffered persecution and massacre and the outlawing of their
books, found refuge and help among the Blefuscudians. Now
the Lilliputians sought Gulliver's aid. Here again he played
the benevolent oversized child-god, manipulating the
enemy's fleet, but in such a way as not to destroy it. He
simply waded into the channel, fastened a cord to each
Blefuscudian ship and hooked it to a long crossbar big
enough to be the lead for the entire fleet. Then cutting the

individual anchor cables, he could draw the entire fleet after him like a child dragging a number of toys.[7]

With a Swiftian passion for fairness, however, Gulliver did not permit his services to the Lilliputian Emperor to be exploited for the destruction of the Blefuscudians. At this point he had, because of his great size, a chance to do a further service to the Lilliputian monarch. This was by the adaptive use of the most primitive and impressive function at his disposal. Thus the royal household was saved from complete destruction by fire when Gulliver, having been well dined and especially wined by the Blefuscudians, found himself, in the heat of the fire, to be the generator of extraordinary urinary pressure, and by the adroit use and direction of this heightened ability, he put out the fire in three minutes. Although urinating within the palace grounds was ordinarily a capital offense, naturally under these conditions of emergency use, this behavior would be expected to bring praise and congratulations. Yet the Empress reacted with such horror (and envy?) that she vowed revenge.

Certain customs and value scales among the Lilliputians are described by Gulliver, especially the emphasis on morals rather than ability. The system of education was founded on the principle that parents begot children purely from drives of biological instinct. Consequently children were considered to owe their parents nothing, and the parents to be ill chosen to educate their children. The educational system[8] provided schools of different ranks, which were also separate for the two sexes. Boys were brought up by men, with older women performing only the most menial tasks. Parents might visit for two hours throughout the year, but must give no indica-

---

[7] This appears as another variation of the fish screen memory of Swift, amplified to the hat story of Gulliver.

[8] Surely all this is a satirical attack on Swift's own early life, a statement of his separation from his parents, the emphasis on being good rather than on his ability in his personal training, and his ever-present need to deny the difference between the sexes.

tion of endearment. At no time might the boys converse with any servant. Girls were educated after the fashion of boys, only by their own sex. They were, however, schooled "to despise all personal ornaments beyond decency and cleanliness." No difference was permitted to exist in the training of the two sexes, under the maxim that a wife "should always be a reasonable and agreeable Companion, because she cannot always be young." These communal training centers were supported by levies upon the parents, for the Lilliputians considered nothing so unjust as people who would bring children into the world and leave the burden of supporting them on the public. In this highly moral country, however, Gulliver found himself about to be impeached, since the court people were afraid of his abilities. He escaped then to Blefuscu, and from there sailed homewards.

The Second Voyage was undertaken (June, 1702) within two months after Gulliver had returned from the First. Again the ship was diverted from its course by storms, and after a complete year of wandering (no account is given of the drain upon the provisions), the entire crew landed on a new continent. Here, separating himself from the others, the better to view the lay of the land, Gulliver found himself permanently separated from them, as they had swum back to their boat and returned to the ship, after being frightened by a monstrous creature found wading in the water. Thus Gulliver finds the tables exactly turned, with a reversal of the situation in which he so recently waded into the channel himself and gathered up the entire fleet. Indeed he finds that he is now a tiny person in the land of giants, fears being trampled under foot, cut by their scythes, or even eaten up by them. This is the land of Brobdingnag.[9] Here the contact

[9] It is interesting here that the initial "L" of Lilliput also is the first letter of "little," and "B" the initial of Brobdingnag, begins "big." More will be said later regarding Swift's peculiar relation to words; neologisms with repetitive syllables, rhyming, punning, the "little language" of the *Journal to Stella,* and the dash language of the letters to Vanessa.

with children, nurses, and small animals (large in this land of oversized creatures) played a much greater part than had been true in Lilliput, and the fear of being eaten or mistreated by them is a recurrent theme. The appearance of the nurse as an important figure is also significant. Two types of nurses appear: the revolting adult nurse who bared her dry nipple to quiet the baby offering him suck and, in doing so, reminded Gulliver of how the Lilliputians had found his skin revolting with its monstrous pores and stumps of hairs; and the little girl nurse who protected him and taught him the language[10] and called him "mannikin." The impression of the revolting breast was later reinforced by the sight of a woman with a cancerous breast where the holes were so great that Gulliver could have hidden in any one of them.

When Gulliver suffered a passive exhibition, being shown as a curio at county fairs, his young nurse carried him in a kind of doll cage dangling from a cord around her waist. He was taken to the Royal Court, purchased by the Queen, and scientifically examined by the King and the wise men, one of whom at first considered him a clockwork toy, then suggested that he might be an embryo[11] or an abortion; and finally decided he was a *lusus naturae*, a sport or freak of nature, although Gulliver protested that he came from a country in which he was a standard product. Particularly difficult in this monstrous country was the behavior of the oversize insects who left unpleasant trails upon his food or carried it away with them.

Ultimately, too, the Queen prepared for him a secure small closet in which he might ride on horseback strapped to the

10 The juxtaposition in the text, of the recurrent fear of being eaten, with the revolting sight of the nurse's breast suckling the infant, followed by the emergence of the little girl nurse who taught Gulliver the language, seems significant.

11 The order of the narrative has been faithfully reproduced in this summary. Any analyst will see the implied preoccupation with pregnancy, an erection, the comparison of penis and breast, the fear and revulsion from the female genitals culminating in extreme castration fear.

belt of the rider, or in a sedan, upon the lap of the child nurse who remained with him. In this manner he traveled on sight-seeing tours over the country, being himself also the object of much curiosity even as had been true in Lilliput. Interestingly enough, however, he was unimpressed by the tallest steeple tower in the land, and computed its height to be relatively less than that of Salisbury steeple in England. Gulliver also found himself in situations of extraordinary mutual exposure with the Maids of Honor, to whose apartments he was taken by his child nurse. Here they stripped themselves and him, and held him close to their bodies until he could scarcely endure the smell, though this too forced him to recall that the Lilliputians had sometimes complained of his body smell. These maids certainly used him for their own erotic amusement, one of them setting him astride her nipple—which completely disgusted and horrified him, as did their copious urination.[12] In the next paragraph we have the report of how he was prevailed upon to witness the execution by beheading of a murderer, in such a manner that the blood spurted prodigiously.

Two incidents following this are also of some import: the Queen provided Gulliver with a small pleasure boat especially fitted to his size, and ordered the building of a trough filled with water, in which the boat might be propelled, sometimes by oars, and sometimes by the breeze from the ladies' fans, thus giving pleasure to both himself and them.[13] A further indication of this unexpected relationship to one of the ladies, governess to his nurse, is given in an anecdote as follows: This lady lifted him up to place him in the boat, but he slipped through her fingers and plunged downward, his fall being stopped by a corking-pin that stuck in the gentlewoman's stomacher, the head of the pin passing be-

[12] There is the suggestion of a reversal of the sexes.
[13] Cf. the symbolism of "the man in the boat" (clitoris). This would suggest the identification with the female phallus or clitoris, which has been thought to be characteristic of the male transvestite (4).

tween his skin and the waistband of his breeches. He was thus suspended in the air, more or less attached to the governess, until he was rescued by his little nurse. At another time he was attacked in the trough by an odious frog which deposited slime on him while hopping over him.

During this period in Brobdingnag, Gulliver suffered three near kidnappings, all by animals. First a dog took him in his mouth and carried him to his master, the gardener, who returned him to his little girl nurse. A little later, a kite hovering over the garden swooped down and would have carried him away, had he not saved himself by running under an espalier. Finally, some time later a monkey came chattering to his box home and, after spying him from every angle, reached in and grabbed him out. Holding him "as a nurse does a child she is about to suckle"[14] and "squeezed . . . so hard that [it was] more prudent to submit." The monkey is described as a male monkey who probably took Gulliver for a young monkey, and being startled, ran out of the palace and to the roof of an adjoining one, where he sat on the ridgepole, holding Gulliver with one hand while he crammed food into him with the other, squeezing the food out from a bag on one side of his chaps. Finally the monkey became frightened by pursuers and let Gulliver drop upon the ridge tile until he was rescued by a young boy, footman to the child nurse. Gulliver was so sickened by the stuff which had been put into his mouth by the evil monkey, that the dear little nurse had to pick it out with a needle. When the King later chaffed him about this, Gulliver was forced to see how really diminutive a figure he was in the land of these giant people, and how much even his misfortunes became a matter of diversion among the Big Ones. Finally, in an effort to be impressive despite his minute stature, he gave the King an account of English laws and customs, but found to his dismay

[14] It is to be recalled that Swift was actually kidnapped by his nurse at the age of one year.

that the King had only become convinced of the ignorance, idleness, and vice prevailing in England, and hoped that the traveler had profited by being so much away from his own country. Gulliver felt extremely badly about this, and explained that he had really tried most artfully to elude the King's careful questioning and make his answers as favorable as possible.

In a final effort to convince the King of the glories and the power of England, Gulliver told him of the invention of gun powder and how it might be used, offering to him the secret of its composition. But the monarch, horrified by the proposal, replied that "he was amazed how so impotent and groveling an Insect . . . could entertain such inhuman Ideas" and appear so unmoved by them. In spite of the shortsightedness of this view, it was to appear that the country was not without its own impressive show of might, and that the members of the militia, spread out in a field twenty miles square, would on command all brandish their swords at once, producing an effect of ten thousand flashes of lightning in the sky. (A reversal, certainly, of Gulliver's situation with the Lilliputians.) Gulliver ultimately found that even this isolated country had suffered from "the same disease to which the whole race of mankind is subject: the nobility often contending for power, the people for liberty, and the King for absolute dominion."

The traveler, having been about two years in the land of Brobdingnag, began to wish to return home, especially as the King was eager to find him a mate his own size with whom he might found a family. Unable to bear the thought of propagating a race so diminutive that it would inevitably be laughable, he sought to escape. In this he had the unexpected co-operation of an eagle, which swooped down upon his box house while the pages had wandered away, and kidnapped him in it, carrying it by the ring that was fastened to its top. After approximately two hours of flight, the bird, being chased by other eagles, dropped the box into the sea where it was tossed about by the waves until it was sighted and taken aboard an English vessel, on which Gulliver returned to England, not before the sailing captain had questioned him carefully to see whether he had committed some great crime for which he was being cast away to perish at sea. This return voyage took exactly nine months.[15] On board the ship and for some time after his return home, Gulliver suffered from a kind of sensory unreality feeling, due to the discrepancy between the sensory impressions of those around him and those giants with whom he had lived for two years. He thought his wife and children had starved because they were so small, and at first thought he was back in the land of Lilliput. He had arrived home early in June, 1706. His residence was at Redriff.[16]

While the First Voyage had been undertaken for economic gain, the Second one was frankly because of Gulliver's "insatiable desire of seeing foreign countries," and was begun only two months after the return from the First. At this time he left his wife, his son Johnny and his daughter Betty, then of school age, and embarked on a vessel called the Adventure.[17] Gulliver opens his account of his Second Voyage, that to Brobdingnag, with the statement that he was "condemned by nature and fortune to an active and restless life." When

[15] The symbolism of the enclosure in a box cast in the water for nine months, before being taken onto land, is strongly suggestive of a rebirth fantasy; while the position of this in the entire account of the travels and its being accomplished by a kidnapping, is suggestive of its representing the return to Ireland, which is now fused with the original flight from Ireland.

[16] Cf. this with Whitehaven, the town in which Swift lived with the nurse.

[17] It is worth noting that one account of the nurse's flight with Swift to England (his first voyage) was that it was for economic gain, when his own mother was under extreme financial pressure, and that this attitude was repeated by Swift when he "abducted" Stella, with a nurse, to Ireland, where her legacy would go farther. Even Vanessa's return to Ireland was rationally motivated by the claiming of an estate and the dream of greater economic freedom.

Gulliver returned from his Second Voyage, he was confused, due in large measure to the difficulty in focusing his vision and accommodating to the idea of being the same size as other people. His wife was concerned about him and begged him never again to return to the sea. But "she had not the power to hinder" him and in ten days he was again under the influence of the "thirst . . . of seeing the world" and was negotiating with the Captain of the Hopewell, planning a voyage to the East Indies.

Consequently, on August 5, 1706, Gulliver set out on this Third Journey. Only a few days out at sea, the ship was attacked by Dutch and Japanese pirates in two ships. He spoke so imprudently to them that they cast him adrift in a canoe. This led to his discovery of a peculiar, exactly circular island up in the air, which was suspended over the body of a continent. The island, which rested on a lodestone so delicately balanced that a little child's hand could manipulate it, could be moved at will "to raise or sink or put it in progressive motion" by the inhabitants. This was the Island of Laputa, and might be described as the Island of Abstract Fantasy without Reality Testing.[18] The movement of the Island, directed by the King, depended much upon mathematics and music. Ideas were often expressed in geometrical figures, although there was great contempt for practical geometry. Even the meat was cut in geometrical shapes rather than according to the principles of anatomical structure. The Laputians were chronically anxious and fearful of total destruction of the earth, the planets, and everything. The Island was also a place of peculiar marital relations. Here Gulliver stayed a month or more, feeling greatly neglected because the Laputians, being so absorbed in their geometry, paid him scant attention. The women, however,

[18] This Voyage, which is probably the least known of any of the *Travels,* can probably be well understood in its sequence in the series. The unconscious meaning of this will be discussed later in the interpretation of the *Travels* as related to Swift's own life and character.

were mostly unsatisfied and restless, a condition which Gulliver likened to that of England.

Through the intervention of the stupidest man on the Island, Gulliver succeeded in getting away to the adjacent continent of Balnibarbi, with a metropolis called Lagado, and a kindly, lordly host, Munodi, who gave the traveler an apartment in his own house. The continent of Balnibarbi had at one time been a substantial and rather noble place, but in the past forty years it had been greatly affected by its local citizens' visits to the Island of Laputa, from which they returned with smatterings of mathematics and "volatile spirits acquired in that airy region." They had attempted to put these exquisite abstractions into practice, but had not completed their projects, and consequently left the country in waste and the people impoverished. It seems to have been a country of energetic promoters of abstractions. Here in the Grand Academy, a kind of Institute of Scientific Exhibits, one man was engaged in extracting sunbeams from cucumbers; another was engaged in an operation to reduce human excrement to its original food; another had written on the malleability of fire. A mixer of paint determined his color choice by feeling and smelling.[19] A physician cured colic by pumping the bowel full of wind which, when released, brought the noxious out with it. On another side of the Academy were projectors in speculative learning. Here there was a machine for the indiscriminate mixing and grinding of words with which to produce books in philosophy, poetry, politics, law, theology, and mathematics. In another place there was a scheme for abolishing words altogether, which was considered an advantage in health, for each word uttered was held to be a diminution of the lungs by corrosion and conse-

[19] These illustrations suggest synesthesias or substitutions of one sense for another, such as one finds in certain psychotic or severely neurotic states. It is closely related to a condition of prolongation of the polymorphous-perverse state of early infancy.

quently might shorten life.[20] Thus it was considered advisable to supplant words by the *things* which they symbolized, which must then be carried by each person. Only the women rebelled and insisted on using their tongues. Further, a kind of lobotomy[21] was practiced as well, but with the advantage of an interchange between individuals, of the amputated lobes. In this progressive country, Gulliver recommended a department made up of spies, informers, discoverers, accusers, witnesses, etc. Here it would be first agreed what suspected persons should be accused of, then all care was taken to procure all their papers and letters and to put the criminals in chains. The anagrammatic method was used in evaluating the evidence.

This country made Gulliver homesick for England. He seemed convinced that this Kingdom really might extend to America and to the land of California. He decided to go further to the Island of Luggnagg, but on his way had an involuntary stopover of a month, and went to the tiny Island of Glubbdubdrib, inhabited by sorcerers and magicians. The servants here were all ghosts, called up for a single stretch of twenty-four-hour duty, once every three months; but they might be dismissed into thin air by a twitch of the Governor's finger. Here fantasy could be readily and magically converted into reality. In his ten days' stay, Gulliver materialized as serviceable ghosts many illustrious people such as Alexander the Great, Hannibal, Caesar, Pompey, and others (incidentally, all men), as well as unmasking the villainy and wretched foulness of many of the supposed great.[22]

The next stop was Luggnagg, where he arrived on April

[20] The equating of speech to other body discharges and essentially the fear of depletion through seminal losses is strongly indicated here.

[21] These descriptions are too close to satirical attacks on cybernetics, semantics, symbolic realization, and the various lobotomizing techniques of today, not to give the present reader a feeling of somewhat eerie familiarity.

[22] Is this some vision of recalling and overcoming the dead father?

21, 1709. There a _man_ interpreter helped Gulliver[23] who was then informed he might proceed to the King, where he could lick the dust before the royal footstool. Although this performance of a ritual was made antiseptic in honor of the visiting traveler, it was ordinarily a way of his majesty's dealing with his enemies. In the consummation of the ritual, the visitor was directed to say certain strange words signifying "My tongue is in the mouth of my friend."

After three months, Gulliver's lust for travel gave way to a desire to see his wife and children. Before he left, however, he was introduced to a strange group of immortals, the Struldbruggs, special variant creatures, human but not subject to death, distinguishable by a peculiar circular mark over one eye. To his disappointment, he found that these people lived like mortals till the age of thirty, then became increasingly dejected until they were eighty. But instead of then fading gracefully, they became opinionated, covetous, morose: envy and impotent desires supplanting affection until they sank into unending senility. The King wished to send a few Struldbruggs with Gulliver to arm the people of England against the fear of death. The traveler left Luggnagg in May, 1709, for Japan where he stayed but briefly and returned thence to his native England, arriving on April 16, 1710.[24]

In August, 1710, having remained at home four to five months and his wife being already well advanced in another pregnancy, Gulliver decided to go, not as a surgeon, but as Captain—again of the Adventure. After some months of sail-

---

[23] This is in contrast to his having previously been nursed and taught by girls, women, queens, and princesses.

[24] This was approximately the date of the death of Swift's mother. It is interesting that the Fourth and the most terrible Voyage is placed in time as beginning August 10, four months after his return. Gulliver reported that he left his wife big with her pregnancy. Swift probably wrote or planned much of the Fourth Voyage during the four months in which he wandered on horseback after Vanessa's death. Thus death is followed by birth, even as it was in Swift's own infancy.

ing under adverse conditions, the sailors mutinied, held their captain prisoner, and deposited him abruptly in a desolate land inhabited by strangely evil and by noble creatures. The former were dirty, hairy, nightmarish animals that scampered about and climbed trees, persecuting and tormenting the traveler by letting excrement drop upon his head. In contrast to these were the reasonable, gentle horses who were the natural aristocrats of the land. Soon he was taken in charge by a pair of them who taught him much of the language and gave him a home. From them he learned that the dirty creatures were called Yahoos and the horses were Houyhnhnms. From the way in which the various Houyhnhnms looked at his face and hands, he observed that they considered him some sort of special Yahoo, although they marveled at his cleanliness, his teachableness, and his civility, as these qualities were opposite to the character of the Yahoos.

At one time they discovered him at night when his clothing had slipped off, uncovering especially the lower part of his body. Now they were sure he was a Yahoo, as earlier his clothing had caused them to think him at least somewhat different. However, a complete examination of Gulliver's body convinced the Houyhnhnms that he was really a very perfect Yahoo, distinguished by his fine white skin, a characterization which did not entirely please Gulliver, and aroused him to protest against it. His subsequent attempts to explain to his benefactors the nature of the customs and laws of the country from which he came only verified their impression of his Yahoo origin. They considered that in some respects he was even at a disadvantage, compared with the hardier Yahoos of their own country. However, after a year's residence in the country of the Houyhnhnms, Gulliver resolved not to return to human-kind. The master Houyhnhnm explained that *"the Yahoos were known to hate one another more than they did any different species of animals; and the reason usually assigned was the odiousness of their own shapes, which all could see in the rest but none in themselves.*" The greediness and lack of discrimination in their appetites was truly appalling. The sexuality of the Yahoos was aggressively foul, as was their system of medicine, the sick depending for cure on the eating of the body excreta. Gulliver himself, attempting to study the Yahoos, confirmed their unteachability but attributed it interestingly enough to a perverse, restive disposition rather than to inherent defect.[25]

After Gulliver had been in the country three years, he became convinced of his own indubitable Yahoo origin when a Yahoo girl of eleven fell in love with him when she saw him bathing, and was so energetic in her embraces that he had to be rescued by his sorrel nag.

In contrast to this Yahoo passion, the Houyhnhnms were governed entirely by reasonable justice and friendliness, educating their own offspring out of reasonableness rather than love, and showing no preference for their own young over those of their neighbors. The number of offspring was also equably determined and couples remained together only until the required number of young was produced, but during the period of the marriage the relationship was one of mutual friendship and benevolence, which was, however, no greater for the mate than for all others of the species. It was noteworthy that the Houyhnhnms trained their youths by exercising them in running up and down hills,[26] and in competitive races.

It is thus apparent that in this land the Houyhnhnms embodied completely equable reason and impersonal good will, while the Yahoos were the creatures of primordial hate and passion. The Houyhnhnms showed minuteness and exactness in descriptions, and a justness of similes in their poetry that

[25] In this they certainly resembled the young Jonathan Swift of uncertain teachability at Kilkenny and Trinity.

[26] Compare Swift's habit of training himself, and his recommendations of exercise almost as a panacea.

was truly remarkable. Further, when they died, which came about through the passage of time resulting in painless decay, and not as the result of disease, there was no mourning or show of emotion, and the dead person was said to have "retired to his first mother." Before this reasonable departure from earth, the dying ones called upon all their friends, meticulously repaying past visits.

Gulliver, having been forced, by the behavior of the Yahoo girl, to recognize his own Yahoo identity, settled down to stay in this extraordinary country, hating himself more than any ordinary Yahoo, contrary to the fashion among them, and meanwhile taking on, by a kind of primary emulation, the speech, behavior and attitudes of the noble Houyhnhnms. But after he had been there five years, he found his stay terminated by the decision of the Houyhnhnms' General Council, many of whom feared him as a special and potentially most dangerous Yahoo. He was therefore forced to leave, and aided by his constant benefactor built a boat in which he got away. He was ultimately picked up by a Portuguese vessel whose captain regarded the exiled Gulliver as a man quite out of his mind, especially when he heard the traveler's account of his experiences. Gulliver was then only desirous of retiring to a solitary island to spend the rest of his days, but the captain prevailed upon him to return to his wife and children. Still under the influence of the noble and reasonable Houyhnhnm ideals, Gulliver could not bear the thought that he had cohabited with a Yahoo and even produced Yahoo children. Indeed, he recoiled from the affection of his wife, and so odious an animal did he feel her to be that he fell in a swoon, and it was more than a year before he could tolerate so much as to eat in the same room with her her and the children. Never afterward could he tolerate their drinking from the same cup with him, or allow them to touch his hand. He perpetuated the memory of the reasonable Houyhnhnms by the purchase of a pair of horses which, with their groom, became his favorites and lived in amiable friend-

81

ship with him; the smell of their stable invariably reviving his sagging spirits.

No account of *Gulliver's Travels* in relation to the life of Swift would be reasonably complete without a reference to the forecast of the *Travels* which was written as early as 1711-1714. At this time Swift, together with Pope, Gay, Oxford, Parnell and Arbuthnot, formed a club, first called the Tory Club, later the Scriblerus Club, whose members planned to write in collaboration a comprehensive satire on the abuses of learning (5).[27] In these writings Scriblerus, who is frankly identified as Swift, reveals certain fantasies concerning his birth, his grandiose ideas, and his attitude towards his own genius. Swift projects the *Travels* (later given to Gulliver) as the *Secession of Martinus Scriblerus* and outlines quite clearly the Four Voyages in a way that indicates he has definitely in mind the First Voyage to the land of the pygmies, the Second to the giants, the Third to the land of the philosophers and mathematicians (which at this time are conceived of as beneficial), and the Fourth, in which there is a "vein of melancholy proceeding almost to a Disgust of his Species." At this time, too, he forecast his cannibalistic scheme for relieving the conditions of the poor, which was not to be actually written until 1729.

[27] Memoirs of Scriblerus in *Satires and Personal Writings by Jonathan Swift*. Edited and Introduction by William A. Eddy.

While these memoirs of Scriblerus were the result of collaboration, certain sections and perhaps the major part were written by Swift. A further condensed and more satirical version of the memoirs was found among Swift's notes and seems to have been prepared by him or by someone who knew his manuscripts. These were entitled *Memoirs of the Life of Scriblerus* and were never reprinted until the Oxford Edition (1932) of Swift's *Satires and Personal Writings*. In this second form, Scriblerus' name is changed from Martin to Tim. In this version too, Swift makes great fun of himself and his own literary genius and productions. In both of the Scriblerian memoirs, Swift makes it very clear, in manifold ways, that Scriblerus is himself. The other collaborators also accepted Swift as Scriblerus. As early as 1711, Oxford nicknamed Swift "Dr. Martin," justifying this on the basis that a martin was a swallow, and a swallow was a swift. Scriblerus and Gulliver alike started on their travels in 1699, Gulliver having previously spent three years aboard the Swallow as Ship's Surgeon.

3.

THE CLINICAL PICTURE

Swift was essentially a homeless child. Born fatherless, in considerable poverty, so that his mother was incessantly preoccupied with consolidating her meager resources, he probably never had as much attention from her as a frail, fatherless child needed. The story of Abigail Swift is ambiguous indeed, and her reported attitude about his kidnapping and return to her, her leaving for England so soon thereafter, her long absence from him—all these may have resulted from dire necessity, but are contrary to the usual strong protectiveness which a mother feels in an immediate way toward her young child. These events do not harmonize with the accounts of her character, nor entirely with the relationship which grew up between her and her son later in life. They constitute the greatest evidence, thinly circumstantial though it is, that there was something (more than is clearly known) askew and hidden about the circumstances of his birth. It is conceivable that it was nothing more than the gossip inevitable to the posthumous birth of a child to a long-ailing father. Except indirectly, in cursing his birth, and in the one autobiographical bit which he wrote, Jonathan Swift made almost no references to his father, a condition the more surprising in that fatherless or motherless children are peculiarly prone to cherish aggrandizing fantasies of the lost parent. Nor was Swift particularly partial to his Uncle Godwin, who certainly made some effort to provide for him and placed him in the best school in Ireland.

The character and circumstances of the kidnapping nurse

who cared for him during the formative years, from one to four or so, must have been extremely important in molding the beginning of personality in this little boy.[1] From the age of one until his manhood, he was not in contact with any member of his immediate family, and from the age of six, he had but little family life of any kind. Nor was he ever able to establish this for himself in his adulthood. We can guess that the nurse valued him highly and that she expressed this in teaching and training him carefully. But at best a kidnapper is in a pathological relationship to the kidnapped child, and the situation is one of mystery-breeding fantasy in the child himself and in those around him. Thus before he was five, Swift had two mysteries: that of his paternity due to his being posthumous, and the other, of parenthood in general, attendant upon the kidnapping. If he was warmly and demonstratively loved during this early period in England, it did not light a sufficiently enduring warmth in him to counteract the bitterness and sense of deprivation from his long years of subsequent institutionalization. One may surmise that however devoted the nurse was to the baby in her care, she did not fondle and caress him in the bodily way which every infant needs, but rather emphasized good behavior and cultivated his intellect. For the child developed precociously both in the purely intellectual sphere and in the premature strength of his sense of reality, threatened though this was in a broad way by the mysteries which surrounded him. The man Swift could take care of himself, was not afraid in the world, and had an unusual keenness in perceiving foibles and detecting incongruities. He might retire from the world in stubborn anger and in jealousy, but he was not shy, except in regard to the body. He was body-preoccupied always, afraid of illness, and confused about sex. His continued infantile longing was apparent through the years in his "little language" to Stella,

[1] This idea is also developed in Evelyn Hardy's life of Swift (1).

though with her there was the ever-present protection against intimate body contact.

He spent his school days in a boys' school, and his adolescence and young manhood in a college for boys. His vacations may have been spent among the eighteen children in Uncle Godwin's household, but this must have been close to an institutional life also. He was mostly in contact with his own sex and mentions no girl cousins, though they probably existed. It is most likely that he knew of and daydreamed about the sister from whom he was separated. His childhood was peculiarly lop-sided, devoid of rich personal contacts, but with unique circumstances such as would make him feel a special, mysterious, perhaps distinguished but unfavored son.

Who was the prototype of Stella, the eight-year-old child whom he tutored, abducted, adopted and attempted to turn into a lesser image of himself? Or of the little girl nurse of nine years who befriended Gulliver so amiably? Or of the Yahoo maiden of eleven, who fell in love with Gulliver on his Fourth Voyage, and in so doing, brought him into a knowledge of his own origins? His sexual longing broke through with Varina—only to be severely checked following his disappointment. With Vanessa too—but unwillingly. He treated his sexuality as something to be fought against and crushed if possible, and seemed to feel it as a danger. He did not similarly suppress other appetites and impulses. Uncommonly fond of food and drink, he was a sociable man and a great diner-out, and he was certainly in no sense an ascetic. An exaggerated pleasure in dirt and excreta, most evident in his humor, in his attacks on others, and in his attitude toward the female body, existed side by side with the opposite characteristic, an extreme and almost fanatical cleanliness. Particularly in writing he let his language become foul and his similes became coprophiliac, even when he was inveighing against these qualities in others.

Perhaps one of the most interesting problems in Swift's life was the special relation between his sexual and his aggressive drives. There seems little indication that there was any experiencing of a full sexual relationship for Swift, and certainly no development of any rich love life with a woman. He distorted Stella to serve as a defense against just such a possibility, so that she became a kind of solid intermediate figure, neither predominantly male nor female: she never lost many of her womanly qualities, but had no fulfillment, and was trained to a kind of pseudo masculinization, which would comfort and reassure Swift by her mirroring of him in a nondemanding way. With Vanessa, this was not possible, although he came to her when he had already tried to shut himself off completely from this kind of passion in life. But he was not entirely successful in his emotional self-immolation, with the result that he tortured them both. The self-realization which was denied him through his failure with women, he sought instead from the satisfaction of power, and the acclaim or at least the responsiveness of the group. Time and time again, when he was wounded by some personal failure of relationship, he would emerge, after a period of angry retirement, to find himself again through support of some righteous battle. If he could not be a lover, he could become, at least temporarily, a hero! But this substitution of fame for love is a dangerous business: lacking the gratifying enrichment and check of personal mutuality, fame tends more and more to increase the scope of its requirements, in a sense feeding upon itself and creating exaggerated rewards and commensurate sensitivities.

It is clear from Swift's writing that he suffered a peculiar fascination with and horror of women's bodies, likening their sexual organs to the lower bowel and seeing them always as dangerously contaminating and yet in some way enticing. This is certainly not an uncommon impression, arising from the peculiarly confused anatomical observations and logic of early childhood. But in Swift's life there was very little opportunity for correction either in this specific respect, or in a greater general ease and familiarity with girls and women which most boys experience in their family relationships, or in other contacts of later childhood. In the special type of his withdrawal from women, he denied himself further some of the tenderest experiences of life, those with children. It appears that starting with no father, he forever craved one. But, perhaps out of the very intensity of his demands, was unable to find a sufficient relationship with any man who might have filled this role for him. Sir William Temple came nearest to fulfilling a father ideal, but Swift's very emotional hunger probably caused him so to magnify slights that he turned away in bitterness. There was some reconciliation, but it could not be what he had hoped. When Temple died, he wrote, "He died at one o'clock this morning, the 27th of January 1698-'99 and with him all that was good and amiable among men." Swift could not find a father, and neither could he become one.

In addition to the fairy-tale appeal of *Gulliver's Travels* which is so wide, Swift is best known for his humor, mostly satirical in nature. This is apparent in the *Travels* and characteristic of much of his other writing. He is virulent in his attack, and fierce in his reduction by ridicule. His uncommonly sharp eye for that which was hypocritical, inconsistent and unsound, and his facility with words could render his opponent vividly ridiculous in short order. This also pervaded his practical joking, in which he showed a rare slapstick finesse, with an incomparable combination of subtlety and shocking broadside.

4.

AN INTERPRETATION

Swift had problems of identity and of identification which were inherent in the strangeness of his birth, with his father dying almost as he was conceived. They were increased by the relative personal isolation of his childhood, and again reflected in the stories of his declining years when with senility already engulfing him, he showed an interest in his mirrored image and remarked, whether in renunciation or self-definition, "Poor old man!" and "I am what I am. I am what I am." In addition to the strangeness of his birth, the kidnapping made complications for his settling in the gradual way of most children the problem: "This is I. My name is such and such. I live here with my mama and papa." Then just at the most vulnerable epoch of a child's life, the oedipal period, he was returned to his mother in a different country, only to have her disappear again in a few months. The security of continuity of relationship, whether to people or to surroundings, was not his by Fate. Rather he was the center of a Family Romance,[1] determined by reality, which might otherwise have remained only a powerful fantasy.

His position throughout childhood was always somewhat anomalous, both in school and in his uncle's family; he was not quite a first-class member of the family. At twenty-one he

[1] The Family Romance is a term used for the frequent childhood fantasy that the child is not born of his own parents, but has been adopted, and is really a waif or a kidnapped baby, whether of high or low origin.

visited his mother and at twenty-two he took a position, not clearly defined, in the household of Sir William Temple. It must have been rather difficult for this young man, who had never lived regularly in a family to find himself in this large and varied menage, kind and considerate though the Temples were. Twenty-two is hardly the optimum time to be initiated into family relationships and young Swift had many difficulties; although he remained with the Temples off and on for ten years, he can hardly be said to have been thoroughly at home there. It could not make up for the vacuoles in his early life.

It is to be expected further from the peculiar circumstances of his first years that Swift would have grave distortions of his oedipal development and of his castration complex. These clinical results which we could predict from the barest events of his life are indeed borne out by his character, his writings, and the course of the later life which he carved out for himself.

Swift's physical health and physical symptoms are worthy of notice. It was said by some that he was a premature, frail infant; but these are general statements and not clearly documented. The mother's struggle with poverty was definite, however. She was not superhuman, and we must conclude that there was some disturbance in her relationship to the infant whose birth so complicated her fortunes; but in just what direction is unclear.

That there was a two-mother situation between the own mother and the nurse is also apparent from the basic facts. That there was a two-father situation in rumor and in fantasy was indicated by the reports of illegitimacy running parallel with remarks that the father never knew of the son's conception. One would surmise that the question of paternity might well have been raised and was to reappear forty-eight years later in the never-solved mystery of Swift's alleged marriage, reputedly interrupted by someone revealing that Swift and

Stella were brother and sister, both the natural children of Sir William Temple. Nowhere is there any evidence, nor does any one of the Swift biographers support the idea that there is real truth in this story. Indeed, it can be proved from historically established facts that Sir William Temple was in another part of the world at the time of the conception of Jonathan Swift. That the Temples, both Sir John Temple and his son Sir William, knew the Swifts and that Sir John was often in Dublin and was instrumental in getting the elder Jonathan Swift an appointment as Steward at the King's Inn is also clearly established. This correction to the story does not, however, dispose of it in its entirety. Even if it is the gossip incident to the peculiar life constellation and character of Jonathan Swift and the outcome of the human weakness for malicious speculation and drama, still its occurrence and even more its persistence has some significance, which cannot be thoroughly abolished by objective correction. It is not clear who is supposed to have made the revelations, though the guess was hazarded that it was Rebecca Dingley. The important aspect of the situation would seem to be that the the story was probably known to Swift in one form or another. In other words, it either sprang from his fantasy primarily or so corresponded to his latent fantasy that he made no apparent effort to investigate or refute it. This matter of the Family Romance and the way in which it fits into Swift's symptomatology will be taken up again later.

In the *Memoirs of Scriblerus,* Swift brings out more play of fantasy about birth than is true in his biography of *Gulliver.* In both Scriblerus accounts (1), the parents had difficulty in begetting a child. In one instance, the pregnancy with Martin was preceded by an abortion of a female child; in both, they had to resort to magic aid. Once the sorceress advised that if the father took seven sheets of paper and wrote upon each with seven alphabets of seven languages, in such a way that no one letter stood twice in the same posture, then clipped all the letters apart and put them in a pillow which would be used by the helpful wife to support her in a certain position, pregnancy would follow. This fantasy might indicate an ironic suggestion of origin from magic thought and/or from perverse relations.

Both *Scriblerus Memoirs* report that on the eve of giving birth, the mother had a dream that she had given birth to a monstrous thing like an inkpot which spirted black liquid in many rivulets throughout the room. The sorceress interpreted this dream to mean that the "innumerable streams are the types or symbols of [the infant's] Genius, and the Extent of it; by them are signifiy'd the great Variety of Productions in human Learning, that will render him the Admiration and Surprize of all the Universe; as to the Spout, it betokens the Sex, and that it will be a Son." When the infant was born, he especially enjoyed the rattling of paper, and dabbling in ink. Later the nurse announced joyfully that the baby had said "Papa," but the father soon determined that the word really was "paper." Thus was launched the child who was to be the Genius of the Age.

To return to the matter of Swift's early health, when physical comfort so strongly interplays with emotional development—there is little knowledge of the period immediately after birth, except the implication that his health was not generally good, as it was reported that when Abigail Swift discovered the whereabouts of her kidnapped son, she sent word that he should not be returned until he was well enough to bear the strain of travel better. But *when* this is supposed to have occurred is obscure, and our chief source of information is Swift's own scant account which puts as good a face on everything as possible. He gave no account of illness in his boyhood. Yet by his late adolescence or early manhood he had instituted ritualized walking to demonstrate and improve his strength. The pictures of him in his maturity show a man of unusually fine physique, handsome and stalwart. By the age of twenty-two, he was rather frequently complaining of ill-health: weakness, pains, stomach-aches (sometimes physical pains and sometimes figurative statements of aversion), headaches, and rather diffuse body pains. He also developed attacks of dizziness with deafness, thought to be Méniere's disease; but attributed by him to the eating of "stone fruits."[2] Many of his complaints had to do with gastrointestinal disturbances, although he was a hearty eater who liked good food. He was extremely fearful of insanity from a quite early age; and was reiterating his defiance of death so strongly that he seemed to be protesting too much. An oft-repeated statement was that life was not worth retaining, but health was. In the Third Voyage of Gulliver, the problem of the fear of death and its cure is presented in the loathsomeness of the immortal creatures, the Struldbruggs.

Swift apparently suffered from severe anxiety and diffuse hypochondriasis of the type which so often accompanies an unusually severe castration complex, in which pregenital determinants are strong. Another characteristic of Swift's hypochondriasis was that it always increased when he was confronted by sickness in others. Then he frequently turned away, in seeming callousness, but generally felt worse himself at once. While some of these situations were such as to suggest that the illness of another made him feel guilty and that he was not a man who could face much guilt, there is further the question whether the sight of suffering did not cause him to take it onto himself through a process of primary identification. This is defended by Swift in a bitter poem *Life and Character of Dr. Swift* (2), written in 1731, in which he states "I could give instances enough that Human Friendship is but Stuff, Whene'er flatt'ring Puppy cries You are his Dearest Friend . . . he lyes.—" and later "True Friendship in two breasts requires The same Aversions and Desires;

---

[2] Jane Swift suffered from progressive deafness also and during her later years was almost totally deaf.

My friend should have, when I complain, A Fellow-feeling for my Pain." A friend should identify completely, be a mirror image of one's self.

What was written so large and so conspicuously in all of his impersonal writings, and was dealt with very delicately in his letters, was his vivid preoccupation with the affairs of the lower bowel.[3] Gulliver recounts the time, conditions, and utilization of his toilet functioning, especially his defecation, with a fidelity worthy of a young child on a trip and a little confused about how to go about these essential duties. In the Fourth Voyage it is quite clear that the foul Yahoos represent the dirty, unrestrained sexual people while the Houyhnhnms are the idealized, gentle, reasonable ones, the super-ego figures, possessing all of the reaction formations against the primitive animal instincts. In some of Swift's poems he was particularly outspoken concerning the filthiness of the female body.[4] In the Second Voyage of the *Travels*, it is the older nurse (who suckles the year-old child who has in turn been threatening the tiny Gulliver) who is described as the most loathsome of all creatures. It is at this point in the *Travels* that Swift through Gulliver splits the nurse image into two, creating an overgrown foul and smelly wet nurse and a preadolescent protective and charming little girl nurse. In general, Gulliver, like Swift, found body apertures, even the pores of the skin, disgusting. That this hostility is particularly focused on nurses is apparent in other productions as well. In his *Directions to the Nurse* (5), he writes: "If you happen to let the child fall and lame it, be sure never confess it; and if it dies all is safe. Contrive to be with child as soon as you can, while you are giving suck, that you may be ready

[3] In one of his letters to Charles Ford, Swift complained bitterly of hemorrhoids, but in general he was personally reticent about the state of his bowels in contrast to his complaints of other bodily infirmities (3).

[4] For a few examples, see *A Pastoral Dialogue, The Lady's Dressing Room, A Beautiful Young Nymph Going to Bed, Strephon and Chloe,* and others (4).

for another service when the child you nurse dies or is weaned." In the *Memoirs of Scriblerus,* there are similar invectives against the "accursed nurse" who, among other things, made the infant's ears "lie forever flat and immovable."[5]

A second theme, rather overproduced in Swift's writing and in his life as well, is the confusion—determinedly rationalized—between the sexes. This appears specifically in his open wish to make boys of both Stella and Vanessa; further elaborated in his various treatises on Education. Never is there any reference to the preparation of girls for motherhood or even for the social demands of the day. But there is the often-repeated requirement that their minds should be as much like the minds of men as possible, and always the exhortation to be cleanly, reasonable, and dispassionate. The confusion of the sexes is further apparent in the (several times repeated) description of low-hung breasts and nipples, which approximate the male genitalia. With his tendency to the polarization of characteristics he tended to deal life into pairs of opposites. He would see women as essentially emotional and men as reasonable, temperate and just. It was the women who were the dangerous seducers and the destroyers of reason. In the country of the Houyhnhnms, the horses were male and female, and so were the Yahoos; yet predominantly the Yahoos seemed to represent the evil, dirty, sexual, female elements, and the horses the honorable, just, deliberate, and gently male elements of character. In a letter,

[5] Probably a reference to impotence—both genital and auditory. I. F. Grant-Duff points out (6) the connection between the ears and the genitals in a passage in *A Tale of a Tub*—"if there be a protuberancy of parts in the superior region of the body, as in the ears and nose, there must be a parity also in the inferior; and therefore in that truly pious age, the males in every assembly—appeared very forward in exposing their ears to view, and the regions about them, because Hyppocrates tells us that when the vein behind the ear happens to be cut a man becomes a eunuch; and the females were nothing backwarder in beholding and edifying by them." That almost any part of the body might temporarily become phallicized is apparent in other passages of the satire.

Swift even referred to Stella as a Yahoo. To make an advance to no one was one of his stated principles of behavior, neither to man nor woman. In order that he might be quite safe, others must always take the first step toward him.

Swift was a stalwart, well-built man, with striking blue eyes that were sometimes cold and penetrating, and again sparkling and merry. Pope described Swift's eyes as being azure as the heavens. He was possessed of unusual charm and wit; a suave, adroit man, he was sought after in social affairs and as a diner-out, a favorite of both men and women. His driving curiosity and ambitions, expressed in his many interests, and his furious activities which made him time and again the focus of all attention were so thoroughly knit into his character that one is likely to forget how much these result from primitive scoptophilia and exhibitionism which continually alternated and interplayed, the very contrasts increasing the dramatic quality of the man. It was to be expected that a posthumous child would inevitably be a special child, as much or more than is the child with the caul. Certainly too, the kidnapping and the life in the home of the nurse in England would tend to make him an object of great interest and curiosity. A woman who kidnaps a child is in some way a pathological person, with a too intense interest in the child whatever its meaning to her may be. Further, while there was gossipy rumor about the possible illegitimacy of the infant, born so long after his father's death in Ireland, it is only reasonable to assume that such gossip would be even stronger in England when the nurse, whether married or not, returned with this baby after a prolonged absence in Ireland.

In the *Travels,* active and passive voyeurism is ubiquitous. Not only were the voyages undertaken out of a lust of the eye, intuitively forecast by Gulliver years before their beginning was rationalized as being motivated by economic considerations, but it is also clear that the seagoing surgeon found the pressures of family life irksome in the extreme. In the First Voyage, Gulliver is an enormous figure of over-whelming importance, cast up out of the sea, and endanger-ing those around him by his very existence. This may very well express the primary narcissistic omnipotence of the in-fant who did threaten the welfare of those who cared for him. In the Second Voyage, he is reduced to a small size among giants, expressive of the helplessness of the child and the awareness of his small size which must become apparent to an infant between a year and eighteen months.[6] In both Voyages, Gulliver is put on exhibit for the populace and him-self is engaged in noting everything that goes on around him. The specific reference to genital exhibitionism has already been noted. In general, however, it is conspicuous that the exhibitionism is largely expressed in excretory rather than in genital sensual or reproductive terms. In the Third Voyage, the voyeurism is almost wholly active and in any event is expressed largely in social and not in personal corporeal terms. Gulliver does reciprocate, giving a short account of the wonders and activities of England.

Perhaps the most fascinating problem of Swift's develop-ment was the configuration of his oedipus complex. He had no real father on whom to play out his oedipal development. Indeed his oedipal crime was accomplished by his very con-ception, after which his father died while the son lived, and possessed his mother, at least in infancy. Whether or not he found a substitute father during the years with the nurse in Whitehaven, he was again confronted clearly with a father-less state precisely at the height of the developmental oedipal period. That there was an attempt to find a father by an interest in his English ancestors, especially his English clergyman grandfather, is probable. The nature of his oedipal crime may well be expressed in the Second Voyage of Gulli-

---

[6] A further possible determinant of this will be suggested in the recon-struction of the Whitehaven period of Swift's childhood.

ver in which he is given a temple as a place to stay, which had been defiled by the murder of a man many years before.[7] Gulliver's recalling of the heroic ancestors of history on the Island of Glubbdubdrib belongs here.

At the time when most boys are giving up their sexual longings for the mother, Swift's mother left him, and he was presented with a collective homosexual existence. It is evident that such a concatenation of events would enormously increase feelings of guilt from whatever source; and might lead to a reinforcement of righteousness and increased effort in the direction of spirituality, together with a strong rebellion against the unfairness and hypocritical attitudes often encountered in the church. Other determinants of this attitude will be dealt with in connection with the discussion of the Family Romance.

His attitude toward the church resembled much the disillusion which children ordinarily feel in their parents, and certainly the church was quite literally bound up with Swift's forefathers. After the age of five, Swift had institutions instead of parents, as he passed from school to church to society in general. It is no wonder that having "killed" his father by his conception, and lost mothers three times before the age of six, he should have accepted the protection of the school with chronic suppressed rage and the appearance of low-spirited compliance. What were the explanations regarding his mother and sister made to him during this period? What accounts did he hear from Uncle Godwin and his cousins? These influences in his childhood are most mysteriously hidden. The early death of the father—prehistoric as far as the child was concerned—could not help but increase the boy's fear of death for himself, according to the law of talion; a

---

[7] Since he further attempted to make some substitution of Sir William Temple for his lost father, only to come to bitterness, it is possible that this temple of Gulliver's is an unconscious reference to this. Not only had Swift "killed" his father by his birth, but Temple's son had committed suicide—i.e.. murdered himself.

fear which he met repeatedly by the denial that life was worth having. While he cursed his birth picturesquely, he celebrated his birthdays for himself and the people close to him faithfully; and he lived beyond the Biblical time allotment.

That the boy Swift, lonely and disappointed, should have suffered from masturbation worries is not surprising. Swift, the man, wrote seldom of any genital sensuality, but there are at least two places in which he makes clear and extensive references, and in several others, indirect statements regarding masturbation fantasies and castration fears. Most outspoken of these is a report of the sagacity of Dr. Martin Scriblerus in treating a young nobleman at court who suffered from distempers of the mind (7). This young man began to show affectations of speech, to talk in verse, to exhibit a whimsicality of behavior, and to seek odd companions. Scriblerus diagnosed him as being in love, but since there was no woman involved and the young man talked to himself, the doctor determined that the patient was blindly in love with himself. "There are people," he said, "who discover from their youth a most amourous inclination to themselves," adding later, "There are some people who are far gone in this passion of self-love: they keep a secret intrigue with themselves and hide it from all the world besides. This Patient has not the least care of the Reputation of his Beloved, he is downright scandalous in his behavior with himself. . . ." Scriblerus then proceeds to describe the sort of remedies which Swift so often recommended for himself and others: that he should give up extravagance; that he should travel in relative hardship; look at himself in "naked truth," and purge himself weekly. In short, the sufferer should do those things which Lucretius had recommended as a cure in the case of women. If all this did not avail, nothing was left, said the Doctor, but to let the man marry himself and when

98

he had tired of himself, he might drown himself in a pond. What a complete version of Narcissus!

It is to be remembered that the other traveling surgeon had his preliminary training under a master named Bates. To quote again from Gulliver's own story, "My good *Master Bates,* dying in two years after and I having few friends, my business began to fail; for my conscience would not suffer me to imitate the bad practice of too many among my brethren." There is the question whether this apparent pun in words can possibly be significant. Swift's peculiar and varied relation to language in which punning has a conspicuous place lends support to the notion that this might even be a sly conscious trick of self-revelation. This seems the more probable in that the location of this explanation in the Gulliver account corresponds so closely to that in the *Memoirs of Scriblerus* of the story of the young-nobleman-in-love-with-himself. In the earlier *Scriblerus* version, the confession is more explicit but is disowned through the device of attributing the disturbance to a patient; in the Gulliver account it is admitted but concealed in the pun. The further question might be raised whether the word *masturbation* was known to Swift. From the fact that it had appeared as part of a title of a book only a few years after Swift's death, we may surmise that it probably had some fairly wide usage before this.[8]

The greatest exposition of the masturbation fantasies appears, however, in the Third Voyage. Here, after a glorious start, Gulliver was much reduced by the pirates, set adrift in a canoe, and fell into great despondency. He finally came to an island which was perfectly round in shape, four and one half miles across, and floated in the air, rising and falling above the body of the continent from which it sometimes shut out the sun. Many of the people on this island were so

---

[8] *Masturprate* and *masturprator* appear as early forms of the word, of uncertain derivation. *Masturbation* appears in the title of a book by Hume in 1766.

taken up with intense speculation that they forgot to speak or pay attention to those around them. Consequently, they kept "flappers" who tapped them on the mouth, eyes or ears, with blown bladders which were attached like flails to the ends of short sticks and contained small quantities of dried peas or pebbles. As has already been described, this island moved up and down to a height of four miles, being balanced so delicately on a lodestone that the tenderest hand could move it.[9] The island also somewhat controlled the fate of the continent of Balnibarbi beneath it, but since it was a place of intense speculation without reality it had exerted a deleterious influence upon Balnibarbi, whose capital city contained a museum of magic and fantastic inventions all in a state of incompleteness, while the country roundabout was impoverished and miserably wasted. The senates and councils were troubled with "redundant, ebullient, and other peccant humours, with many diseases of the head and more of the heart; with strong convulsions, with grievous contractions of the nerves and sinews in both hands, but especially the right—" etc. etc. Gulliver offered suggestions for further additions to their activities, in the establishment of a department of informers, spies, prosecutors, witnesses, etc.

9 Professor Marjorie Nicolson has given us a most interesting picture of the scientific background of these constructions, and states "This was no haphazard or fortuitous piece of fancy; the constructive and rational mind of Swift never worked more coolly than during its composition" (8). The utilization of those current scientific fantasies of Swift's day seems to us absolutely in keeping with elaborated masturbation fantasies, which may occur detached from masturbation or with the peculiarly prolonged and sometimes incomplete masturbation of the latency period in children who have especially little resolution of the oedipus complex. The child, in the latency period, is especially involved with understanding the mechanics of the world around him, and when this is combined with his unresolved masturbation urges, the fantasies of the mechanics of the body are combined with unusual intensity with similar ones regarding external objects and surroundings. Such thinking may last throughout life and is sometimes valuably productive. That Swift saw the dangers of these ruminations limited to masturbatory states is obvious from his descriptions of the Laputans.

100

Swift's early life would certainly predispose to the development of a stunting bisexuality, as indeed his mature years showed. That there was further a fixation at the anal level and an extreme impairment of genital functioning is indicated in his character and his writings. In addition, he tended to absorb friends into his service in a demanding and possessive fashion—the infantile oral quality of these relationships being partly obscured by the man's real genius which could fascinate and command many of those around him, so that they wanted the more to *be* absorbed by him, but were likely to find themselves considerably burdened after a time. Even Charles Ford, devoted to Swift to the end, seemed ultimately to put geographical barriers between himself and the older man. Two additional developments within this setting are of particular interest, viz., the influence of his special anal character on the texture of the Family Romance, which fate determined in reality and stimulated in fantasy, and the special nature of his relationship to his sister, which in turn left a strong mark on his relations with other women.

On the one hand, he had a prenatal oedipal situation which was finished decisively even before his birth, and on the other, the events of the postnatal years made it impossible for him really to reach, much less to conclude, any substitute oedipal relationship at the appropriate period of his development. Parents seemed simply to disappear at the most critical junctures of his life. There seems little doubt but that the young child was aware that he was not the son of the nurse during his early stay in England, a situation in which fantasies about his origin would inevitably have arisen. On his return to Ireland, to his mother and sister, he must have had memories and fantasies regarding the family he had left in England. And again in a few months, he had neither of these families and was left only with the memories of both. No wonder then that he was resentful of his uncle and became a depressed, unproductive, and submissive child.

The anal stamp of his character can only have been established during the period with the nurse in England. It appeared vividly and compellingly throughout his life, in a direct form in his writing and in strong reaction formations of excessive cleanliness and stern ideals in his personal life and speech—so stern, however, as to destroy any acceptance of that margin of genitophallic interest which would otherwise have survived the prohibitive oedipal situation. It is amply clear from the illustrations already given that Swift considered the spoken word and the written word as miles apart. The spoken word was airy, pure, and of the spirit, a quality which he attributed further especially to vowels. The written word was often discharged in secret and disclaimed until it had proved itself—and appeared "fathered by another," as he once wrote. He considered the vowels as "airy little creatures all of different voice and features" (9). By contrast the proper names in *Gulliver's Travels* are heavy with repeated consonants and duplicated syllables overburdened by consonants, e.g., Glubbdubdrib, Luggnagg, Traldragdubh, Clumdalclitch, Clumegnig. These words suggest an onomatopoeic derivation from the sound of drippings and droppings, possibly originating in the overly intense preoccupation with toilet functions, which seemed for the child Jonathan to engulf and then to color his important infantile philosophies.

In addition to these klang and repetitive associations, one should note the great tendency that Swift had to play with words, to pun in a way that would conceal and tell at the same time. He clearly made combined identifications through names which function as in dreams to condense associative connections. The original *Journal to Stella* (1710-1713) which has been much edited in most of its published forms reveals Swift's language in its most infantile oral qualities of endearment, in which "you" is "oo," "dearest" is "dealest," r's and l's get strangely mixed up, and the effect is of a lisping child saying good night in a seductive way, as for example: "Nite dealest richar M.D. Sawey dealest M.D. M.D. M.D. FW, FW, FW ME, ME Poo Pdfr. Lele, lele, lele." The *Journal* is replete with such passages. We shall not translate it all. Swift himself said, "When I am writing in our language, I make up my mouth just as if I were speaking it" (10). "Our richar Gangridge" is "our little language." Of the abbreviations, "M.D." stood for "My dears," "FW" meant either "farewell" or "foolish wenches," "ME" stood for "Madam Elderly" (i.e., Dingley); "Pdfr" was "poor dear foolish rogue" Swift, and "Ppt" stood for "Poor pretty thing" Stella.[10] The "little language" was predominantly baby talk, mixed however with simple code and "pig Latin" contrivances so characteristic of the prepuberty years.

It seems possible that the names "Yahoo" and "Houyhnhnm" are peculiarly condensed "nonsense words," having profoundly to do with Gulliver's effort to find himself, i.e., to achieve some integration of his own identity; and that Yahoo signifies "Who are you?" and Houyhnhnm, the sound of which is close to that of "human" contains also suggestions of the pronouns "you" and "him" and "who" in a jumbled pig Latin fashion. It is on this voyage that Gulliver is forced to admit his primitive dirty attractions, but attempts to save himself through adopting the rationality of the Houyhnhnms.

The Family Romance has been regarded as occurring in children who are especially strongly attached to the parents and are sexually active and imaginative, yet full of resentment and retaliatory impulses against the parents who have been prohibiting the child's sexual practices. Seeing that the parents indulge in precisely these activities, which had been labeled as bad and punished in the child, the child suffers disillusionment and is moved to repudiate the parents. He then adopts new, unsexual and lofty parents, to fortify the self and devaluate the parents. There is then a kind of

10 For discussion of the "little language," see Ehrenpreis (11).

masked reversal of the generations out of revenge, but as Freud (12) remarks in his original article on this subject, the ennobled or elevated "adopted" parents really represent the original estimate of the own parents.

It has been the observation of the author that the Family Romance has been furthered in a particularly severe and sometimes malignant form in children whose genital development and oedipal problem have been gravely distorted by severe anal fixations, and also in those who have had such overpowering and usually anxious mothers that the development of the early ego has been possible only through an early negativistic attitude, an ego organization through opposition, which follows an overly strong attempt at absorption by the mother. In some instances indeed, the early ego negativism and the anal fixation combine—exactly the same sort of anxiously demanding and protective mother tending to promote both in a basically strong and well-endowed child. We will return to this again in the discussion of possible reconstructions of Swift's early years in England.

Children with emphatic theories of anal birth, like Swift, and with nursery ethics based on approval focused on matters of the toilet, not infrequently utilize their interest in the stool and its smell or gaseous image (as thought or memory) as representative of bad and good, dirty and godly, black and white, low and high, etc. This dichotomizing joins directly with the Family Romance. The foundling, the adopted child —the one not born of the real parents—is either the child of the gypsies abandoned by them or the royal child that has been stolen by them. This theme recurs so often in literature as to bear witness to its universality and its importance.[11] Swift almost never wrote or spoke of his father, other than to remark that the father lived long enough to secure his mother's reputation. Obviously the fantasy of bastardy is here at hand, under the mask of humor. His own father had been

[11] Cf. *Prince and the Pauper* and *H.M.S. Pinafore.*

unsuccessful and abandoned his family by death and by poverty. Neither did Swift write of the nurse except in the indirect ways already quoted. On the other hand, Sir William Temple, the ambassador and man of the world emerges quite clearly as the noble, illustrious father, with Swift's own clergyman grandfather as an earlier and less satisfactory version.

It is known that Swift's relationship with his mother remained cordial throughout and that he visited her even at the expense of making tedious trips on horseback or by stage on his journeys to England. In spite of this she plays little part in his letters, and the one preserved anecdote is an indication of her reversed oedipal attachment to her son. The year of her death, when he was forty-two, Swift began his *Journal to Stella*, a curious mixture of the memoir type of chronicle of worldly activities and a highly personal communication involving the "little language" which was made up partly of baby talk and partly of abbreviations.

In all the biographies, Jane Swift appears as but a shadow in her brother's life. She was about two years older than Jonathan. We first get a definite statement about her, however, when it is mentioned that she was a member of the Temple household along with Jonathan when he was twenty-two. One of Swift's cousins mentions hostility between the brother and sister, and praises the mother's attitude of fairness between the two. Yet it seems likely that some fantasied image of his sister influenced Swift in the selection of the three women who were to play important parts in his life. The first girl to whom he was definitely attached, and the only one whom he wished to marry, was named Jane and was the sister or cousin[12] of a college friend. The other two,

12 It is not clear whether the supposition that Jane Waring was the sister of Swift's roommate at Trinity (which is stated as a fact in the earlier biographies), was due to the assumption of the biographers or to Swift's referring to her in this way. Examination of the accounts of the Waring family indicate that she was probably a cousin.

Stella and Vanessa, both actually named Hester, were the daughters of widows, even as the first Jane (Varina) and his sister Jane were. Although all three young women were considerably younger than he, he tended to state the ages of Stella and Vanessa as two (or more) years older than they were, and also occasionally made them younger. His attachment to them contained a very large degree of identification, as is shown in his wish to make boys of them both, and his repetition of his own history with them: playing the teacher nurse who must instruct them in cleanliness, in reading and writing, and improve their minds generally. With Stella, he even so closely reproduced his own situation as to abduct her in charge of a nurse so that she would live near him in Ireland. In the meantime, he sent his widowed sister Jane to live with Stella's mother in England. It seemed that some change overtook Swift after his break with Jane Waring (which came at the time of Temple's death). With the denial of any hope for this marriage, the identification with the woman or with an intermediate sex became stronger. (Such identification is certainly more frequently the outcome of a disastrously strong oedipal attachment with the deformation of character and ideals occurring either at about six years or at puberty. In Swift the whole problem was delayed and complicated.) Possibly complete impotence overtook him then. This, to be sure, is not certain, but is suggested by a few references and especially by his behavior. Stella and Vanessa were both named Hester—which seems possibly an extra determinant for *sister*, this being the more probable since Swift was so moved by alliterative sounds and puns. The sister theme is unmistakably clear in the account of the blocking of the marriage between Swift and Stella, which was to be a marriage in form only, anyway.

Reconstructive interpretations regarding the events of the life, especially events of the first years of a man who has been dead more than two hundred years, may offend many.

Yet the offense probably consists in the suggestion by deduction that certain actual events did occur, as indicated by the known characteristics, problems and repetitive actions, supported by the memory traces which remain in so many disguised forms. We are generally less cautious and less perturbed concerning the reverse, namely speculations regarding the effects of known experiences—perhaps because we have such a respect for the objectivity of "factual" data (although it is often misremembered and subjectively distorted) and are less respectful toward the personality traits and attitudes, which must be described rather than enumerated. Yet sometimes these characteristics are of such a nature that the experienced psychoanalyst knows just as definitely as the internist observing later sequelae of tuberculosis or poliomyelitis, that the deformity is the result of specific attacks upon the young organism, not by invading bacteria, but through the agencies of those who have nurtured and trained the infant.

So it was with the "anal quality" of Swift's character: his great personal immaculateness, his secretiveness, his intense ambition, his pleasure in less obvious dirtiness, his stubborn vengefulness in righteous causes. Such traits of character develop only where the early control of the excretory functions has been achieved under too great stress and often too early. The effect is of a stratum of anxious preoccupation with these functions and their products and derivatives throughout the entire life.

We are justified in concluding that the kidnapping nurse, however devoted to her little charge, was in some way overly conscientious and harsh in her early toilet training, and left this stamp of the nursery morals of the chamber pot forever on his character. That she was ambitious for his intellectual development is indicated by Swift's own belief that on his return to England at about four, he already could read any chapter of the Bible. Whether or not this was literally true, we must probably accept it as an indication both of the child's basic endowment and of the nurse's readiness to develop precocious intellect in him. A kind of linking of the written or printed word with the excretory functions—the two were being mastered and gotten into usable order at the same time—is dramatically apparent in Swift's writing as in the illustrations already given. But when these educative achievements of intellect are being urged or forced before the emotional energy is sufficiently freed from attention to bodily preoccupation, the latter invade the former and the two are indissolubly linked. Words then become endowed with animate qualities, have magic and personalized meanings, and the functioning of speech, reading, and writing may become precociously overly emotionalized and consequently vulnerable to conflictful problems, which produce blockings. We are used to seeing this in spoken language, in the vicissitudes of stuttering and other speech defects; but with Swift it is clear that such an emotional battleground was shifted to the written and the printed word. "I am very angry," wrote Swift to Arbuthnot in 1714, "I have a mind to be very angry and to let my anger break out in some manner that will not please them, at the end of a pen" (13). When Swift was angry but trying to please "them," as in his school days at Kilkenny, he did not break out with a pen, but was compliant, depressed and even thought to be a little stupid.

That the infant Jonathan lived in close bodily intimacy with the nurse, to such a degree and with such continuity as to produce a tendency to overidentify with the woman is strongly indicated, the problem of anatomical differences never being solved with any ordinary degree of stability, and met later by fear of the female body or attempts to endow the girl with masculine attributes, if she is to be in the least either desirable or endurable. This was spoken and written boldly by the adult Swift in his rearings of Stella and of Vanessa, in his admonitions to other young ladies seeking his advice, and in his frequent dissertations on education. This demand that the girl should be masculine could be outspoken in the realm of the mind and emotions, but could not be as specifically stated concerning the body. Here it appeared clearly in a negative form: the emphasis on the dirtiness and repulsiveness of the body apertures, of which the woman possesses one more and that a conspicuous one, than the man. To Swift, every body aperture, even the pores of the skin, became on occasion a suggestion of anus. That in unconscious or preconscious fantasy Swift sometimes tended to phallacize the woman and to identify the entire body of the child with the female phallus, is apparent in a careful reading of *Gulliver*: the oversize maidens make sport with the tiny man by setting him astride their nipples and bouncing him there; the women similarly have their fun by blowing him in his canoe back and forth upon a narrow channel which has been constructed for him; the little girl nurse carries him in a box on her lap; one time he slips through the fingers of a lady who is handling him and falls in such a way as to get caught in her stomacher from which he dangles in a peculiar position.

This identification of the male with the female phallus is characteristic of the transvestite. While we have no indication of Swift's showing any well-marked transvestite pressures, it is possible that his accepting the robes of the Anglican priest included such a hidden tendency in a way which was acceptable and could be fairly well integrated into his life. Certainly his almost ritualistically compressed demands of the women who were to be close to him, that they should be of intermediate sex, eschewing feminine adornment and cultivating masculine minds; his attempts to convert them somehow into replicas of himself as a child, while he played the part of the nurse, teaching them how to read and write and keep cleanly bodies—all this has the stamp of fetishism.

although he was probably not a fetishist in the ordinary sense of the word.

That Swift was continually obsessed with body imagery which formed the almost ever-present backdrop for his moralizing satire can be readily demonstrated. Such a quotation as that given by Bullitt at the opening of his book is significant:

> To this End, I have some Time since, with a World of Pains and Art, dissected the carcass of Humane Nature, and read many useful Lectures upon the several Parts, both Containing and Contained; till at last it smelt so strong I could preserve it no longer. Upon which I have been at great Expense to fit up all the Bones with exact Contexture and in due Symmetry; so that I am ready to show a very compleat Anatomy thereof to all curious Gentlemen and others [14].

It is quite appropriate that Bullitt's book on Swift is subtitled "The Anatomy of Satire." Swift wrote satirically to prove that the stomach is the seat of honor.

> I will say that a writer's stomach, appetite and victuals may be judged from his method, style and subject as certainly as if you were his mess-fellow and sat at table with him. Hence we call a subject dry, a writer insipid, notions crude and undigested, a pamphlet empty and hungry, a style jejune,—and many such-like expressions, plainly alluding to the diet of an author—[15] . . .
> [Or:] Air being a heavy Body and therefore . . . continually descending, must needs be more so, when loaden and pressed down by words; which are also Bodies of much Weight and Gravity, as it is manifest from those deep Impressions they make and leave upon us, and therefore must be delivered from a due altitude, or else they will neither carry a good aim nor Fall down with a sufficient force . . . [Swift's satirical account of the "System of Epicurus"].

That somewhere in the course of the intimate association of the infant Jonathan with the anonymous nurse, things took a marked turn for the worse in the development of the child's attachment is probably indicated in the Second Voyage of *Gulliver*: here, it will be remembered, Gulliver is no longer the oversize important and threatening figure which he has been on his First Voyage, but is now diminutive, helpless, and himself endangered among giants. It is in this land of Brobdingnag that the disgusting nurse appears and, to quote *Gulliver*, she was carrying

> a child of a year old in her arms, who immediately spied me and began a squall that you might have heard from London Bridge to Chelsea after the usual oratory of infants, to get me for a plaything. The mother, out of pure indulgence, took me up and put me toward the child, who presently seized me by the middle and got my head in his mouth where I roared so loud that the urchin was frighted and let me drop. I should infallibly have broke my neck if the mother had not held her apron under me. The nurse to quiet the babe made use of a rattle . . . but all in vain.—She was forced to apply the last remedy by giving it suck. I must confess no object ever disgusted me so much as the sight of her monstrous breast which I cannot tell what to compare with, so as to give the curious reader an idea of its bulk, shape, and color. It stood prominent six foot and could not be less than sixteen in circumference. The nipple was about half the bigness of my head, and the hue both of that and the dug so varified, with spots, pimples and freckles that nothing could appear more nauseous: for I had a near sight of her, she sitting down the more conveniently to give suck, and I standing on the table. This made me reflect upon the fair skins of our English ladies who appear so beautiful to us—only because they are our own size, and their defects not to be seen

but through a magnifying glass where we find by experiment that the smoothest and whitest skins look rough, coarse, and ill-colored.

It was after this that Gulliver was adopted and protected by the little girl nurse, not yet at puberty, who so charmingly carried him every place with her in a small box made for him.

The passage just quoted depicts rather bitterly Gulliver's plight of finding himself with the tables turned—small, threatened, not only by the adults but by a year-old child, suckled by the loathsome nurse. The description of the breast certainly contains elements of breast awe and envy turned to loathing and with the consequent aim of degrading it. The age of the threatening infant is just the age at which Swift himself was kidnapped and the age at which according to Swift's *Modest Proposal*, the infants of the poor should be eaten by the rich. It is not chance either, that the tiny Gulliver is in danger of being eaten by the infant, or that he scrupulously recalls in the next breath, as it were, that in the days of his bigness, his own pores and his stubbly beard were seen as disgusting. What would appear to be back of this remarkable passage is that the nurse became pregnant after her return to England and in due time had a child whose suckling upset the infant Jonathan, and aroused in him intensest jealousy, biting resentment and cannibalistic feelings toward the infant—projected by Gulliver as felt toward him by the infant. This too is connected then with Swift's *Modest Proposal* with which he was to fight the battles of the depressed Irish families with satirical fury nearly sixty years later. This thought of benign cannibalism was, however, in the background of Swift's mind quite consciously for many years, as he refers to it in the Scriblerus period (1711-1714).

The image of the disgusting nurse's breast carried with it fear, and a sense of its similarity to a pregnant abdomen and to an adult phallus. That this combined image is rendered less dangerous by being degraded and fecalized is suggested in the passage already quoted. It appears that when Swift refers to the nipple as the *dug*, which he does when he is disgusted, the word itself is very close to the word *dung*. Later, in the Second Voyage, the bad nurse reappears and in a male form, as the evil, kidnapping monkey who drags the diminutive Gulliver out of his little house, and holding him "as a nurse does a child she is going to suckle," squeezed him very hard, stroked his face, and probably mistook him for a very young monkey, later cramming food into his mouth from a bag at one side of the monkey's chaps and patting him when he could not eat—the whole spectacle appearing so ridiculous that the onlookers burst into laughter; the vile stuff having to be picked out by the amiable little girl nurse. Gulliver was exceedingly sick after this, and the monkey was executed by royal decree. This appears clearly to be a homosexual fellatio fantasy, the reverberation of which appeared in Swift's own life in his sickness from "too much stone fruit" at a time when he was first drawn to Sir William Temple.

Two other assaults were made on the helpless Gulliver by evil male creatures, in this same period: one by a deformed dwarf encountered in the Queen's garden and unwittingly insulted by Gulliver, who naively commented on his bodily distortion. The dwarf in revenge shook the apple tree under which Gulliver sat so that the enormous fruit knocked him flat as he was stooping over. Another time, a huge frog hopped into Gulliver's little boat as he was navigating it in his trough, and hopping back and forth over him, deposited its odious slime upon his face and clothing. The largeness of the frog's features made it appear the most deformed animal that could be conceived. Gulliver finally fought with this ugly creature and succeeded in ridding himself of it. Gulliver himself was not without responsibility for some of his animal encounters in this period, especially those with birds. On one occasion he grabbed a swan-sized linnet by the neck with both his hands. The enraged bird beat him around the head with its wings, but was subdued with the help of one of the Queen's servants and subsequently served for dinner. All these adventures are suggestive of further homosexual fantasies and possible incidents, first involving a confusion of breast and phallus, and later taking on other configurations of contact.

This study of Swift was stimulated by an interest in fetishism and the part played in its development by sensations of instability of body size (16). It is pertinent then to make some brief further references to these questions here. There is no indication that Swift was an overt fetishist, although he shares much in the structure of his personality with those who develop the manifest symptom. The anal fixation was intense and binding, and the genital response so impaired and limited at best, that he was predisposed to later weakness. A retreat from genital sexuality did actually occur in his early adult life, probably beginning with the unhappy relationship to Jane Waring, the first of the goddesses. After this he never again seemed willingly to consider marriage, while his expressed demands were that the women who were closest to him should be as much like boys as possible. His genital demands were probably partly sublimated through his creative writings, but even these showed the stamp of his strong anal character. He did not need a fetish because he resigned from physical genitality. In a sense, his converting of the women of his choice into boys fulfilled a fetishistic need. Especially Stella was to be the faithful, dependable, unchanging bisexualized object, a cornerstone for his life. With her death he began to go to pieces.

Lemuel Gulliver went a step further than his creator in that he was a married man, who was however continually escaping from his marriage which was so predominantly disgusting to him, though his periodic sojourns at home sufficed sometimes for the depositing of a child with his wife. From his descriptions, however, this hardly seemed an act of love or even of mutual interest. The *Travels* appear as the acting out of Lemuel's masturbatory fantasies, which, like the character of Swift, are closely interwoven with anal preoccupations and ambitions rather than with genital ones.

The problem of changes in body size (expressed as fact in the *Travels* rather than merely as sensations) based on phallic functioning are reflected characteristically onto the total body,[13] much reinforced by observations of pregnancy, and especially by the theme of reversal of the generations which is very strong. There is less substitution of other body parts for the phallus than is to be seen in *Alice's Adventures in Wonderland*, although there are some disguised references in the Third Voyage, in which the phallic problems are expressed in the medium of thought rather than in that of the body itself. A further discussion of these themes is undertaken in Part III, where Swift and Carroll are compared.

[13] This was especially emphasized in Ferenczi's early article on the "Gulliver Fantasies" (17).

PART TWO

LEWIS CARROLL

LEWIS CARROLL AS A YOUNG MAN

1.

THE LIFE OF
CHARLES L. DODGSON

In the summer of 1843, safe in the reign of Queen Victoria, a boy of eleven played with his brothers and sisters in a pleasant rectory garden in Yorkshire. He was a gentle and ingenious child, active yet dreamy, the oldest boy (and third child) in the brood of ten, with two sisters older and five younger, the youngest of all just having been born. Two brothers were then five and seven years old, and a third brother was not to appear for another three years.[1] The rectory at Croft was bigger and

[1] In some of the biographies of Lewis Carroll, it is stated erroneously that he was the oldest child in the family. This may be due to the fact that the first biography of him written by his nephew Stuart D. Collingwood gives the date of the parents' marriage as 1830 instead of 1827. Charles (Carroll) was born in 1832, and had two older sisters.

So far as I have been able to ascertain, the vital facts of the Dodgson family were as follows: Charles Dodgson, later Archdeacon, and his cousin Frances Jane Lutwidge were married April 5, 1827. They had eleven children. Frances Jane, born in 1828, was christened February 6, 1829; Elizabeth Lucy, born in 1830, was christened July 23, 1830; Charles Lutwidge, born January 27, 1832, was christened July 11, 1832; Caroline Hume born in 1833, was christened September 18, 1833; Mary Charlotte, born in 1835, was christened June 4, 1835; Skeffington Hume, born in 1836, was christened December 25, 1836; Wilfred Longley, born in 1838, was christened October 28, 1838; Louisa Fletcher, born in 1840, was christened July 26, 1840; Margaret Anna Ashley, born in 1842, was christened February 27, 1842; Henrietta Harington, born just before the move to Croft in 1843, was christened July 23, 1843. Edwin was born at Croft in 1846.

the garden more ample than the one the children had recently left, for the family had but just moved from a country parsonage on the edge of the village of Daresbury, a place of real rural isolation in Cheshire. As is the case in most large families, it is probable that this one broke itself up into smaller units, subfamilies, and that the older children shared many of the responsibilities of parenthood. The household was a quiet one, sustained and perhaps somewhat overcast by the Christian doctrine of love. Indeed, the little boy, Charles, constructed a crude railway train to journey around the Croft garden for the pleasure of the younger children. It was conceived and built mainly around a wheelbarrow, strung together with various other garden appurtenances, but it had its regular route, with way stations for boarding and refreshment. The wheelbarrow, strangely enough, he conceived of as looking like himself, as he was to reveal in a note some years later (1).[2] The name of this railroad was

---

One is impressed with the repetitiveness in the names of the children, of variations of Charles and Louis: Lucy, Charles Lutwidge, Caroline, Charlotte, Louisa. (I am indebted to the Rev. Canon, W.L.M. Protheroe of Daresbury Vicarage, in Cheshire for verifying the christening dates for me.)

[2] In a letter to Magdalen Millard, of December 15, 1875, Carroll explained the wheelbarrow. There are also references to wheelbarrow attributes in *Sylvie and Bruno.* His letter is so charmingly Carrollian that it is quoted in full:

My dear Magdalen.

I want to explain why I did not call yesterday. I was sorry to miss you, but you see I had so many conversations on the way. I tried to explain to people in the street that I was going to see you, but they would not listen; they said they were in a hurry which was rude. At last I met a wheelbarrow that I thought would attend to me, but I could not make out what was in it. I saw some features at first, then I looked through a telescope and found it was a countenance: then I looked through a microscope, and found it was a face! I thought it was rather like me, so I fetched a looking glass to make sure, and there to my great joy I found it was me. We shook hands, and were just beginning to talk, when myself came up and joined us, and we had quite a pleasant conversation. I said, "Do you remember when we all met at Sandown?" and myself said, "It was very jolly there; there was a child called Magdalen," and me said, "I used to like her a little: not much, you know—only a little." Then

Love, and it was equipped with carefully written rules. One of the most important, added to the original list, defined the procedure for requesting and administering first aid to any passengers, sick from the speed of the Love train: to wit, such a passenger must lie quietly where he has fallen and allow himself to be passed over three times by the engine of Love before he may ask to be aided (2).

The boy was Charles Lutwidge Dodgson, later to become world famous as Lewis Carroll, the author of *Alice's Adventures in Wonderland* and *Through the Looking Glass,* two of the most appealing nonsense books in the English language, both devoted to the adventures of a little girl, of about seven or eight, in a mysterious and magic garden. Charles had been born in Daresbury, where the family lived from the time of the marriage of the parents to the move to Croft, which was a definite advancement. An early picture of the father (3) shows a young man with large, sensitive, even startled-looking eyes in a face generally strong and massive with big, well-chiseled features. In a later picture, however, when he had become Archdeacon of Richmond, this father appears amiably stern in mien but relaxed in posture, and the face has lost any trace of the early apprehensive wistfulness.

The father was Charles Dodgson also, and had married his cousin Frances Jane Lutwidge, for whom the first child was

---

it was time for us to go to the train, and who do you think came to the station to see us off? You would never guess, so I must tell you. They were two very dear friends of mine, who happen to be here just now, and beg to be allowed to sign this letter as your affectionate friends

Lewis Carroll and C. L. Dodgson.

This is the only letter signed with both names. More frequently Mr. Dodgson preferred to keep his identity separate from that of Lewis Carroll. One may deduce from the context of the letter and the uniqueness of the signature that the wheelbarrow represented some particularly strong projected state of depersonalization, occurring in the course of overcoming panic.

121

named. The father came of a line of Anglican clergymen, only the grandfather breaking this professional succession. Very little detailed information regarding the mother remains, except that she was a quiet devoted mother, much occupied with and by her babies.[3] In one letter, record of which remains, written when she was called away to the sickbed of her father, she wrote most tenderly to her darling Charlie and sent him a billion kisses, a gift which he repaid many times over later in life, when in writing to little girls usually of seven to eleven, he would in turn send them many kisses, often measured and weighed, lest they prove too heavy for proper delivery. Kissing was the only form of physical affection which Carroll is known to have permitted himself in later years also. The letter with the billion kisses was obviously treasured by the child, who wrote a warning on its back, "No one is to touch this note for it belongs to C.L.D." and to fortify this further, added "Covered with slimy pitch so that they will wet their fingers" (6).

Dodgson's earliest known letter, reproduced in Derek Hudson's recent book (7), was addressed to his nurse and read

> My dear Bun,
>   I love you very much, & tend you a kitt from little Charlie with the horn of hair. I'd like to give you a kitt, but I tan't, because I'm at Marke. What a long letter I've written. I'm twite tired.

[3] She is described by her grandson, Stuart Collingwood, who quotes an unnamed friend as "one of the sweetest and gentlest women that ever lived, whom to know was to love. The earnestness of her simple faith and love shone forth in all she did and said: She seemed to live always in the conscious presence of God. It has been said by her children that they never in all their lives remember to have heard an impatient or harsh word from her lips"—the gentlest of mothers (4).

Derek Hudson, who has evidently had access to some of Mrs. Dodgson's letters not earlier uncovered, remarks that she wrote in a sensitive swiftly running hand; was clearly a very busy person, in a "tearing hurry." He sums her up as a practical angel who lived effectively on this earth (5).

The note is addressed on the back "For dear kind Bun, from little Charly." This infant communication is obviously written by someone else, or possibly by the child with his hand held by an adult. (We may remember how the White King feels his pencil being held and directed by someone else, when Alice plays this practical trick upon him and forces him to record something about the White Knight.) But the spelling too obviously reproduces an adult's phonetic representation of the child's lisping pronunciation, in which "s" and "c" are replaced by "t." There are two significances here of interest in studying Carroll's later writings: the similarity to the cute baby talk treated as a precious indulgence with the baby talk of the loved Bruno in *Sylvie and Bruno,* and the transformation of the *kiss* into *kitt.* Carroll had a special liking for cats and kittens as will be discussed later in this study. One must be aware of the possibility that the *kiss* as a *kitt* may have been a family pleasantry, which was one facet in the growing fancies of the boy Charles.

Appealing anecdotes persist of the little boy's communion with the small animals of the garden, and of his predilection for slimy, repulsive ones, snails and toads being favorites. One may conjecture that these were exactly the animals little girls would like least, and through which the boy could find some defense against the bevy of sisters. It is said that he entertained the ingenious plan of supplying earthworms with small pieces of pipe for weapons and then encouraging them to civilized warfare. Later in life, not only were his famous nonsense tales full of humanized animals and bestialized people, but in his other character of the Oxford don, he wrote letters to the newspapers and tracts against vivisection, and the sacrifice of animals for humans. The conflict between childish impulsiveness and the straight jacket of obligatory and dutiful love may further have been responsible in part for the boy's stammer, which troubled him all of his life, and for a certain awkwardness of movement, although he was adroit and skillful in the use of his hands, and always an energetic walker. All of the children had some disturbances of speech and two or three of them had definite stammers. Some biographers have reported that Charles was left-handed (and there are passages in his stories which would harmonize with this), but it is recently denied by the Editor (8) of his *Diaries*.[4] Certainly, however, he was preoccupied with the left and right, as with right and wrong, and was an accomplished mirror writer. He used tools well, once constructing a very tiny set of tools, all in a little case, for one of his sisters. But above all else he was possessed of a searching eye, and a keen sense of the dramatic. He was a marionettist and sleight-of-hand artist. He not only made the marionettes, but wrote the plays and gave the performances. His love of the theater was to last throughout his life and come into sharp conflict with his overly rigid moral, social and religious code. He probably dazzled his sisters who later held him in almost reverential awe.

He was a questioning boy. "Please explain" is quoted as a byword. He was continually trying things out, constructing puzzles and games of wood and paper, conundrums and plays upon words in the medium of language. He made puns and rhymes, played at anagrams, and word-letter arrangements, drew pictures which somehow turned out to be caricatures, and often wrote a meticulously even hand. One gets the impression that many of his puzzles and conundrums were but

[4] Mrs. Florence Becker Lennon has said that Louisa, one of the younger sisters, was left-handed. She learned this from one of the Misses Dodgson, nieces of Charles. Her informant, although recalling Louisa's left-handedness clearly, was very uncertain that Charles shared the trait (personal communication). In the original Carroll-illustrated version of *Alice's Adventures in Wonderland* there is a drawing made by Carroll of Alice's hand extending out of the window of Mr. W. Rabbit's house (9), in which Alice is clearly left-handed. Tenniel converted Alice to right-handedness. Charles was fairly adept at mirror writing, a talent which is frequently associated with left-handedness or ambidexterity.

scantily concealed versions of his endless ponderings about nature and creation.

There may have been a preoccupation with punning, possibly obsessional in force. This is suggested at least in certain passages in *Through the Looking Glass* in which a voice from an invisible source keeps whispering possible puns into Alice's ear in an annoying way. "You can make a pun about that," says the voice repeatedly. Indeed, sometimes Carroll's tendency to punning had a similar insistence. He became adept at what might be called the slow pun—a somewhat ponderous and labored punning depending not so much upon klang associations or rhyming as upon the same word having quite different or contrasting meanings, some of which might not readily come to mind. The use of the pun thus served the purpose of puzzling rather than of flashy wit or repartee. One might call it the pun with the delayed surprise. Some of these puns seem bizarre, because they betray unexpected and unusual preoccupations and consequently could not be readily appreciated by the listener. The pun here is a combination of joke and riddle. It is probable, too, that most of his punning was in writing; with his stammer, the spoken pun would indeed have been grotesque. It is said, however, that he used his stammer to enhance the suspense of a well-climaxed joke. Much of his early versemaking was parody.

From all reports, he was a good child, whose angers were controlled by an early and very strong conscience. There are no early pictures available, but even in his young manhood his face was overly sober and childlike, an expression which later took on a quality of feminine gentleness (10).

At twelve, on being sent away to school, he wrote long letters home to the other children, one of his first to his six-year-old brother, as follows: "My dear Skeff, 'Roar not, lest thou be abolished—Yours—" This is as much of an expression of aggression as appears directly in his personal writings. The early letters to his sisters were signed, "Your affectionate brother Charles." Later he kept a formal distance from them and signed only "C. L. Dodgson." At school he began to write Latin verse and short stories for the school magazine.

The estimate of him given by Mr. Tate, the headmaster of Richmond School, is interesting: that the boy had an uncommon share of genius, was possessed of clear reason, and so jealous of error that he demanded absolute accuracy in solution of mathematics and all other problems that seemed obscure. With words, however, he was distinctly playful and too lenient about their use, being "marvelously ingenious in replacing the ordinary inflexions of nouns and verbs as detailed in our grammars, by more exact analogies or convenient forms of his own devising"(11). Here already evident was the antithesis between mathematics and literary fantasy which was to persist and increase throughout his life, until of one man there became two: the meticulous, overexact, boring and probably bored mathematician, the Oxford don, Charles L. Dodgson; and the storyteller of grotesque nonsense fantasy, the famous Lewis Carroll. One feels that Lewis Carroll was the truer descendant of the boy in the garden telling stories or making fancy tricks for the sisters. As though to continue this garden play, his later stories were told mostly to little girls of seven to eleven years of age. Mr. Dodgson, on the other hand, was the deacon-mathematician, a shadowy version of the official character of the elder Mr. Dodgson who was an Archdeacon with a special love for mathematics. The one was the guardian of the other, until the fantasy teller broke loose and overcame the don. Mr. Tate, however, was on the side of the clerical mathematician and ventured the prediction that the fault (of too great freedom with words), although flowing freely just then, would soon exhaust itself. When he left Richmond, Charles was given the highest praise by the Headmaster, who described him as a gentle, intelligent and well-conducted boy, exacting peculiar interest from his teacher. Next he went to Rugby.

126

That the elder Mr. Dodgson had a side which, too, had a strong Carrollian tinge has always been suggested by the fact of his reputation as a raconteur. It seems that this side was considerably developed and may have colored the children's whimsies. Derek Hudson's recent book (2) contains a very valuable early letter from the elder Charles Dodgson to the little boy Charles at the age of eight.

> I will not forget your commission. As soon as I get to Leeds I shall scream out in the middle of the street. *Iron mongers—Iron mongers—*Six hundred men will rush out of their shops in a moment—fly, fly in all directions—ring the bells, call the constables—set the town on fire. I *will* have a file and a screw-driver, and a ring, and if they are not brought directly, in forty seconds I will leave nothing but a small cat alive in the whole town of Leeds, and I shall only leave that because I am afraid I shall not have time to kill it.
> Then what a bawling and tearing of hair there will be! Pigs and babies, camels and butterflies, rolling in the gutter together—old women rushing up the chimneys and cows after them—ducks hiding themselves in coffee cups and fat geese trying to squeeze themselves into period cases—at last the Mayor of Leeds will be found in a soup plate covered up with custard and stuck full of almonds to make him look like a sponge cake that he may escape the dreadful destruction of the Town . . . At last they bring the things which I ordered and then I spare the Town and send off in fifty waggons and under the protection of 10,000 soldiers, a file and a screw driver and a ring as a present to Charles Lutwidge Dodgson from his affec[nte] Papa.

One can fairly reconstruct the situation which stimulated such a letter—the earnest demands of the eight-year-old boy that the father, on his visit to Leeds, should not forget or overlook the so strong and so important needs of the child

127

for the tools with which to work in the remote Daresbury Vicarage. The letter itself burlesques the terrible importance of the child's wants, so that the whole town shall be torn down before the father will go back empty-handed. The father's affectionate pride in the earnest child shows through, however, at every turn. Equally important is the great similarity to Carroll's own trial scenes in the *Alice* books—the burlesque of world-shaking devastation, the rise of metaphors combining such contrasts as to heighten to an extreme the sense of the ridiculous: ducks hiding in teacups, fat geese squeezing into pencil cases, and the Lord Mayor served up as a sponge cake. It is apparent that Lewis Carroll had a firm foundation of his sense of fantastic fun in the early years in Daresbury before the father had become so austere and important a clergyman.

At Rugby, Charles made a distinguished academic record, winning prizes and high recommendations from another headmaster Tait, who had succeeded Arnold at the famous school. It seems that he did not have many happy memories of the place, however; as he wrote later, he must have made some progress in learning, but he spent an incalculable amount of time doing penalties, and none of his learning was accomplished with love. He suffered from the lack of privacy in dormitory sleeping arrangements, and somewhat from the hazing, but there is little definite knowledge of his specific troubles. Those of his letters that remain and are reported in his nephew's biographical account of him (13) are largely documentary offerings of accomplishments as recommendations to his father. It was only later that, with a hint of bitterness, he wrote that he would never again voluntarily live through such a three years. This reminds us of his chronicles of the utter dreariness of the usual family Sunday afternoon —recorded as an aside in *Sylvie and Bruno* (14), although the official attitude toward his own childhood was either noncommittal or positively approving.[5]

During the period at and just before Rugby, however, he began to write and illustrate home magazines for the sisters and younger brothers. These probably began about 1845 and continued until 1849 or 1850. Among these journals were *Useful and Instructive Poetry* and the *Rectory Umbrella,* consisting largely of short stories and poems, humorous essays, parodies of prose and poetry, and caricature drawings. There are bizarre qualities in these early drawings; conspicuous body distortions, especially the tendency to draw figures with a ghastly-sharp thinness, or a ballooning obesity (17). The women are frequently, though not universally, portrayed as gaunt and starved appearing, and the men as overly rotund. There is evident also a considerable preoccupation with food, with eating and being eaten, themes which reappear so conspicuously in the *Alice* stories. Crude as his drawings were, he succeeded in giving many of his sketched figures a hollow, anxious look, most apparent in and around the eyes—a look somehow suggesting damnation and abject hunger. This is a peculiarly and grossly exaggerated version of the appearance of mild searching apprehension so haunting in the face in the early photograph of the elder Dodgson. The conflicts, the violent fights and trickery between sib-

[5] Carroll makes it clear that he is actually quoting the letter of a lady friend and a speech made by a child friend. This is incorporated into the text as an argument for humanizing Sunday. "The child had said 'On Sunday I mustn't dig in the garden!' Poor child, she has abundant cause for hating Sunday." The lady had been even more detailed and explicit (15).

Hudson's recent biography (16) gives a facsimile of Charles L. Dodgson's signature in a schoolbook during his Rugby days, in which the "C.L. Dodgson" written by Charles is followed by the words "is a muff," written in another schoolboyish hand. Hudson thinks the indications of Charles' misery at Rugby are such as not to "encourage a biographer to investigate his Rugby years at all closely." It seems to me, however, an erroneous idea that one should not look into the miseries and conflicts of the great in any understanding and appreciation of the total stature of accomplishment.

lings are the subjects of fun, and pun making, but the illustrations are sad or a bit horrifying rather than frankly funny. The frontispiece to the *Rectory Umbrella* is especially arresting: it shows a young person reclining on the ground, holding aloft an open umbrella (18).[6] This person has long, shaggy

Frontispiece to *The Rectory Umbrella*

[6] Hudson's interpretation of this figure is that it represents a jolly old poet. He also considers the possibility that Charles may have been influenced one way or another by the recently published nonsense rhymes and illustrations of Edward Lear (9). Lear was some years older than Carroll and had at this time published his *Book of Nonsense.* Carroll at no time mentions Lear, and does not specifically acknowledge any copying of the older man. In *The Storm,* in this early book, Charles spells "leer" as "lear," which may be a hidden or unconscious acknowledgment. One must realize, however, that many of Carroll's poems were parodies, not specifically acknowledged because he took it for granted that the originals were known to his readers. In addition, there is the possible fact that Lear's epilepsy was known to Carroll, who had a somewhat phobic reaction to fits. Although he showed

hair and beard, and a face not unlike that of a good-natured, smiling lion. The dress is that of a little girl, the skirt suggesting the appearance of a closed umbrella. The open umbrella is labeled *Tales, Poetry, Fun, Riddles, Jokes.* This male-female umbrella person is beset by two orders of small figures: those nearest seem to be female fairies with long gowns and flowing hair. Each brings a gift—the assortment including *Liveliness, Knowledge, Good Humor, Taste, Cheerfulness, Content* and *Mirth.* From a little distance overhead six imps are hurling down rocks labeled *Woe, Spite, Ennui, Gloom, Crossness,* and *All-overishness.* These imps are frenzied, with hair standing on end;[7] they are nude with predominantly male body cast but without other distinguishing anatomical differences.

Between *Useful and Instructive Poetry* and the *Rectory Umbrella* were several other journals which lived through only a few issues each. According to their editor's own account (21) written in 1855, these were produced mostly in the years 1848 to 1850, and were concluded with *Misch-Masch.* Certainly the journal writing was roughly coincidental with the period at Rugby and before entrance to Oxford; and probably furnished outlets for the struggling Rugby student. All this is of some interest, because it is an indication of the already existent cleavage between the good and compliant student faithful to his prizes, and the caricaturing imp who wrote fantastically and drew strange pictures. But about the years 1849 to 1850, there is some obscurity. It is a period somewhat elided in the biography of S. Dodgson Collingwood, a nephew, published in 1898. A later biogra-

---

a preoccupation with them—in abstract and impersonal ways—there was more than ordinary fear of them. It is conceivable that this combination of fear and fascination would promote exactly the result of a repeated attempt to *abreact* with repetitive copying and unconscious denial.

[7] Later on (20) Charles made an unsuccessful attempt to photograph a little girl being given an electric shock, hoping to get an actual picture of hair standing on end.

pher (22), Florence Becker Lennon, points out that there "is no documentation for Charles' doings between the end of 1848 and his entrance to Oxford in January 1851." The last record of prizes brought from Rugby was for Christmas, 1848, and since at this time he had been at Rugby almost three years, it may be that he left Rugby in 1849 and did not actually enter Oxford until January, 1851. He wrote of the period at Rugby as though it were three years, probably 1846-1849.[8]

In January, 1851, when almost exactly nineteen years old, Charles L. Dodgson became a resident at Christ Church College, where he was to continue in residence for almost forty-seven years. His mother died only a few days after his going to Oxford, but the nature and duration of her illness are unrecorded: whether or not it had anything to do with the gap between Rugby and Oxford cannot be told. But that it had a profound effect on the young man is reasonably certain. In some ways she must have seemed a young woman for she left a child, Edwin, only five years old. Charles, always parsimonious in direct expressions of feelings, wrote little of her, but one poem, which has been cited as evidence of his having fallen in love and lost his loved one, may be seen on careful reading probably to refer to his mother. This poem, *Stolen Waters* (24), describes his seduction to a stolen delirious love, and his betrayal by the loved one:

> And unaware, I knew not how,
> I kissed her dainty finger-tips,
> I kissed her on the lily brow,
> I kissed her on the false, false lips—
> That burning kiss, I feel it now!

[8] A letter written from Rugby in the early spring of 1849 indicates that he remained there at least that long. Green states in his "Introductory" to the Diaries that Charles suffered from whooping cough and from mumps while at Rugby—and that the latter left him deaf, although he had earlier had an attack of deafness also. How severe or prolonged these illnesses were is not described (23).

"True love gives true love of the best:
Then take," I cried, "my heart to thee!"
The very heart from out my breast
I plucked, I gave it willingly;
Her very heart she gave to me—
Then died the glory from the west.

In the gray light I saw her face,
And it was withered, old and gray.
The flowers were fading in their place
Were fading with the fading day.

Forth from her like a hunted deer
Through all the ghastly night I fled,
And still behind me seemed to hear
Her fierce unflagging tread.
And scarce drew breath for fear.

Yet marked I well how strangely seemed
The heart within my breast to sleep;
Silent it lay, or so I dreamed,
With never a throb or leap.

For hers was now my heart, she said,
The heart that once had been mine own:
And in my breast I bore instead
A cold, cold heart of stone.
So grew the morning overhead.
— — — — — — — — — — — — —
They call me mad: I smile, I weep.
Uncaring how or why;
Yea, when one's heart is laid to sleep,
What better, than to die?
So that the grave be dark, and deep.

This was written by a young man of thirty who had lost
his mother on the brink of manhood. His clear portrayal of
his loved one as the young-old woman is not the statement

of a youth who has lost a young sweetheart. To this writer, it seems a clear statement of the intensity of the unresolved oedipal love for the mother.[9] The latter part of the poem contains an equally clear description of the encapsulation of his own emotions as well as a review of his childhood, ending with the prophetic admonition:

> Be as a child—
> So shalt thou sing for very joy of breath—
> So shalt thou wait thy dying.
> In holy transport lying—
> So pass rejoicing through the gate of death,
> In garment undefiled. . . .

This was the cry of a man who seemed never to love another woman, but to live as a child, still in the magic garden, devoted only to little girls not yet across the mystic bar of puberty. That this remained a taboo throughout his life is clear when at forty-eight he recorded in his diary that having kissed a little girl, whom he took to be less than fourteen, and having discovered that she was sixteen, he had written a letter of apology to the mother assuring her that this would not happen again.[10] It may be significant that the girl's mother took the matter of the kiss rather seriously, also.

Closely connected with the intense, frustrated love of the little boy for his mother is of course the intense, unconsummated love of the man for the little girl Alice, and the myriad of other little girls who followed and represented her. Charles' mother must have been a young woman when he was born, with an age difference between her and her son not so very different from that between Charles and the little Alice Liddell, i.e., about twenty years. This reversal of the unresolved oedipal attachment is quite common. It is sug-

[9] This is also stressed by Mrs. Lennon (25).
[10] Diary entry of February 5, 1880 (26).

gested further by the Carroll poem *Faces in the Fire* (27), which begins with a clear reminiscence of his birthplace:

> The night creeps onward, sad and slow
> In these red embers dying glow
> The forms of Fancy come and go.
> An island farm—toward seas of corn
> Stirred by the wandering breath of morn
> The happy spot where I was born.

A succession of pictures follow: a childish form with red lips pouting for kisses; a grave and gentle maid half afraid of her own beauty; a matron with her boys, and finally,

> Those locks of jet are turned to gray
> And she is strange and far away
> That might have been mine own today
>
> That might have been mine own, my dear,
> Through many and many a happy year—
> That might have sat beside me here.
>
> — — — — — — — — — — — —
>
> The race is o'er I might have run
> The deeds are past I might have done
> And sere the wreath I might have won.
>
> — — — — — — — — — — — —
>
> The pictures with their ruddy light,
> Are changed to dust and ashes white
> And I am left alone with night.

This was written in January, 1860, the month that Carroll was twenty-eight years old (about the age of the father, coincidentally, when he was married) and when he had made an unusually good beginning in his academic life and had already begun to emerge as Lewis Carroll, the writer. Alice Liddell was then between seven and eight. While Carroll was already a little uneasy about the interpretation put on his relationship with the Liddell children, the break with the Liddells had not yet become an open one,[11] and would not for several years.

After his mother's death, young Dodgson gave little outward sign of his mourning but threw himself into dogged application to his studies. He wrote home of being up late, until past midnight, and of oversleeping so that he had no time for breakfast before Chapel—a statement which interestingly betrays no indication of the profound sleep disturbance which was to beset him during many years of his life. In the Fall of 1851, he was awarded the Boulter scholarship, the first of a series of honors distributed throughout his life at Oxford.

A few weeks later, on Christmas Eve, he was nominated for a studentship, corresponding rather to our teaching fellowships, by "the terrible Dr. Pusey," Canon of Christ Church, an old friend of the elder Dodgson, who had been in correspondence with him since the time of Charles' matriculation, possibly with a view to promoting just such recognition for the young student. It is reported that the Canon had had a rigidly disciplined childhood, at the hands of extremely compulsive parents. He had waited long for marriage and then lost his wife by death after a few years,

[11] As early as May 17, 1857, a diary entry reveals that his notice of the Liddell children had been construed by some as attention to their governess, Miss Prickett; and out of consideration for her, he was resolving to avoid taking any public notice of the children in the future. Unfortunately the diaries for 1858-1862 have been lost and only those extracts early quoted by Collingwood remain. Mr. Alexander Taylor (28) has regarded Alice Liddell as the one love of Carroll's life and believes that Carroll definitely wanted to marry Alice. He interprets the poem as an anticipation—something which Carroll and the Liddells somehow made come true in later years. The force back of this unconscious demand to love inappropriately and to lose seems quite surely to be the lost love for the mother. Whether or not there was any little sister who was also involved in this, is hazy, to say the least. That the age of seven to eight was an important one for Carroll is evident—it is the age of *Alice* in *Wonderland* and the *Looking Glass*. The sister, Louisa, born when Carroll was eight, was the only one who shared his mathematical interest and was in certain ways a favorite, but other evidence is missing.

and by the time he was Canon of Christ Church, he had long since become a gloomy, moral sadomasochist, reaffirming his early statement: "I love my grief better than any hollow joy." He had been a friend of Newman's but did not quite go overboard to the Roman Road (29). A contemporary of the Canon's, the Reverend William Tuckwell, wrote of him (30), "The habit of reacting toward others as a confessor seems to have generated a scientific pleasure in religious vivisection. He made an idol of celibacy. His obscurantist dread of worldly influence begot the feeling that no young woman was safe except in a nunnery, no man except in Holy Orders." He urged young men to take orders as early as possible, i.e., at twenty-three. Orders first and controversial thought and reading later, was his prescribed programme. This is the man to whom Charles' father recommended him.

The studentship carried a stipend which eased the young man's economic pressures, and the teaching duties were not well defined. But the other conditions, that the student should remain unmarried and should proceed to Holy Orders, doubtless reinforced the neurotic walls with which the young man was anyway buttressing his position. The father wrote of his "feelings of thankfulness and delight" at the honor which Charles, not quite twenty, had won for himself. Charles' early life was certainly not like that of the Canon, whose mother, conscientiously cultured, sat on a hard chair, reading a *good* book with a watch beside her.

Yet his life seems to have been straightlaced and garden-bound by the tenderest admonishing of love and peace from his mother, ever busy with a new baby, and by the firm and reasonable moral precepts of his father, who had a sense of humor, however, and was something of a raconteur. From Charles' own reminiscences, it seems probable that he, as the eldest son, was thus drawn into precociously mature and responsible behavior, devising endless games and entertainments for the younger children, and was encouraged to an

137

early and too complete suppression of his jealousies and resentments of the growing brood, and the baby which must so often have separated him from his beloved mother. Certainly in the *Alice* books the baby receives no gentle care being tossed about by the Duchess, tied in a knot by Alice, and ultimately becoming a little pig running off sobbing into the woods.[12] In the *Diaries* of Dodgson too, recently published, he gives little attention to the recording of the births of nieces and nephews, and such enthusiasms as were expressed were entirely about little prepuberty girls, with whom he formed quick infatuations. He marked such days "with a white stone." He seemed to carry always a longing to continue in the idyllic charms of childhood, especially of the period between six and twelve, which is least beset with sexual pressures. And he was ever attempting to obliterate, forget, or ridicule what seemed ugly to him in nature. This very compulsion to repeat endlessly the prettinesses of childhood bespeaks loudly the horrors of the jealous conflicts within, portrayed in his crude sketches and in his early verses (31). Only so could he attempt to merit the billion kisses of his devoted mother, who had betrayed him so often with another baby. Certainly an examination of much of his later poetry and his prose, especially *Sylvie and Bruno*, would indicate something of the kind. (The special structure of this remarkable piece of literature will be discussed later.) The florid cruelty of the scenes in the *Alice* books is masked and softened by the mild and puzzled characteristics of the little heroine.

Thus at nineteen he lost his mother, left home permanently, attained appreciatively the first steps toward economic independence, and looked definitely in the direction of a life of celibacy. At the same time his father was rising in prominence in the Church, and in 1853, when Charles was

[12] It will be recalled that in the letter of the elder Dodgson to the eight-year-old Charles, pigs and babies were grouped together (see p. 127).

twenty-one, the father became one of the Canons of Ripon Cathedral. His undergraduate course was marked by a succession of honors, so that in 1854 young Dodgson, tired of being congratulated, wrote, with unconscious self-revelation, "There seems to be no end to it. If I had shot the Dean, I could hardly have had more said about it" (32).

He wrote long letters to his sisters, perhaps out of lonesomeness, but also seemingly with definite relief through writing. The letters to his father were frank in their presentation of his own successes, with more than a hint that his prizes were offerings for his father's rejoicing. He took his Bachelor of Arts degree in 1854 when twenty-two, and the next year saw him made sublibrarian, given a Bostock Scholarship, and made "Master of the House," in honor of the appointment of the new dean, Dr. Liddell, who with his family was to become so important in his life. These awards made him economically independent.

Meanwhile he had had verse published in the *Comic Times*, and in the *Whitby Gazette;* and in 1856-1857 he contributed to *The Train,* which had been founded by the editors of the *Comic Times*. It was at this point that the writer Lewis Carroll emerged. He first thought of using the name Dares, undoubtedly appropriated from the name of his birthplace. But one suspects a pun, also—for when did he refrain from a possible pun? At any rate, when his publisher disapproved, he did not dare to insist, and suggested instead a choice of one of four names: Edgar Cuthwellis, Edgar U. C. Westhall, Louis Carroll, and Lewis Carroll. The first two of these were constructed from rearrangements of the letters of his two Christian names, Charles Lutwidge, and the latter two were variant forms of those names, reversed in order. These tendencies to reverse the order, to write backward, to turn time backward, to bring the mirror image to life, and to take things apart, whether concrete objects or words, and to rearrange the parts into new objects, new words, or new names, were always with him. He seemed repeatedly to be asking, "Do the same materials arranged differently make a different identity?" This may have contained the question about what made the differences between the siblings, all children of the same parents. In connection with the name Lewis Carroll, it is interesting to note that Caroline was the sister born the year after him, and that Louisa, born when he was eight, later shared an interest in mathematics with him. The shadows of the question of identity and of the possibility of changing identities with another were present in many puns, conundrums, puzzles, stories, and in some of the jokes in his letters to his little girl friends.[13] Later he made a stalwart effort to keep separate the identities of Charles L. Dodgson, the mathematics don at Oxford, and Lewis Carroll, the creator of *Alice,* being quite annoyed when addressed by one name when he was in the character of the other.

As Dodgson he continued to teach and study mathematics at Oxford. His contributions in this field did not prove extensive or profound; and after some years he was writing gently satirical and witty articles concerning Oxford affairs, expressed in mathematical language and academic form. Among these were *The New Method of Evaluation as Applied to* π, with a dedication to Jack Horner (1865) (34); and *The Dynamics of a Parti-cle* (1865) (35).

The latter has much of the Reeling, Writhing, and Fainting in Coils sort of humor. Neither was Dodgson, who had suffered from the lack of love in learning in his own school days, a remarkably good teacher. He did not seem to make a real contact with his students, who respected him but regarded him as eccentric and withdrawn. Many have asked why the young man, undoubtedly talented and with an early start in his academic career, did not really "work himself into the main stream of mathematics rather than eddy around in little pools by the shore" (36). Perhaps the answer

[13] See letters to Gertrude Chataway in connection with the *Snark* (33).

lies in the fact that a mathematician does not progress far unless his mathematical ability and his imagination work in harmony[14] and that for Carroll-Dodgson the mathematical interest was generally opposed to the imagination, probably carrying too much the burden of a neurotic compulsive defense against the nearly mad imagination of Carroll. The two-men-in-one struggled along in some mutual bondage, and as one man kept a respected place upon the Oxford faculty; but it was only when Carroll escaped from Dodgson's restraints that he wrote with deep fidelity to his emotional as well as to his intellectual self, and his writing came out as particularly beguiling nonsense.

In *Reminiscences of Oxford* (37), Rev. William Tuckwell describes Carroll as follows:

> Of course he was one of the sights of Oxford:—[visitors] begged their lionising friends to point out Mr. Dodgson and were disappointed when they saw the homely figure and the grave repellant face. Except to little girls he was not an alluring personage—austere, shy, precise, absorbed in mathematical reverie, watchfully tenacious of his dignity, stiffly conservative in political, theological, social theory, his life mapped out in squares like Alice's landscape, he struck discords in the frank, harmonious college camaraderie. The irreconcilable dualism of his exceptional nature, incongruous blend of extravagant frolic with self-conscious puritan repression—cut him off while living from all except the "little misses" who were his chosen associates.

Professor Frederick York Powell was somewhat more tender toward the young don, and refers (38) to the quiet humor of his voice and his occasional laugh, and especially

---

[14] "It is true that a mathematician who is not also something of a poet will never be a perfect mathematician." Karl W. Weierstrass, quoted by Lennon, p. 270.

emphasizes his patience, his "rigid rule of his own life, and his dutiful discharge of every obligation that was in the slightest degree incumbent upon him." Powell considers him always modest, a good teller of anecdotes and very skillful in the management of the life of the Common Room.—Perhaps these two versions are but different aspects of the same picture; or possibly the Rev. Tuckwell was recalling Carroll only after he had become famous and correspondingly more retiring.[15]

In the first years of his establishment at Oxford, however, the young man's life was outwardly successful and mildly monotonous. His teaching obligations increased and required daily preparation. He lived a rather cloistered life, rowing on the river, studying, reading, amusing himself with an occasional excursion and gradually opening a little the doors of the literary world. He met Tennyson and Ruskin, and he began a correspondence with the surgeon, Sir James Paget, to whom he wrote concerning medical and surgical questions which puzzled him. Walking along the street near the college one day in 1856[16], he saw a young man having an epileptic fit and was impressed with his own helplessness in the situation. That this sight of the convulsion also stirred him deeply unconsciously is apparent from his preoccupation with fits in his nonsense poetry and prose. This seems to have begun earlier, but was intensified by the sight of the fit. It has been said that after this unhappy event he bought some human bones and attempted to study anatomy from them, to prepare himself the better to meet another such emergency. If this is true, it is an extraordinarily clear indication of how deeply and unconsciously the convulsion was associated with problems of anatomy in his thoughts and queries. This will be discussed further in connection with the *Hunting of the Snark* (40), which was described as a poem in Eight Fits.

[15] Also quoted by D. Hudson, p. 212.
[16] Diary entry of March 1, 1856 (39).

Fit was also written as *fytte,* the old English word for *Canto.*
This nicely completed Carroll's pun.

He was enamored of the theater; saw the young actress,
Ellen Terry, in *A Winter's Tale* (1856) and was delighted.[17]
Subsequently she and her sisters Kate and Marion became
his friends.[18] His interest in the theater together with his
stammering were considered serious obstacles in the way of
his taking Holy Orders, a course to which he was more or less
committed if he was to retain his studentship. The Bishop of
Oxford, Wilberforce, had stated unequivocally that the determination to attend the theater was a disqualification of
Holy Orders. Carroll's comments on the theatrical performances which he saw, as recorded in his diaries, are common-
place, and give no indication of the nature of the deeply
unconscious and intense response to the theater which he
undoubtedly experienced. Indeed, the *Diaries* (or those parts
of them which have survived and recently been published)
would seem to have been written by the carefully restrained
Mr. Dodgson and not at all by Carroll. Finally, however, with
the partially supporting advice of Dean Liddon, he found a
way out of the dilemma of the pull between theater and
church by becoming ordained as a Deacon, in December,

[17] Ellen Terry was only eight when she appeared in the *Winter's Tale*
playing the part of the boy Mamillius. At ten, she played Prince Arthur in
King John.

[18] The idea that Dodgson was in love with Ellen Terry is dealt with at
some length by Hudson (41), who indicates the possibility that the long
friendship may have contained elements of an autistic love affair, but
certainly unexpressed. Hudson quotes Dodgson's niece, Miss F. Menella
Dodgson, as having obtained from her cousin, S. D. Collingwood, a statement that when in his biography of Carroll he stated he believed Charles
to have suffered from a disappointment in love which cast a shadow upon
his life, he was referring to the opinion of his aunt Fanny (Charles' oldest
sister) that Charles had been in love with Ellen Terry. There is no other
evidence. It is true, as Hudson points out, that a wistful fantasy love might
have developed, never openly expressed and possibly only permitted because it was really impossible for him to marry her. Such shadowy love
affairs are the frequent concomitants of unresolved oedipal attachments. In
addition Ellen Terry's nature was one which might well have inspired such
an autistic romance.

1861, probably with the plan of not undertaking ministerial duties. At any rate, he was never ordained as a priest, and never undertook regular parochial work, although he preached an occasional sermon.

About 1856, Carroll became acquainted with photography which soon became an absorbing interest to him; with the result that he became one of the outstanding photographers of his time. He was interested largely in photographing prominent people and little girls. In reading his *Diaries* with frequent references to his photography, one gets the impression that the taking and the development of the pictures was a real triumph to him, and that in the pursuit of this avocation, with a certain amount of lion-hunting, he permitted himself more boldness than was possible for him in ordinary contacts with others. His photography and his photograph albums gave him contact with many people from whom he would otherwise have shied away, but his zeal seemed primarily in the work of photography itself. At the beginning, he took a number of photographs of skeletons of animals and other biological specimens. But this was about the time of his encounter with the epileptic man and with his consequent desire to study the deeper structures of anatomy. In his portrait photography his liking for the pretty, and the precision of the posing of his subjects was noteworthy. He enjoyed having his little girl subjects pose in various character costumes and kept something of a wardrobe to use on these occasions. Later in life he took pictures of little girls in the nude, a fact which is slyly revealed in his Diaries, when he refers to taking a picture of a child "in the usual clothes"—the *usual* being the bare skin in contrast to the varied and unusual costumes which might otherwise be supplied.

While any special significance of this interest in the nude girl has been denied by some on the ground that it was the custom of the time to take photographs of children in the

PHOTOGRAPH OF A YOUNG GIRL BY LEWIS CARROLL

nude, it would seem that it was really most unusual to extend this to a period beyond infancy. Indeed, it seems possible that it was the objection to this on the part of the little girls' parents that led Carroll to abandon his photography abruptly in 1880 and never return to it. This was about the time, too, when the sixteen-year-old girl's mother did *not* accept his apologies for the kissing incident, and he was sufficiently perturbed to seek definite advice from others.[19] Photography then was supplanted by a return to sketching which he now did in the studio of Miss E. Gertrude Thomson, an illustrator of children's books, and under whose instruction he could continue to study little girl models. Carroll's work and life as a photographer have been admirably presented by Mr. Helmut Gernsheim in a small book, *Lewis Carroll, Photographer* (43).

In the Collingwood biography, Carroll is given some praise as an artist (44): He "possessed an intense natural appreciation of the beautiful, an abhorrence of all that is coarse and unseemly, which might almost be called a hyper-refinement, a wonderfully good eye for form, and last but not least, the most scrupulous conscientiousness about detail. On the other hand, his sense of color was somewhat imperfect and his hand was almost totally untrained, so that while he had the enthusiasm of the artist his work always had the defects of an amateur." This was written immediately after Carroll's death and by a nephew. It would seem to us, however, that the outstanding merit of the Dodgson-Carroll sketches lay in an extraordinary and incessant caricature in which evil is frequently unconsciously and subtly suggested, but never presented directly. His sketching shared characteristics with his writing: being devastatingly sadistic but in so veiled and hidden a form as to produce tickling sensations rather than clear awareness of attack. The body distortions and incongruities are prominent in the sketches, as in the writing, in

[19] *The Diaries,* February 5, 1880 (43).

contrast to the photography, which was limited largely to idealized subjects: little girls and famous people. It would seem that the photographs were to capture and hold as incontrovertible fact the precious moments in time and space occupied by his ideal and adored subjects, whereas in his writing and in his sketches, forms do not stand still or stay put, bodies change in size and proportion even as time flows irregularly and sometimes unpredictably. Surprise is frequently the order of the day. Further, he was more or less body-bound: in that he rarely photographed or drew landscapes or objects other than human beings or animals.[20]

Neither was he greatly interested in affairs outside the gardens of Daresbury, Croft and Oxford. The latter seemed indeed a larger, more complex version of the rectory garden. He played his part in its affairs with conscientious zeal and concern, being, in addition to mathematics don, sublibrarian, curator of the Common Room, including supervision of the wine cellar—this last assignment utilizing extensively his penchant for collecting, classifying and cataloguing. He was deeply concerned with the rebuilding and rearrangements in the university and earnest in his expression of opinion—sometimes accomplished through witty and parodying pamphlets. He did not seem to be clearly interested in affairs of the world, outside the university, although references to politics and science are sometimes reflected in a half-hidden way in some of his writing.

He traveled little. In 1867, there was a two months' tour to Moscow with Henry Liddon (later Dean of St. Paul's) in which they included Brussels, Cologne, Berlin, St. Peters-

[20] How much Dodgson thought in body terms is apparent from a rather striking entry in his Diary for November 24, 1857. "Finished the first volume of De Quincey: it is perfectly delightful reading and full of information of all kinds. I want to organize some regular means, by which all valuable reading may be made available afterwards—i.e., that I may be able in a moment to refer to any part of it. This must be done by various 'indices' which, like the absorbent ducts in the human system, shall each mechanically take up and secrete what belongs to its department" (45).

burg, Warsaw, Breslau, Dresden and Paris. Liddon was probably acting as unofficial ambassador from Wilberforce to the Greek Orthodox Church, and the observations regarding the visits to the various churches and cathedrals comprise a large part of Dodgson's *Russian Journal,* which on the whole is a disappointingly schoolboyish reportorial account of his travels (46). This was his only journey outside of Great Britain. Otherwise he spent some holidays at Sandowne on the Isle of Wight or at Eastbourne, but generally visited with his maiden sisters at Guildford. He had been to Scotland in 1857 and returned in 1871 and 1882. There is an account, unsubstantiated but carefully cherished by the local people, that he spent the summer of 1862, 1863 or 1864 in Llandudno, Wales with the Liddell family. This seems to have been the extent of his traveling.

From his boyhood on, he was a faithful diarist. Unfortunately, many of the journals have been lost. Although the early biography by Collingwood quotes from the journals which have subsequently been lost, there are no diaries and very scant letters or other records for the years 1849-1851. Although most of the Diary entries are factual recordings, as though to support memory rather than to preserve ideas, indulge speculations and ruminations, or even to give vent to emotional reactions, there are occasional statements of modest self-deprecation interspersed with earnest prayers "that God would forgive him the past and help him to perform His Holy Will in the future" (47). These occur especially at the end of a year and the beginning of a new one. Yet his life was one of sad and desperate immaculateness.

At Christ Church College, the library looked out over the garden, where the Liddell children often played. Dodgson, inevitably eavesdropping on their play in their very early childhood when he was acting as sublibrarian, must have been reminded of the gardens at Croft and Daresbury where he amused and played with his sisters and brothers. He had already shown some propensity to develop attachments to children of about seven to eleven, but these early friendships were about equally with boys and girls. The intensity of these friendships diminished when the children reached adolescence. It would seem that he could not endure the sexuality of the developing body at puberty, and that he perpetuated, or unconsciously attempted to perpetuate, the idyllic garden memories with the brothers and sisters, when he had been forced to abandon them as he passed into puberty and went away to school at twelve.

The three little Liddells, Lorina, Edith, and the famous Alice, became the favorites among all his child friends. He devised games and riddles, told them stories, took them for boat rides on the river, and took innumerable photographs of them. It is interesting that while the three sisters are immortalized in the *Alice* books, there were actually ten little Liddells coming along in the deanery during the next years, to remind him quietly and implacably of the ten other children of his own family, one of them not yet born when he had left the Croft rectory garden for the schools outside. That there was a conscious or unconscious identification of this family with his own brothers and sisters seems inevitable. It is interestingly apparent from his Diaries, however, that in his earliest attachment to the Liddells, the oldest child Harry played a prominent part. Undertaking to tutor Harry in mathematics, he found him a not very apt pupil. Still he records many pleasant afternoons with Harry. This may have been partly due to the fact that his sensitivity to misinterpretation and gossip regarding his attentions to the little girls and their governess caused him to retreat somewhat to the safety of excursions with Harry. Still, it is evident that during these years (roughly those of the '50's) he was not as acrimonious toward little boys as he became later. His Diaries during this early period sometimes comment on

THE LIDDELL SISTERS: EDITH, LORINA, AND ALICE

the beauty of this or that boy child—usually boys between seven and eleven also.

On July 4, 1862, approximately six months after his ordination as a deacon by the relentless Wilberforce, he invited the three little Liddells to go rowing on the Isis River, accompanied and chaperoned by Canon Duckworth. On this excursion he unfolded the *Alice's Adventures in Wonderland* story, extemporizing as they rowed along. The story was not created entirely new at this time, for there is evidence that some of its incidents had been in his mind for some time. He had a way of going over and over his fantasies, elaborating, condensing and putting them together in new arrangements, much in the fashion of repetitive dreams which are remodeled from time to time to include details of current happenings.[21] Indeed, the idea of the *Looking Glass* world which

21 The growth of Carroll's stories seemed to occur as naturally and as slowly as that of a tree. If one reads all of his writings, one finds bits and fragments produced here and there many years before they are woven into the fabric of a definite tale. The idea that *Alice's Adventures in Wonderland* go directly back to the gardens at Croft and Daresbury is given rather uncanny support by a collection of small articles uncovered from a secret cache in the nursery floor of the Croft Rectory when it was remodeled in 1950! The story in the family of some secret hiding place proved to be more than a fantasy, for under the floor boards was a miscellaneous assortment of children's toys, including a thimble, a child's white glove, and a child's left-foot shoe. These relics seem probably part of nursery play which is reproduced in the lost glove of the White Rabbit in *Wonderland*, the thimble which Alice carried in her pocket and which was again presented to her by the Dodo (Dodgson), and was also used by the Mariners in the *Hunting of the Snark*. The "left-hand shoe" appears again in the *Aged Aged Man* song. . . . It seems that the nursery floor was renewed and strengthened in 1843 when the Dodgsons first moved to Croft and in the remodeling more than a century later, three pieces of the floor were seen to be inscribed in pencil. On one was written, possibly by the hand of the youthful Charles Dodgson, "This floor was laid by Mr. Martin and Mr. Sutton June 19th 1843." On one board the writing was not decipherable, while a third, clearly written by Charles said:

> And we'll wander through
> the wide world
> And chase the buffalo.

The buffalo too reappears in the song of the *Aged Aged Man* and in the song of the mad gardener. One suspects that this little cache in the new nursery at Croft may have been something of a cornerstone laying, carrying over relics from the nursery play at Daresbury (48).

was not published until 1871 had seemed to occur to him first definitely in connection with another Alice, his distant cousin Alice Raikes, about 1868, and already by this time he had related many of the *Looking Glass* incidents to Alice Liddell; and so with *Wonderland* too—or as it was first called *Alice's Adventures Under Ground.* Still the excursion of July 4, 1862 must have done much to crystallize these fantasies into a definite pattern.

The little jaunt is reproduced in the *Wonderland* scene, where the animals are caught in a pool of water: the Duck, the Dodo, a Lory, an Eaglet, and Alice were admittedly Canon Duckworth, Dodgson, Lorina, Edith, and Alice Liddell. Even this, however, was combined with the memories of another excursion, three weeks earlier, when he had also been accompanied by his sisters, Fanny and Elizabeth, and the whole party had been caught in a rainstorm and had to seek shelter to dry out.[22] In this scene, certainly there is evidence of the combination of the little Liddells with the maiden sisters, the little Liddells almost surely representing an earlier charming version of these sisters before their spinster days. The Liddell children were really beautiful, as is evident in the Dodgson photographs; and among them Alice was the favorite, keenly imaginative, full of humor and appreciation. Of her and to her Carroll was to write a dedication of his tale, *Through the Looking Glass,* at a time (1871) when she was almost grown up and he had seen very little of her for some time.

> Child of the pure, unclouded brow
> And dreaming eyes of wonder!
> Though time be fleet and I and thou
> Are half a life asunder,
> Thy loving smile will surely hail
> The love gift of a fairy tale.

[22] Diary entry, June 17, 1862 (49).

I have not seen thy sunny face
Nor heard thy silver laughter
No thought of me shall find a place
In thy young life's hereafter—
Enough that now thou wilt not fail
To listen to my fairy tale.

There is a curious mystery about the excursion on the Isis of July 4, 1862. All of those who participated have described the day as one of brilliant sunshine and heat, whereas the weather records of the time indicate that the afternoon was overcast and somewhat cool. It seems probable that the recollections are really fusions of the July 4th excursion with other similar excursions, and it is possible further that the memory of sunshine is enhanced because the little event with its uniquely and universally significant content had something of a screening function in the memories of the various participants. Hudson refers to this aptly as "bottled sunshine" (50).

By the time of the writing of *Through the Looking Glass*, Alice Liddell had passed beyond the barrier of puberty into young womanhood. In addition, there was some sort of estrangement between Carroll and the Liddells, which seems to be reflected in the dedicatory verse. The basis for this has been a matter of some thought and conjecture. Reading as much as is published of his journals, one is impressed with an uneasiness on Carroll's part regarding the interpretation of his attentions from a quite early time in the friendship and there are the slightest hints of gossip of some kind. Certainly the Diary entries indicate that Carroll spent much time with the children in 1856-1857. Then there are four missing (lost) years of the Diary, but in 1862 up to and for a time after the July 4th expedition, he seems to have been on free visiting terms with the children. During the Fall of 1862, there are notes of his consulting Dean Liddell regarding his possible obligation to take Priest's Orders. Only a week later (October 28, 1862) he records his efforts to get Mrs. Liddell to permit an artist, who was to color some of Dodgson's photographs, to call on the children in order to get good likenesses; and he concludes, "She simply evaded the question. I have been out of her good graces ever since Lord Newry's business" (51). While this is not explained, it seems nonetheless to mark the recognition of a definite rift which was not at first wide but gradually became so. By the end of 1863, he remarked after a pleasant evening with the Liddell children that it had been nearly six months since he had seen anything of them. Some have thought that Mrs. Liddell, beautiful and ambitious, found burdensome the devotion of the stammering and eccentric Dodgson to the growing Alice. Certainly she destroyed the letters which he wrote to the children, especially to Alice, and did much to prevent the continuation of the friendship. That Dodgson was an earnest kisser is apparent in his letters, his poetry and his anecdotes as well as from the reminiscences of his little girl friends. It may have been that this in itself was sufficient to stir the little girl and set the mother on edge, but what Lord Newry's business was is still obscure.

There was obviously later a considerable amount of gossip at Oxford concerning the relations between the Liddells and Dodgson, which became the subject of lampooning by the Oxford undergraduates. Some humorous verse entitled *Cakeless* was composed by Rev. John Howe Jenkins and published in 1874. It is devoted to ridicule of Mrs. Liddell's snobbish matchmaking and among the characters Dodgson is represented by *Kraftsohn,* who protests during the wedding of Psyche, one of the daughters of Apollo and Diana. The little pamphlet was suppressed and its author "sent down" or "rusticated" as indicated by the penciled marginal note on the copy still extant in the British Museum (52).

On the day of the rowing party (July 4, 1861), however, Dodgson recorded faithfully in his journal, "I made an expedition up the river to Godstow with the little Liddells; we had tea on the bank there and did not reach Christ Church till half past eight," adding somewhat later, "On which occasion I told them the fairy tale *Alice's Adventures Under Ground* which I undertook to write out for Alice." This title was subsequently changed to *Alice's Hour in Elfland* and then (1864) to *Alice's Adventures in Wonderland.*

The original manuscript was carefully copied by its author and presented as a Christmas gift to Alice Liddell in December, 1862. It was only subsequently that he was persuaded by George MacDonald, author of *At the Back of the North Wind*, to seek publication which was then arranged with Macmillan with illustrations by Sir John Tenniel. Publication was accomplished in July, 1865, three years to a day after the famous river outing. The first edition proved somewhat faulty in its printing and Dodgson, ever exacting concerning details but withal saving, had this withdrawn and a new edition substituted, the imperfect first edition being subsequently released to the American trade.[23] The book was immediately a considerable success and before many years was translated into several languages and was furnishing an appreciable income to the surprised author.[24] Carroll and

[23] There is some indication that the real objection was from Tenniel who complained that his illustrations had been badly reproduced (53).

[24] Most of the reviews were favorable, but the critic on the *Athenaeum* wrote caustically on December 16, 1865, "This is a dream story—but who can, in cold blood manufacture a dream, with all its loops and ties, and loose threads and entanglements, and inconsistancies and passages which lead to nothing, at the end of which sleep's most diligent pilgrim never arrives? Mr. Carroll has laboured hard to heap together strange adventures, and heterogeneous combinations and we acknowledge the hard labour. Mr. Tenniel, again, is square and grim and uncouth in his illustrations, howbeit clever, even sometimes to the verge of grandeur, as is the artist's habit. We fancy that any real child might be more puzzled than enchanted by this stiff overwrought story."

Carroll had a phobic reaction to reviews later in life, simply avoiding reading them, as he confessed in the Preface to *Sylvie and Bruno Concluded*. Unfavorable reviews made him cross, he stated, and favorable ones made him conceited. Neither result was desirable.

Alice were simultaneously famous, world figures in fact. If anything this worsened the relationship between Dodgson and the Liddells, but broadened his contacts in the literary world.

In 1867, Carroll contributed a small story, "Bruno's Revenge," to *Aunt Judy's Magazine*. This must have been about the time of his visit to Russia, and it is an interesting speculation whether the name Bruno, so strange among Carroll's other child names, was in any way connected with the idea of the Russian Bear. At any rate, this little sketch was the beginning of Carroll's longest work *Sylvie and Bruno*, which was written in fragments over a period of nearly thirty years, being published in two sections: *Sylvie and Bruno* appearing in 1889, and *Sylvie and Bruno Concluded* in 1893. It is a curious, rather sweetly tedious book, suggesting in its elision of time and of character identities, a somewhat confectionized version of the shifting from unconscious to conscious activities so fantastically reproduced in the novels of Franz Kafka. As literature it is boring; but as a revelation of the psychic structure of the author, it is enormously valuable. It is the one story of Carroll's in which the main character is a boy, and sympathetically dealt with.

Archdeacon Dodgson died rather suddenly in the summer of 1868. There is little direct record of the son's immediate reaction, although in a letter written nearly thirty years later, and toward the end of his own life, he referred to his father's death as "the greatest blow that has ever fallen on my life." He spent the summer at Croft, arranging things and preparing for the family's move which was accomplished in the fall, to a house called the Chestnuts at Guildford, where they continued throughout the rest of his life. At this time, none of the children had married, but his sister Mary married the Reverend Charles Collingwood in the following April (1869); in August, 1871, Wilfred married Alice Donkin, and not until June, 1883 was there another marriage, Skeffington

to Isabelle Cooper. These events, important as they must
have been to Charles, the elder brother, are but scantily recorded and with almost no comment. Only once in the published *Diaries* does Charles permit himself to record thoughts
of marriage for himself, and then it was to deny them.[25]

In November, 1868, a few months after the death of the
father and roughly coincident with the moving of the family
to Guildford, Charles himself made one of the major changes
in the arrangements of his life in that he moved into rooms
in the Tom Quad in Oxford, a relatively spacious apartment
with room for his photographic work as well. Here he was
to remain for the rest of his life—i.e., nearly thirty years. The
year 1869 saw the publication of *Phantasmagoria,* followed
in 1871 by *Through the Looking Glass* which had been in the
process of evolution for some time.

Whether influenced by the death of his father (1868),
the marriage of his sister Mary (1869) and the birth of his
godson, later his biographer (1872), he was by 1872 again
preoccupied with the problems of anatomy, physiology,[26]
pain, and ghosts (55). It is interesting that he did not specifically mention the birth of this first child of the next
generation of the family, but only recorded, ". . . I found
Charles Collingwood [Mary's husband] waiting for me, and
we drove together to Southwick, where I found Mary, Elizabeth, and my little godson Stuart." Wilfred's first son (second child) was almost as tersely recorded under date of
March 23, 1876. "Birth of a son at the Moor. I received the
first finished sheets of *The Snark.*"[27]

25 Diary entry of July 31, 1857 (apropos of discussing insurance with his
father): "My present opinion is this: that it will be best not to effect any
insurance at present, but simply to save as much as I reasonably can from
year to year. If at any future period I contemplate marriage (of which I
see no present likelihood) it will be quite time enough to begin paying
premiums then."
26 Diary entry for December 26, 1872 (54).
27 What Dodgson did not write in his Diary, Carroll did write in his
verse: In October, 1871, he wrote the prologue for two private theatricals

As far back as 1856 in the early days of his studentship at Oxford, when he had first seen the epileptic man in a fit in the street, Dodgson had been greatly concerned to assure himself that he would be able to offer good help in such a crisis and had sought to prepare himself by the study of anatomy. The same year he had been horrified to see "a mouthing idiot, like the evil genius of the spot" in the courtyard of the inn at Bowes, where the original of Dickens *Dotheboy's Hall* still stood, and he asserted emphatically in his Diary:[28]

> Next to a prison or a lunatic asylum, preserve me from living at Bowes

---

given at Clevedon House on November, 1-2. The plays were *The Loan of a Lover* and *Whitebait at Greenwich*. Following a gossipy and critical discussion of the play by two hypothetical characters, Miss Crab and Miss Verjuice, the speaker continues:

> What! Acting Love!! And has that ne'er been seen
> Save with a row of footlights placed between?
> My gentle censors, let me roundly ask
> Do none but actors ever wear a mask?
> Or have we reached at last that golden age
> That finds deception only on the stage?
> Come, let's confess all round, before we budge
> Where all are guilty, none should play the judge:
> We're actors all, a motley company,
> Some on the stage, and others—on the sly,
> And guiltiest he who paints so well his phiz
> His brother actors scarce know what he is,
> A truce to moralizing: we invite
> The goodly company we see tonight.
> To share the little banquet we have got,
> Well dressed, we hope, and served up hot and hot.
> *Loan of a Lover* is the leading dish.
> Concluding with a dainty course of fish,
> Whitebait at Greenwich in the best condition
> (By Mr. Gladstone's very kind permission)
> *Before the courses will be handed round*
> *An entree made of children nicely browned.*
>
> Quoted from *Early Theatricals at Oxford*, by Fred B. de Sausmerez [56]. [Italics added.]

[28] Diary entry for August 30, 1856 (57). Derek Hudson sees in this scene only evidence of Dodgson's unashamed, hearty laughter (58).

and described quite clearly how mirth and laughter evolved from the horror of this scene and the subsequent encounter with an objectionable guide in the form of a hermit.

> I was immediately seized with a fit of laughter, which I only just succeeded in stifling, and sat for ten minutes or more looking fixedly out of the window, in a state of agony, and longing for escape . . . the relief of getting into the garden was indescribable—we almost lay down and rolled—I think he must have heard our shouts of laughter, all the more violent for having been pent up so long.

This is a significant picture of a psychological pattern characteristic of Carroll, but more frequently expressed in a less noisy way in his writing. In the very next Diary entry he recorded that he had finished *Upon the Lonely Moor,* a parody on Wordsworth's poem about the leech gatherer, and had sent it off for publication. This was an early version of the poem *A Sitting on a Gate* which was finally to be completed in *Through the Looking Glass* (the inner connection between this theme, the idiot, and the epileptic is discussed later).

About a year later, in December, 1857,[29] he was again testing himself, concerning his ability to meet a crisis helpfully. His Diary records then that he had attended an operation at St. Bartholomew's Hospital with his friend and photographing companion Southey. The patient's knee joint had to be cut into, and when it was discovered that there was a considerable destruction of bony tissue, an amputation above the knee was decided on. "The chloroform took several minutes to act fully, producing first convulsions, and then stupor like that of a man dead drunk." Dodgson expected to be ill at the sight, but was surprised to find that he could bear this quite well though the operation lasted more than an

[29] Diary entry of December 19, 1857 (59).

hour. He decided that this endurance was only possible because of his awareness that with chloroform the patient was suffering no pain, and concluded, "This is an experiment I have long been anxious to make in order to know whether I might rely on myself to be of any use in cases of emergency, and I am very glad to believe that I should not enjoy seeing much of it." It is unlikely that the chloroform actually produced a convulsion, but more probable that some twitching was so interpreted by the overwrought watcher. This matter of the fit and its connection with pain was a repetitive concern. Ten days later he was writing characteristic New Year's resolutions: chiefly to study more assiduously mathematical and theological problems, and to memorize poetry.

By 1871, *Upon a Lonely Moor* had gone through several changes and emerged in the *Looking Glass* as *A Sitting on the Gate.* One suspects there is a relationship between the old man on the gate with his foolish movements and suggestion of senselessness, the white knight who falls in every direction including upside down, and Father William who both balances an eel on the end of his nose and stands on his head—these three on the one hand, and the mouthing idiot, the patient under chloroform, and the epileptic man, on the other. The horror of the last three is being converted into the humor of the fictitious characters, much in the fashion of the rolling on the grass in the garden is a release from the impression of the idiot boy at Bowes.

In 1872,[30] Carroll had acquired a set of bones and was again studying physiology and anatomy, so assiduously that he felt he had little spare time for anything else. In the same Diary entry he mentioned reading Charles Darwin's *Expression of Emotions in Man and Animals* and after various other

[30] Diary entry for December 26, 1872. It is interesting to note that each time that Dodgson became interested in anatomy and physiology he also made an effort to cure his speech. The disturbance of speech in drunkenness, idiocy and epilepsy is of course frequently conspicuous (60).

158

memoranda he ended the day's notes with "Wilfred and Alice are here with their baby, and as Mary's two children are still here, the house is busy enough." The christening of Wilfred's first baby, Edith, had been noted in a sparse entry on October 20, 1872.

Dodgson had been interested in magic since his puppeteer[31] and sleight-of-hand days at Daresbury, but during the years following his father's death, a period of death, marriages, and births, roughly from 1868 to 1876, he became more seriously concerned with occultism. He was for some time in contact with an artist, Mr. Heaphy, who had painted a picture of a ghost whom he claimed to have seen; and although Dodgson "considered the tale curious and inexplicable, he thought the ghost lovely."[32] It seemed he could neither completely affirm or deny his belief in these supernatural phenomena, and from its beginning in 1882 until 1896 or 1897 he was a member of the Psychical Research Society. In this same period too (1875) he wrote a letter, "Vivisection as a Sign of the Times," which was published in the *Pall-Mall Gazette*. This was a subject which had long been troubling him. It was against this background that the *Snark* arose—by spontaneous conception, it seems, for Mr. Carroll related that it was on July 18, 1874 that, while walking alone on a hillside near Guildford, the line "For the Snark was a Boojum, you see!" came into his mind. At the time he was not aware of its meaning, but wrote it down. Four days later he had composed a stanza, using this as the line, as follows:

In the midst of the word he was trying to say
In the midst of his laughter and glee
He had softly and suddenly vanished away
For the Snark *was* a Boojum, you see.[33]

---

[31] There is probably some relation here of the puppet to the effigy, the use of which preceded portrait caricature (61). See Part IV of this book.

[32] Quoted from Alexander Taylor's *The White Knight* (62).

[33] To this author, this stanza by itself might be an expression of the panic at the root of and reproduced in his stammering. This is further described

Gradually the rest of the poem evolved. By November of that year he was consulting Henry Holiday about illustrating it, and consulting Ruskin about Holiday. All of Carroll's descriptions of the Boojum were quite unimaginable to Mr. Holiday, and Carroll wished them to remain so. Ultimately in 1876, the *Snark* was published, a poem of agony in eight fits. Still the author claimed to have no idea what a snark was like, although he described the word itself as a portmanteau word, containing snail and shark. When pressed further as to what a snark really was, he would explain that "the Snark *was* a Boojum, you see."

The popular legend that Carroll was a great mathematician seems to have been sadly untrue. That he had uncommon ability in mathematics is very probable. But his mind here was generally conservative rather than imaginatively exploring. His Diaries show repeated vows and determinations to do further reading in mathematics and theology rather than a spontaneous and lively interest. In his earlier years of teaching these pious wishes appeared as New Year's resolutions.[34] These two subjects certainly belonged to his

---

in an earlier stanza of the finished poem, written Carroll-wise, however, after this concluding stanza. The poem, completed, has other unconscious themes as well, though all converge in the state of combined panic and awe which ends the poem and came first to the solitary pedestrian on the hillside.

[34] Thus at 11:30 P.M. on December 31, 1856, he wrote ". . . As to the future, I may lay down as absolute necessities *Divinity Reading* and *Mathematics Reading*. I trust to do something this vacation but most of the Long Vacation must be devoted to work, and I think my best plan will be to take lodgings wherever [Bartholomew] Price has his reading party and so get occasional help from him." On December 31, 1857, he recorded a list of things (Poetry; Elements of Mathematical Subjects; Proofs of Formulae of Mathematical Subjects; Formulae Themselves; Chronology for Memoria Technica; and Geometrical Problems) to be learned by heart and kept up at such times as railway traveling, etc. He proposed for the New Year "1) Reading for Ordination at the end of the year 2) Making myself a competent Mathematical Lecturer for Christ Church 3) Constant improvement of habits of activity, punctuality, etc."

Even as late as July, 1881, he recorded in his Diary the work he planned for the summer holiday, and began with "Finish Euclid II; Euclid and his Modern Rivals; Limits of Circle-Squaring etc."—but now he was writing

father, and his full realization in either of them seemed inhibited, although his dutiful pursuit was predestined. After the 1860's, his resolutions about work and study of mathematics somewhat diminished. He was publishing occasional mathematical articles, but as one writer (63) has said of his mathematical problems, they "can interest almost nobody because the techniques are too involved for the layman and the problems too trivial for the mathematician." He did not seem to take great interest in mathematical research, in spite of being in contact with Bartholomew Price and H. J. S. Smith, two of the most brilliant mathematicians of the time. Neither was he described as a good teacher. He was probably perfunctory rather than zealous with his interest gradually going more and more into other fields: his photography until 1880, the theater, his writing, and always his little girls.[35]

Indeed, he was gradually coming to the decision to give up teaching (lecturing) as he approached his fiftieth birthday, in favor of writing without any fixed obligation. On November 30, 1881, he wrote in his Diary that his journal (in years past) recorded that he had given his first Euclid lecture on Monday, January 28, 1856, and that of twelve students assigned, nine had actually attended; and that now nearly twenty-six years later he was giving his last lecture with an attendance of two out of a possible nine students. He

rather than just preparing by study. A distaste for his lecturing is shown in his Diary entry of November 23, 1881, in which he planned "Euclid I and II, as a chatty book for boys, with illustrations though not definitely *comic*, but to make it interesting." This was just at the time that he was relinquishing his lectureship, and "going on without any fixed occupation."

[35] Mr. Warren Weaver, writing in the *Princeton University Library Chronicle*, 1951, says of Dodgson: "There were twenty-one books on mathematical subjects. It had better be admitted gracefully and at once that Dodgson was not a very good mathematician. He was chiefly concerned with defending Euclid from any sacrilegious attempt to question him or modernize him. He did some useful work in formal logic, but not at a profound level. But he was as good as you would expect when he concerned himself with tricky and witty mathematical puzzles" (64).

161

reflected that there was a sadness at coming to the end of any thing in life. The marriage of Alice Liddell to Reginald Hargreaves, which occurred in 1880, and to which he seems not to have been invited, must have affected him greatly. Characteristically there is no mention of it in his Diary. Sometime later, on hearing that Alice was to have a child, he wrote her asking her to name the baby Alice. She replied, however, asking him to stand as godfather to her son Caryl. He is reported not to have replied.[36]

Dodgson continued to live on at Oxford after his resignation as a lecturer. He read a great deal, wrote, attended the theater, and sketched. He was further occupied with his duties as curator of the wine cellar and with the endless systematic recordings of his own interests: his letters, his dinners, his visits and visitors. He was evidently increasingly subject to respiratory illnesses and "ague-like feverish attacks" and between 1885 and 1891 suffered from several migraine attacks with scintillating scotoma which he described as "moving fortifications" but with scant headache. He worked intermittently on *Sylvie and Bruno*, piecing together the already published fragments and sketches with the aid of "padding" to make what he hoped was a novel, which was eventually published in 1889. His nephew-biographer thinks that this marked an epoch in his life as "it was the publication of all the ideals and sentiments which he held most dear . . . From a higher standpoint (higher than that of artistic and literary value) that of the Christian and the philanthropist, the book was the best thing he ever wrote" (65). During the period of the '80's he was also much concerned with the production of *Alice* on the stage in tableaux, dramatic form, and operetta, and with various adaptations of it in publications for children.

[36] The Account of Captain Caryl Hargreaves, *The New York Times*, May 1, 1932.

In 1888, he records[37] the new experience of sketching a nude model of fourteen—a young girl who had been a model since the age of five. He concluded that a spectator would have to be really in search of evil thought to have any other feeling about her than simply a sense of beauty as in looking at a statue. She seemed a good and modest girl with every prospect of growing up a pure and good woman. His previous sketching of nude girls had been limited, he stated, to two studies of girls of five. Mrs. Shute, the artist in whose studio he worked, later wrote that he confided to her that he preferred the undeveloped (or incompletely developed) female body to the mature one, and that twelve would be his ideal age as "children are so thin from seven to ten." This may have represented some shift in his interest as in the '50's and '60's—i.e., when he was between twenty and forty —there is every indication that seven to eight was the preferred age.

The last ten years of Dodgson-Carroll's life were considerably slowed down. He no longer entertained much and accepted few invitations to dine out. He continued to frequent the theater and to write letters of protest when he thought plays indecent; to work and rework his games and riddles, to give occasional lectures and sermons, and to entertain his child friends. At one time (1893) his sister Mary Collingwood apparently suggested prudence to him, as she had heard some gossip. He replied with asperity concerning the wicked recklessness with which people repeat gossip, and announced the two criteria for his behavior: his own conscience, and the approval of the parents of his little girl friends (67). In 1896 (at sixty-four), he was writing[38] to such a parent to ask if her daughter were invitable and kissable and explaining that he asked this question of mothers of girls over fourteen; but that later when the girl became

[37] Diary entry of January 28, 1888 (66).
[38] See Editor's note to Diary entry for July 11, 1896 (68).

engaged, he did not continue the practice of kissing except with the fiance's permission. On the other hand, he distinctly felt that if he were the fiance he would not consent. Throughout he was a faithful visitor to his sisters at Guildford.

For some reason not quite clear, in 1897, Dodgson took a more decisive attitude toward Carroll and more or less expelled him from Oxford. He had for some time disliked getting the two confused and was known as Dodgson to have turned away visitors to Carroll (including once the American editor, Edward Bok). But now he even refused all mail addressed to Carroll at Oxford and had it returned to the Dead Letter Office unopened with the endorsement "Not known."[39]

Only a few weeks later, while on his usual Christmas visit to Guildford, he fell sick of what first seemed a rather mild respiratory infection, which refused to improve, however. On January 5, 1898 his brother-in-law Charles Collingwood died. Only eight days later, Charles Dodgson succumbed to the attack of bronchitis which had begun so insidiously. He was survived only five days by Dean Liddell. His death occurred almost exactly forty-seven years after the death of his mother.

[39] Diary entry for November 8, 1897 (69).

In 1890, he had circulated a printed pamphlet: "Mr. C. L. Dodgson is so frequently addressed by strangers on the quite unwarranted assumption that he writes under an assumed name, and seemingly in ignorance of what he believes is usually implied in that practice viz that such writers desire to avoid all *personal* publicity and all contact with the outer world—except through their publishers and under their assumed names—that he has found it necessary to print this, once and for all, as an answer to all applications:

He acknowledges no connection whatever with any 'pseudonym' or with any book not published under his own name. Having therefore no claim to retain, or even to read, the enclosed, he returns it for the convenience of the writer who thus misaddressed it."

Quoted from Warren Weaver (70).

2.

THE CHARACTER OF
DODGSON AS REVEALED IN
THE WRITINGS OF CARROLL

Dodgson was regarded as an eccentric by his students and his contemporaries, and although some saw him as dull and boring, the picture in retrospect is interesting and at times colorful. In his boyhood he had been so adept manually that he not only made his own marionettes and theater, but on one occasion he made for a sister a very tiny set of tools, complete in a case, only one inch long. He, like the White Knight, was an inventor —of gadgets, of puzzles, riddles, games, and conundrums, as well as many mnemonic devices.[1] During a great deal of

---

[1] Dodgson "turned out nearly 200 little printed pamphlets, many of which consist of only a single sheet. Nearly 60 were devoted to topics in mathematics and logic, over 30 were concerned with games he invented or were schemes for ciphering. Nearly 50 were related to Christ Church—its little quarrels, its proposals for change, its regulations. . . . Over 50 were devoted to miscellaneous subjects—how not to catch cold, how to score tennis tournaments, on second-hand books, proposals for a new dramatic institute and for a bowdlerized Shakespeare for young girls, how to play billiards on a circular table . . . how to write and register correspondence, common errors in spelling, on the profits of authorship, an advertisement for selling a house, a questionnaire based on the rules for commissions chargeable on overdue postal orders, how to memorize dates, etc. etc. . . . In one series [of pamphlets] he describes an unbelievably complicated variant of croquet, successive editions making it less and less likely that anyone would ever learn the rules." Quoted from Warren Weaver (1).

his adult life he apparently suffered from an intractable insomnia; and he constructed many of his inventions, seemingly, as a way of keeping his mind busy during the long hours of the night. He invented an instrument which he called a nyctograph for making records in the dark. He worked out most of his inventions entirely in his mind, only making a record on completion.

To those who did not know him well he seemed "stiff and donnish" (Collingwood's words), and Mark Twain found him "the stillest and shyest full-grown man" except for Uncle Remus that he had ever met. During several hours of conversation in a group, Carroll contributed nothing but an occasional question.[2] On the other hand, Twain found him interesting to look at. The shyness may have been increased by his stammering and by his deafness (left ear), but it was almost all pervasive, except with his little girls. Only occasionally in some meeting would he flash out with an incisive witticism—and he was generally more amusing when enticed into a monologue than in a conversation. He was slight, stoop-shouldered, and rather drab in appearance. It is said that the two sides of his face did not match. He habitually put his right hand in front of his mouth while lecturing and was sufficiently self-critical that he drew a caricature of himself in this position. As he grew older, his face became more feminine in cast, an effect possibly enhanced by his wearing his hair rather long. His effeminacy was sufficiently obvious that some of his less sympathetic students once wrote a parody of his parodies and signed it "Louisa Caroline."

He disliked garish colors, preferred pinks and grays and is said to have requested one of the little girls not to visit him in a red dress (3). He himself wore unobtrusive clothing, except that he habitually went without an overcoat, wore a tall hat, and black cotton gloves. He stood so straight that he seemed to be leaning backward, and is also said to have

2 See Editor's note in the *Diaries*—under date of July 26, 1879 (2).

Carroll's self-caricature, "What I Look Like When I'm Lecturing"

staggered a little, i.e., veering more to one side than the other. In spite of this he was a tremendous walker—and in 1897, six months before his death, he noted walking seventeen to twenty miles on each of two days with only one day in between.

There was a tinge of the crank inventor in his attitudes. For the most part he carried out his mental researches without much reference to the activities in the outer world, although he was a habitual publisher of his ideas, either in articles, in magazines or by letters to the newspapers. Thus he invented a new method of reckoning postage which he sent to the post-office department; a new method of scoring and eliminating in tennis matches, sent to the Lawn Tennis

Association; a new method of voting when more than two choices are present. In 1876, he invented proportional representation, although it had been invented by Thomas Hare and debated in Parliament in 1867.

From an early age he was interested in Time, and wrote and lectured many times on the subject "Where does the day begin?" and he spent much time writing people all over the world to discover how they dated letters at a specific time; but he paid no attention to the Prime Meridian Conference held in Washington, D.C. to settle the question of the International Date Line. He seemed always to be in some kind of battle with time, attempting to avoid being caught by time or trying to entrap time himself. He often refused invitations for a specific time but would announce his intention to come at a later, unspecified time.

For twenty-one years (approximately 1870-1891), he consistently wrote in purple ink; and then suddenly stopped.[3] The significance of this is unclear. But ink, itself, had great meaning. Throughout his stories it is used as the agent for reviving creatures who faint out of terror or excitement.

Not only was he a compulsive publisher of his ideas, but he was a compulsive indexer. He kept a record of all the letters he wrote or received, cross-indexed for topical content. At the time of his death, this registry contained more than 98,000 items. He was something of a collector too, having a number of music boxes and more than two hundred fountain pens.

[3] Mr. Warren Weaver, who has examined many of Lewis Carroll's manuscripts, letters, and notations writes:
"Every example I have ever seen is written with black ink up to June 27, 1870; in purple from December 16, 1870 to December 7, 1890; and then black thereafter, except
  a) one item dated January 27, 1871, written in purple ink but corrected in black
  b) one item dated June 10, 1872 in black
  c) one item dated June 12, 1872 in black with purple corrections.
Every example I have seen dated February 5, 1891 or later is in black" (4).

168

He frequently carried a little black bag, much like a doctor's bag, filled with safety pins, puzzles, and games of his own making, pencils and paper, handkerchiefs and other articles to aid little girls on railroad trains and at the seashore, and to entice them into a fuller acquaintance (5). One is reminded here of the original railroad whose victims must be thrice flattened by the engine of Love before first aid is granted. Now, Mr. Dodgson being older gave prophylactic help.

With adults he was sometimes pompous. For over forty years he kept a record of all his dinner parties, including a statement of the seating arrangements and the menu for the occasion. He often invited little girls to lunch, with instructions to them to leave their brothers at home. In his middle life he frankly loathed little boys, and refused to stand in church until after the boy choir had passed as he wished to prevent the boys from becoming conceited. He was known to invite a lady to dinner but stipulate that she should leave her husband at home.

His sensitivity to fits and convulsions has already been described. He also had a recurrent preoccupation with cords and knots—not only was the baby tied into a knot by Alice, but the rat's tail was also knotted, as was the Tangled Tale. Carroll also sent Macmillan a diagram of just how all packages to him should be wrapped, how the cords should be tied and where the knots should be placed. In packing for vacation trips, he had a great many portmanteaux (luggage as well as words) with contents wrapped in paper in individual packets, sometimes tied as well. Consequently paper very much increased the size and weight of his luggage.

The illustrators of Carroll's books found him a difficult man to work with: exacting in the extreme, wishing to dictate many details to the illustrator who should somehow reproduce exactly Carroll's own mental picture of the scene, almost as though the artist might photograph Carroll's own imagery. Sir John Tenniel, Holiday and Furniss all found their tasks arduous, and Furniss, a conscious caricaturist, and much younger than Carroll, tried to outdo him in eccentricity and threatened to strike when Carroll became too strongly demanding (6). While Furniss' account (7) has been discredited by some, as burlesquing the situation—and he almost surely embellished his description of it somewhat—yet it is too much in accord with other traits of Dodgson-Carroll to be completely discarded. Furniss, who was the illustrator for *Sylvie and Bruno* worked with Carroll from 1885 to 1892, when Carroll had more and more retired into Dodgson, and his peculiarities had somewhat deepened. He had become more solitary, had given up much of his always moderate social life, abandoned his photography and his teaching, but continued to live at Oxford and work on his manuscripts. He is generally reported to have become increasingly vain, secretive, and even a little suspicious. He rarely accepted invitations to dine, but would "drop in" at a less exactly appointed time; if he did go out to dinner, he sometimes took his own bottle of wine with him. He became more and more burdened by his own prominence and had refused to accept mail addressed to Carroll at Oxford; at the same time that he published frequently and often trivia. According to Furniss' account, Carroll sent him an elaborate document committing him to secrecy about the manuscript. He seemed to wish to make sure that Furniss' wife did not see a picture or look at the manuscript before publication—a stipulation to which Furniss did not agree and so refused to sign the document. But still cautious that others might see prematurely the precious *Sylvie and Bruno* manuscript, which he considered his best work, he prepared the manuscript by cutting it into horizontal strips of four or five lines each, then placed the whole lot in a sack and shook it up. Taking out piece by piece, he pasted the strips down as they happened to come. All strips had already been marked with code hieroglyphics according to which they might be properly reassembled. Furniss reports that he sent the whole batch back with another threat to strike. This jumbled manuscript had been delivered at night.[4] Furniss found that Carroll wanted him to assemble his illustrations from almost as many fragments as were represented in the manuscript. The author would send the illustrator quantities of photographs showing this or that feature which he found inspiring, or would request him to visit friends or even strangers to collect "fragments of faces" which Carroll had thought suitable for the illustrations.

Roger L. Green (Editor of the *Diaries* recently published), in a *Story of Lewis Carroll* (8), neutralizes the Furniss account of the *misch-masched* manuscript, explaining it rather on the basis that the manuscript, which was frankly made up of a number of short stories and sketches, had not yet been properly assembled. That Carroll had a feeling for *Misch-Masch* as well as for order and was constantly taking things apart, jumbling them and reassembling them, cannot be denied.[5] How much Furniss caricatured is an additional question.

Two other preoccupations were so conspicuous both in his life and in his writing as to be clinically noteworthy, viz. (1) special attitudes toward eating and breathing, and (2) his relationship to animals, especially to cats.

---

[4] Compare this with the account of Swift's anonymous delivery of his manuscript at night.

[5] Compare the alleged treatment of the manuscript, with the following stanza from *Poeta Fit, Non Nascitur:*

> For first you write a sentence
> And then you chop it small;
> Then mix the bits and sort them out
> Just as they chance to fall:
> The order of the phrases makes
> No difference at all.
>> In *Phantasmagoria,* 1869 (9).

171

ATTITUDES TOWARD EATING AND BREATHING

Eating (or drinking) and breathing are of course psychologically very close together. In certain respects the latter appears as a kind of ghost or spirit of the former. Both were exceedingly important in Carroll's life. He was himself rather slight in stature. This, combined with his somewhat stiff erectness made him appear taller than he was. He was abstemious, eating and drinking little. A biscuit and sherry constituted his lunch very often. He was somewhat appalled by the healthy appetite of some of his little girl friends. Nonetheless he was greatly preoccupied with eating. His early sketches tended to make people either abnormally fat or abnormally thin. The interest in food and its "nothingness" represented in air is interestingly apparent in one of his early drawings: a sketch of a family taking food in homeopathic doses, in which a butler announces that only a billionth of an ounce of bread is left in the house and that this must be saved for next week, and the mother orders that a trillionth more should be ordered from the bakers. One child asks whether another should have "another molecule" and an older sister deplores that her present glasses have not permitted her to see a nonillionth which has come her way. The whole family party has the grim appearance of those suffering from anorexia nervosa, and the humor has an *Emperor's New Clothes* type of satire, expressed of course in another medium. This cartoon appeared in the *Rectory Umbrella* which dates from Dodgson's period between Rugby and Oxford (10). A complementary cartoon appearing in the same magazine was a sketch purporting to be a caricature of Joshua Reynolds' painting, *The Age of Innocence*. The Dodgson version shows a young hippopotamus, obviously well fed, who "seated under a shady tree, presents to the contemplative mind a charming union of youth and innocence" (Written by Charles L. Dodgson, the Editor of the *Rectory Umbrella*) (11).

The question of eating or being eaten is introduced into the *Wonderland Adventures* before Alice gets fairly down the rabbit hole, with her ponderings as to whether cats eat bats, or bats eat cats. Subsequently eating and drinking magically change her body size; the contents of the "Drink Me" bottle which she finds on the glass table, suddenly shrinks her; whereas the "Eat Me" cake reverses this. Similarly nipping from another bottle near the looking glass in W. Rabbit's house enlarges her and the pebbles that turn into cakes reduce her. And so it goes. She frightens the mouse by talking about Dinah the cat who is such a good mouser, and she finds herself singing about the crocodile who "welcomes little fishes in with gently smiling jaws." Time is suddenly involved when the turning of the earth on its axis gets mixed with the preparation of the soup by the Duchess's cook; and again, this problem crops up in the eternally revolving and mad tea party in which the old subject "When does the day begin?" is revived. Food is the source of trouble and guilt with the Seven of Hearts threatened with decapitation for bringing the cook tulip bulbs instead of onions and again in the grand trial scene when the Knave of Hearts is being tried for having stolen the tarts.

This same gastrointestinal axis to the world's turning appears in some of the early poetry written during Charles' adolescence, especially the moralistic poems dealing with hostility between siblings. *Brother and Sister* (1845) (12), a rollicking rhyme ending with the moral "Don't stew your sister"; and *The Two Brothers* (1853) which relates the tale of a boy who baited his fish hook with a younger brother and so broke their sister's heart "into three" and provoked the lament "One of the two will be wet through and through and t'other will be late to tea" (13). Similarly in parody *The Lady of the Lake* becomes *The Lady of the Ladle* (14).

One can well imagine that sibling rivalry may have been expressed early and drastically among the children of the Daresbury clergyman, in terms of food preference and privileges. Edwin, who was probably the target of the *Age of Innocence* cartoon, was born after the family had moved to Croft and somewhat more affluent circumstances. He was an innocent infant of three to four at the time of the drawing of the cartoon (1849-1850). The caucus race in *Alice's Adventures in Wonderland* in which all the animals, large and small, must have prizes appears as the solution for, or warding off of, such jealousy and rivalry, with Alice rather than the youthful Charles playing the role of arbiter.

In *Through the Looking Glass* changes in body size and proportions are lacking, but the time-space relationship is still puzzling and appears in changes in space appreciation outside the body as indicated by the varying rates of speed necessary to cover apparently similar distances, or sometimes any distance at all. Volcanic explosions seem to have occurred when Alice picked up the White King and Queen and moved them so rapidly that they became breathless. Alice herself floated rather than walked downstairs simply by touching the hand rail with her finger tips. Again there was the eventful race in which the Queen seized Alice by the hand and ran breathlessly and with toes barely touching the ground, but without actually changing their location on the chess board. A little later the Queen said good-bye and vanished seemingly into thin air. Then there was the railroad journey in which the entire train rose straight up in the air, in crossing a brook, and Alice presently found herself talking to a giant Gnat which fanned her with its wings. At this point flying seems to pervade the picture. The Rocking-horse-Fly swung itself from branch to branch while a Bread-and-Butterfly crawled at her feet. People were threatened with the extinction of going out like the flame of a candle; and in the final scene which is a banquet rather than a trial

174

(in contrast to *Wonderland*), Alice finds herself pressed between the two Queens in a way that lifts her into the air, while the candles suddenly shoot upward to the ceiling and all the dishes develop wings. Food was certainly not unimportant in the *Looking Glass* World, only it was not as ubiquitous as in *Wonderland*. In the former, movement through the air appears rather as the reverse of passage of food into the body.

Charles Dodgson considered whether air was healthy or morbid with nearly the same intensity of concern which he gave to food and drink which he catalogued so constantly. His apprehension of infection was great and he had such concern about contaminated or unhealthy air in general that at times he stuffed all the cracks under doors and windows, and had an elaborate system of keeping the temperature equalized throughout his rooms, causing him to make repeated daily rounds of his series of thermometers.

Gertrude Chataway, one of Carroll's little girl friends to whom he dedicated *The Snark*—and it will be recalled that the Boojum Snark caused any onlooker to vanish into thin air—described Mr. Dodgson as follows:

> Next door there was an old gentleman [actually aged 43!] who interested me immensely. He would come onto his balcony which joined ours, sniffing the air with his head thrown back and would walk right down the steps on to the beach with his chin in the air, drinking in the fresh breezes as if he could never have enough . . . Whenever I heard his footsteps, I flew out to see him coming and one day when he spoke to me my joy was complete . . . In a very little while I was as familiar with the interior of his lodgings as with my own . . . He often took his cue [in telling stories] from [the child's] remarks . . . so that the story seemed a personal possession . . . It was astonishing that he never seemed tired or to want other society . . . He

[later] told me it was the greatest pleasure he could have to converse freely with a child and feel the depths of her mind . . . I don't think he ever really understood that we whom he had known as children, could not always remain such.

A letter from Carroll to little Miss Chataway, written October 3, 1875, explains that he will *drink her health* instead of sending her a present. Then finding a pun in this phrase he continued,

But perhaps you will object . . . If I were to sit by you and to drink your tea, you wouldn't like that. You would say "Boo-hoo! Here's Mr. Dodgson's drunk all my tea and I haven't got any left!" I am very much afraid Sybil will find you sitting by the sad sea-wave and crying "Boo! Hoo! Mr. Dodgson's drunk my health and I haven't got any left!" Your mother will say [to the doctor] "You see she would go and make friends with a strange gentleman, and yesterday he drank her health! . . . The only way to cure her is to wait until next birthday and then for her to drink his health." And then we shall have changed healths. I wonder how you'll like mine! Oh Gertrude, I wish you would not talk such nonsense! . . . Your loving friend. Lewis Carroll [15].

Miss Chataway's first description of the man breathing in health with his exuberant sniffing of the sea air is a reverse side of the same picture as that given elsewhere of his elaborate precautions against breathing in contaminated air, specially that emanating from a letter received from one of the Bowman children who suffered from scarlet fever (16). In this Chataway letter, the idea of the gift of drinking the health and the turning by a pun of this intensely positive attitude to the extreme opposite—a destructive vampirish sucking or swallowing up is implicitly suggested, with a merry ghoulishness. It also contains an elaboration of childhood's idea—with its modicum of truth—that our bodies and hence our identities are determined by what we eat.

THE RELATION TO ANIMALS

The animals in the *Alice* books far outnumber the human beings, even as they probably did in the gardens at Daresbury and Croft, and Charles continued always to be in communion with them. He has his favorites and his dis-favorites (To coin a Carrollian word). Among the less loved were dogs. Although an oversized puppy appears amiably enough in the *Wonderland* garden, there is evidence that in actual life Dodgson did not enjoy dogs, and when one rushed violently at him on a visit to the Arnolds, he refused ever to return there unless the dog were destroyed. (One may venture the conjecture that the dog was a male.) He sent the Arnolds an exact diagram of the canine tooth marks on his trouser leg, and when the dog was not abolished, he continued on friendly terms with the family but arranged to see them outside of their own home (17). In general, however, he seems to have been charming with and charmed by small animals and to have treated them in whimsy as somewhat superior to human beings, whom they either replaced or in part represented.

Among all the animals the cat has a special place. Not only were there Dinah, the white kitten and the black kitten (who became royalty), but there was the Cheshire cat as well.[6] In Carroll's letters (about 1863) to another little girl

[6] The Cheshire cat did not originate with Carroll, but is part of the folklore of the county in which he was born. Its appearance in *Wonderland*, however, has made it so famous that its earlier existence is often overlooked. The phrase "grinning like a Cheshire cat" or "grinning like a chessy cat" appears in various writings before 1865. Wolcott (Peter Pinder) wrote in 1792, "Lo, like a Cheshire cat our court will grin." There seem to be two main theories regarding its origin: One is based on the fact that a cheese was formerly made in Cheshire molded like a grinning cat. This has a peculiar Carrollian appeal, as it provokes the fantasy that the cheesy cat may eat the rat that would eat the cheese. It reminds one further of the

friend Agnes Hughes (20), he developed fantasies about cats in quite a significant way. He had sent Agnes many kisses apparently with some instructions for dividing them up, at which the child apparently demurred. He replied:

> You lazy thing! What? I'm to divide the kisses myself, am I? Indeed and I won't take the trouble to do anything of the sort. But I'll tell you how to do it. First you take four of the kisses, and that reminds me of a very curious thing that happened to me at half-past four yesterday. Three visitors came knocking at my door, begging me to let them in. When I opened the door, who do you think they were? You will never guess. Why they were three cats! . . . They all looked so cross and disagreeable that I took up the first thing I could lay my hands on which happened to be the rolling pin and knocked them all down as flat as pancakes: "If you come knocking at my door," I said, "I shall come knocking at your heads." That was fair, wasn't it? Yours affectionately . . .

---

current phrase for a smugly smiling person "He looks like the cat that has eaten the canary," and again we ask with Alice "Do cats eat bats, or bats eat cats?" The explanation for the grin given by Brewer (18), however, is that the cats there knew that Cheshire is the County Palatine, and the idea is so funny that they are perpetually amused by it. (Certainly a cat may look at—and laugh at—a King). Another explanation offered is that a lion rampant being the crest of an influential noble family of Cheshire, a cat's head became substituted for it due to the maladroit work of a painter who made signs for inns and other public places. Thus the cat became associated with Cheshire. The most coherent explanation, offered by Mr. Michael Perkins (19), relates the grinning Cheshire cat to the "witch cat" which began to grin on Hallowe'en in the Isle of Man and frightened observers all the way to Scotland. This cat was probably derived from the Palug Cat which the Welsh Triads record as having been kittened by the sow Henwen under the spell of the magician Coll, at Collfrew, at the Black Stone in Menai Straits. In North Wales, the cat bogey (which reappears in our grinning Jack-o'-Lantern) was a black hog with a "cutty" tail. It seems related then to the Manx cat of the Isle of Man. The Dodgsons made a family excursion to Beaumaris when Charles was a young boy, and the Menai Bridge reappears in his rhymes about the aged, aged man. The cat without a tail, or the manx cat, becomes then converted into the cat without a head, or the head without a body, and is part of the decapitation and body-mutilation theme so apparent in Carroll's writing.

Again one ventures the thought that the troublesome cats were little males (or at least made him aware of maleness); and it is worth noting that the preceding letter to Agnes carried a postscript in which Carroll had sent his love to the little Agnes and his kindest regards to her mother, but "to your fat impertinent ignorant brother my hatred—and I think that is all." It was in turn followed by more cat letters:

About the cats, you know. Of course I didn't leave them lying flat on the ground like dried flowers. I picked them up, and I was as kind as I could be to them. I lent them a portfolio for a bed—they would not have been comfortable in a real bed, you know; they were too thin; but they were quite happy between the sheets of blotting paper, and each of them had a pen wiper for a pillow. Well then I went to bed; but first I lent them three dinner bells to ring in the night in case they wanted anything in the night. You know I have *three* dinner bells,—the first (which is the largest) is rung when dinner is nearly ready; the second (which is rather larger) is rung when it is quite ready; and the third (which is as large as the other two put together) is rung all the time I am at dinner. Well, I told them they might ring if they happened to want anything—and as they rang all the bells all night, I suppose they did want something or other, only I was too sleepy to attend to them. In the morning I gave them some rat-tail jelly and buttered mice for breakfast, and they were as discontented as they could be. They wanted some boiled pelican but of course I knew that would not be good for them. So all I said was "Go to Number two Finborough Road and ask for Agnes Hughes and if it's really good for you, she'll give you some." Then I shook hands with them all and wished them good-bye, and drove them up the chimney. They seemed very sorry to go and they took the bells and the portfolio with them. I didn't find this out until after they had gone, and then

I was sorry too, and wished them back again. What do I mean by "them"? Never mind. How are Arthur, and Amy, and Emily? Do they still go up and down Finborough Road and teach the cats to be nice to the mice? I'm *very* fond of *all* cats in Finborough Road. Give them my love—Who do I mean by "them?" Never mind. Your affectionate friend—

And another letter to Amy, the sister of Agnes, contained the following:

You have asked after those three cats. Ah, the dear creatures. Do you know, ever since that night they first came, they have *never left me?* Isn't it kind of them? Tell Agnes this, she will be interested to hear it. And they are so kind and thoughtful: Do you know, when I had gone out for a walk the other day, they got all my books out of the book-case and opened them all to page 50 because they thought that would be a nice useful page to begin at. It was rather unfortunate, though: because they took my bottle of gum, and tried to gum pictures upon the ceiling (which they thought would please me), and by accident they spilt a quantity of it all over the books. So when they were shut up and put by, the leaves all stuck together and I can never read page 50 again in any of them! However they meant it very kindly, so I *wasn't* angry. I gave them a spoonful of ink as a treat, but they were ungrateful for that and made dreadful faces. But of course, as it was given them as a treat, they had to drink it. One of them has turned black since: it was a white cat to begin with. Give my love to any children you happen to meet. Also I send two kisses and a half for you to divide with Agnes, Emily, and Godfrey. Mind you divide them fairly. Yours affectionately—

These letters are perhaps as self-revealing as anything, except *Sylvie and Bruno,* that Carroll ever wrote. They show readily enough the fluctuating aggressiveness with an urge to cruelty and then to affectionate playfulness; but there are expressed, further, more disguised but equally powerful complex trends which will be delineated in the discussion of the dynamics of the Carroll-Dodgson character formation.

THE MAIN THEMES IN CARROLL'S WRITING

The two Alice books, *Alice's Adventures in Wonderland* and *Through the Looking Glass*, furnish naturally a starting place for the study of the thematic content of Carroll's fantasies; then *The Hunting of the Snark, Sylvie and Bruno*—with of course secondary consideration of his poetry and miscellaneous writings.

Wonderland

Alice in a state of sleepy boredom saw a rabbit run past her nervously looking at his watch and talking to himself about being late. Her curiosity aroused, she followed him down a rabbit hole which seemed very long indeed, but after a time turned into another long passage, which in turn became a long low hall with locked doors all around it. She found a tiny golden key which opened a small door hidden behind curtains, and gave her a view into a beautiful garden which she longed to enter. The story deals with her vicissitudes in getting into the garden and finally with the unexpected events within.

In brief, Alice goes through a series of bodily changes, always induced by eating or drinking something, except in the last instance where her change in form is due to the fan (nosegay of flowers in the first version) which she picks up and holds after it has been dropped by the rabbit.[7] Some-

---

[7] The close connection between the air (which is set in motion by the fan or given special significance when breathed in from the nosegay) and eating and drinking is again apparent.

times she is enlarged and again she becomes too small to reach even the door handle. In two of her enlarged states it is her neck which grows especially long, and she is once mistaken for a serpent as she coils her neck down through the tree branches in order to see underneath them. In her small states, she once suffers from her chin hitting her feet and apparently has no neck at all, and again is threatened with going out like a candle.

She has feelings of alienation both from her body and from her mind, believes that she may have become somebody else and tests her identity with problems in arithmetic, trials of her memory, and school lessons to see if she still knows the things she has learned, as she has repeatedly found herself saying nonsense. The great charm of the tale lies in the panorama of grotesque caricature expressed in the general mixture and fusion of identities of the animals, insects and strange human beings whom Alice meets. Through all this is a cacophony of cruelty so extreme as to be ridiculous: animals eat each other up, a baby turns into a pig and is abandoned to wander away into the forest, decapitation is a general threat, and a Cheshire Cat does appear smiling though separated from its own body. Even words are always changing *their* identities through punning. All this appears against a backdrop of illogical time and spatial relations, and an attitude of gentle puzzlement on Alice's part. In general the irrational changes in size are confined to sudden changes in Alice's own body.

Finally, however, entrance into the beautiful garden, the home of the royal family, is achieved. But the bedlam is, if anything, worse. An animated pack of cards are the main characters: the Spades are the gardeners, the Clubs are the police force, the Diamonds are the courtiers, and the whole garden is ruled by the Hearts. It is interesting to consider here that the suit of cards, the Royal family, has exactly the same number of members as the Dodgson family. There are admonitions of love, but a threat of execution permeates the place, and the Queen of Hearts seems madly lustful for everyone's head. Irritability and rage prevail, only, as the mock turtle explains, the executions, like everything else, are not real. "It's all her [the Queen's] fancy that: they never executes nobody you know!" Finally it develops that the Knave of Hearts is being tried for having stolen tarts made by the Queen, and he in turn is in danger of execution. Alice is surprised to find herself called as a witness, and upsets the courtroom both literally (for she has again become gigantic) and figuratively by her rebellion against the nonsensical course of the trial. A final bit of evidence is produced in the form of an unsigned letter, written in rhyme, indicating that the tarts have been returned. It is a masterpiece of confused identities, expressed in pronouns, and concludes—

> They all returned from him to you,
> Though they were mine before.
> — — — — — — — — — — —
> My notion was that you had been
> (Before she had this fit)
> An obstacle that came between
> Him, and ourselves, and it.

The Queen goes into another fit of rage while denying that she is subject to fits and demands an indefinite sentence. Alice declares a verdict must be given first and finds herself threatened with decapitation by the Queen, and defiantly replies: "Who cares for a pack of cards?" Whereupon the whole pack rises up in the air to hurl themselves against her, and she awakes to find that she had been having a nightmare.

In a curious epilogue to the main tale, Alice recounts the dream to her sister, who in turn dreams the dream over, and in a half-awake state "pictures to herself how this same little sister of hers, would in after time be herself a grown woman; and how she would keep through all her riper years, the simple and loving heart of her childhood; and how she would gather about her other little children, and make their eyes bright and eager with many a strange tale perhaps even with a dream of Wonderland of long ago;"—truly an immortality of innocence as unreal and fantasied as were the executionary threats of the Queen of Hearts.

Looking Glass

This was written nine years after Carroll had told the tale of *Wonderland* to the three little girls on the river and Alice is a little older than she was in *Wonderland*. Its plot follows, with similarities and reversals, that of *Wonderland*. The story opens with the theme of punishment: Alice reproaching her kitten for its faults and threatening punishment only to think of her own fate if her punishments were accumulated and given to her at once. In a final threat to put the kitten through the mantle looking glass, Alice discovers she can go through herself into that land of reversal, only a small bit of which can be seen ordinarily. It is the space behind the clock. Thus *Looking Glass* begins with guilt and possible punishment rather than ending so; and time is involved (in the White Rabbit's watch and the mantle clock) in both adventures. In *Looking Glass*, inanimate objects have come alive; the pictures on the wall move and the face of the clock grins, while the chess pieces on the hearth become the active inhabitants of the land. The motif of the game, expressed in the card game of *Wonderland*, is now experienced more fully as the game of chess, and concern about external space, not merely our own body change, plays a primary role, with the time theme secondary. In fact, in all *Looking Glass* land, Alice never once changes size herself although objects external to her change frequently, and distance has a troublesome way of contracting, expanding, and reversing itself. There is the same wish to get into the garden, but this is achieved early in the tale and without trouble. She floats downstairs so rapidly that she steadies herself by clutching the doorknob at the garden entrance.

The garden is full of pert flowers whom Alice finally threatens to decapitate (pick) in order to subdue them. While attempting to reach a hill from which to have a better view of the garden, Alice encounters the Red Queen of Chess, now grown life-size, whom she has previously seen on the hearth and frightened by lifting her rapidly through the air. There is now a reversal in that the Red Queen forces Alice to run breathlessly through the air with her, but without reaching any place. The rest of *Looking Glass* is involved with Alice's progress through the Chess Game of Life until she can be crowned a queen herself, on attaining the Eighth square. Each square has its own adventures which in general are not so frightfully exciting as those of *Wonderland*. Alice is repeatedly confronted with the facts that space, time, and even memory and cause-and-effect may be reversed and run in either direction, this unreliability causing much confusion. The Red King and Queen are the main characters, much less fierce than the King and Queen of Hearts, and they have counterparts in the untidy but well-meaning White King and Queen. Several fights or threats of fights occur—notably between Tweedledum and Tweedledee, and the Lion and the Unicorn. Finally, Alice encounters the White Knight, who plays a role partly like and partly opposite to that of the Knave of Hearts in *Wonderland*. The White Knight cannot possibly be accused of any crime—he is just too muddled, awkward, and generally impotent. He continually falls from his horse in every direction except over its head, and he carries dangling from his saddle any number of futile contrivances, each of which he owns to be his own invention. Alice has repeatedly to pick him up and get him seated again, and in one final rescue has to pull him out of a ditch where he has plunged head foremost. The knight amiably

185

explains: "What does it matter where my body happens to be? My mind goes on working all the same. In fact the more head downward I am, the more I keep inventing new things." (Thus the White Knight seems to be in a state of chronic partial alienation between head and body, resembling in this the Cheshire cat.) Finally the White Knight sings Alice a song about an old man asitting on a gate which is sung to the tune of "I give thee all, I can no more"[8] and parodies Wordsworth's *Leech Gatherer*.[9] He is disappointed that Alice does not weep. The White Knight then says farewell, foolishly smiling and begging her to wave her handkerchief in good-bye to him by way of encouragement, after which she will go on into the Eighth Square and Queenship, as indeed happens.

As preparation for Queenship, Alice is sent through a course of training by the Red and White Queens—a training and an examination which has a shadowy resemblance to a trial; and she is finally obligated to give a dinner party to celebrate her royal debut—all this under the malicious and officious direction of the Red Queen. The party ends, however, in chaos and confusion, not unlike the end of the trial scene—only again, instead of Alice changing size, the objects on the dinner table become large and animated: the candles shoot up to the ceiling, the plates develop wings, the soup ladle is threatening, and complete pandemonium is about to prevail until Alice, in reaction to the emergency, literally turns the table by pulling the cloth off and dumping the whole mess on the floor. She then turns to attack the Red Queen who had provoked the perversity of the dinner party, but finds the Queen again shrunken to chess-piece size. She awakes shaking the Red Queen only to find she is really shaking her kitten.[10]

[8] Thomas Moore, "My Heart and Lute" in *Poetry and Pictures*.

[9] *Resolution and Independence*.

[10] This whole picture reminds one inevitably of Carroll's attack on the cats of Finborough Road.

While the manifest plots of the *Alice* books are thus similar and simple in structure, it is not their plots which are generally remembered, but their various absurdly irrational incidents with the apparent triumph of sheer but rhythmical nonsense. Perhaps no book except the Bible is quoted as often in unlikely places and by improbable people as *Alice*. For in the account of Alice's experiences there is always some vividly mad vignette which can be used for comparison and relief in most of life's troubling dilemmas. The plot, however, the penetration into the hidden or secret garden and the difficulties encountered there, is in essence the most universal plot of mankind whether stimulated by the vision of the sublibrarian, of the little girls playing in the dean's garden, or from the gardens at Croft and Daresbury traversed by the engine of Love and inhabited by the civilized but combatant worms and caterpillars, or more remotely derived from that garden where Adam and Eve ate of the apple and the serpent of sophistication lurked nearby.

The Hunting of the Snark

This is a heroic nonsense poem in eight fits, describing a voyage in search of a fabulous monster, undertaken by a confused and confusing crew of ten, each of whom has a regular occupation beginning with B: the Baker, the Banker, the Barrister, the Beaver, the Bellman, the Billiard marker, the Bonnet maker, the Boots, the Broker, and the Butcher. The monster, the Snark, is, according to the author, a portmanteau animal and word, in that it contains more than one idea condensed into a single world—in this case *snail* and *snark*. One suspects that the snake has crept into this portmanteau although not specifically mentioned by Carroll. The excursion is the more dangerous in that certain snarks are of a boojum character, and cause the hunter to disappear into thin air at the very moment of sighting them. This fact is not known to the crew, except to the Bellman, at the beginning of the voyage. The expedition has been organized by the Bellman who provides a map which is an absolute blank. His one idea of crossing the ocean is to tinkle his bell continuously—thus resembling the three cats of Finborough Road who tinkled the bells all night (21). The Bellman is so sensitively fastidious about appearances that he has the bowsprit unshipped once or twice a week to be revarnished, and when the time comes for replacing it no one can remember to which end of the boat it belongs, in consequence of which it generally is fastened crosswise of the rudder—"a thing," as the Bellman remarked, "that happens in tropical climes when a vessel is so to speak, snarked."

The Baker, who is chief of the crew, knows only how to make Bride's Cake, the materials for which are not available. He shares other characteristics with the author, in that

> He had forty-two boxes, all carefully packed
> With his name painted clearly on each;
> But since he omitted to mention the fact
> They were all left behind on the beach.

The Bellman does succeed in getting the strange expedition under way. But as they arrive amidst crags and chasms and he is giving an account of the five cardinal characteristics of snarks and begins to speak of a special variety of Boojum Snarks, he no sooner says the word *Boo* than the Baker sinks into a faint, from which he is revived with jam, among other things. He arouses himself to talk of his genealogy and is silenced by the Bellman, but finally recalls that an uncle has told him that the right sort of snark can be caught and eaten with greens, but that anyone who sees a Boojum Snark will at the very moment "softly and suddenly vanish away," a thought which the Baker cannot endure. The excursion has reached such a point, however, that retreat is impossible. Each of the crew has his own dream of the nature and dangers of the hunt, but it is the Baker who finally comes upon the Snark just at night fall. As he announces his find, he follows it with the words "It's a Boo—" and disappears head-long into a chasm.

So much for a prose paraphrase of the manifest story of the *Hunting of the Snark!* Various interpretations have been offered. Carroll himself, as reported by his nephew Colling-wood, said that the poem had no intentional meaning, but it would seem from a further statement that he was at least vaguely aware of an unconscious one. He stated that the first verse which he composed was the last one of the com-pleted poem and that he did not mean anything but non-sense, adding, however, "Still we know words mean more than we mean to express when we use them; so a whole book ought to mean a great deal more than the writer means" (22). One author (23) sees the end of the expedition as a repetition of the eat-or-be-eaten theme and that the Snark has so destroyed the Baker. Another writer (24) presents an interpretation of the whole poem as a satire on the socio-economic conditions of the time, when England had just been passing through a state of economic depression. Others have seen it as a political satire and have offered similar in-terpretations of the *Alice* books. Perhaps in the latter more than in *Snark* there is also possible an interpretation as criti-cisms of education and statements of far-reaching vision of future mathematical developments. While all of these inter-pretations may have some merit, with varying degrees of validity, it is not for these reasons that Carroll's writing has so wide an appeal to children as well as to adults, and to people of all nations.

It is obvious too that the manifest content of *Snark* re-sembles somewhat that of *Wonderland* and of *Looking Glass* in that again it is the tale of an exploration in which the crew of ten suggests the crew of the railway train at Croft when there were almost certainly ten little Dodgsons to travel around the garden, since Edwin was not yet born when the family moved there. The exploration also ends in a state of climactic disturbance, which might be described as the reverse of an explosion—viz., a sudden vanishing annihilation. The references to the boy's stammering—which was shared in some measure by all of the others, has been already commented on. And all of the "B" members of the crew represent facets of the writer as is so apparent in the cases of the Bellman and the Baker. In a similar way, the Dodgson children shared and reflected each other to an amazing degree. All of the boys became ordained—the husband of the only sister who married was a clergyman. The unmarried sisters continued to live together until their deaths. It was certainly a closely knit family.

Charles himself stammered, especially on the letter P. It is possible that his repetitive use of the letter B in the Snark poem was a substitution of B for P, since the poem itself carries such clear references to the speech inhibition. The exact nature of the speech disturbances of his siblings is not known, but at least two are said to have had definite stammers. In his Diary, he refers to recommending treatment for them at the same time that he was seeking to cure himself (25). Before Charles Dodgson found the name of Lewis Carroll, he had signed with B.B. some of his earlier poems, specifically "The Lady of the Ladle" and "Wilhelm von Schmulz" as well as other poems published in *College Rhymes*.

It is to be remembered that the *Snark* was written at a time when, Mary and Wilfred Dodgson having already married and had children, this outcropping of a new generation must have stirred memories in Charles of his own childhood when the younger brothers and sisters were coming along. It was against this background that he had been again aroused to concern about his ability to endure the sight of someone in pain and to aid those in distress, and had renewed both his study of anatomy and his attempts to cure his stuttering. *The Hunting of the Snark* is subtitled "An Agony in Eight Fits." It is noteworthy that there were eight little Dodgsons younger than Charles.

The summer before the publication of the poem had been spent at Sandown on the Isle of Wight where Carroll had become acquainted with little Gertrude Chataway and had spent time on the beach with her and her friend. His obvious fantasy of changing identities with her was clearly written in his birthday letters to her. The idea of birth and the determination of identity then and later was a latent preoccupation. The idea of changing places with the little girl appears again in a letter of July 21, 1876, a few months after the publication of the *Snark* poem, when in true lover-like fashion he wrote to Gertrude from Sandown, "How am I to enjoy Sandown without *you?* How can I sit alone on these wooden steps? . . . You will have to come . . . I shall tell [Violet] to invite you to stay with her and then I shall come over . . . to fetch you. If I do come over . . . I couldn't go back the same day, so you will have to engage a bed for me . . . if you can't find one I shall expect you to spend the night on the beach and give up your room to me . . . I send you seven kisses (to last a week)" etc. (26). It is interesting too that the exchange of sexual identities and the condensation of both in one individual is hinted at in the first lines of Carroll's dedication of the *Snark* poem to the little Gertrude. "Inscribed to a dear child: in memory of golden Summer hours and whispers of a summer sea," the double acrostic poem opens:

> *Gert* with boyish garb for boyish task
> Eager she wields her spade; yet loves as well
> Rest on a friendly knee, intent to ask
> The tales he loves to tell.

> *Rude* spirits of the seething outer strife
> Unmeet to read her pure and simple spright
> Deem, if you list, such hours a waste of life
> Empty of all delight!

Sylvie and Bruno

This "novel" of impressive size, was published in two main sections, *Sylvie and Bruno* in 1889 and *Sylvie and Bruno Concluded* in 1893. It had been begun in 1867 when Carroll contributed a small story, "Bruno's Revenge," to *Aunt Judy's Magazine*. Another bit was added to this in 1872 and yet another in 1874, with stories told to children on some special occasions. About 1874, he thought of making these bits the nucleus of a longer story and began to jot down "all sorts of odd ideas, and fragments of dialogue" that occurred to him with a kind of compelling force and suddenness. Sometimes he felt he could tell from what event or thought of his own they had sprung, but sometimes they came without seeming connections but with some intensity of their own, or were fragments of dreams which possessed this same autonomous force. Carroll collected these messages and heaped them together in what he described aptly as *litterature* and appeared as imminent chaos. It was another ten years, however, before he had succeeded in sorting out these bits and putting them together with sufficient padding, or filling, to cement them hopefully into any continuous structure. In the introduction to the first installment of *Sylvie and Bruno*, Carroll states his ideals for producing several books, "desirable to be written"—first a Child's Bible, to include selected passages according to the principle that Religion should be presented as a revelation of *love* (omitting the account, for example, of the Flood); second, a selection of pieces from the Bible suitable for memorizing; third, a selection, prose and verse, from books other than the Bible; and fourth, a "Shakespeare" for girls well pruned down to meet the needs of maidens ten to seventeen. Carroll was obviously grappling with an anxious sense of the imminence of death, and remarks, "Few more interesting subjects of enquiry could be found by a student of history, than the various weapons that have been used against this shadowy foe." This then is the background of *Sylvie and Bruno,* which he considered his greatest work.

Carroll wrote of *Sylvie and Bruno* that it was based on the assumption that fairies exist and that there are three levels of existence: (1) "real" life, (2) the "eerie" stage in which one sees fairies, and (3) the "trance" in which the body is asleep, but the individual is not and cannot enter fairyland. None of these three states corresponds directly with dreaming. The individual "I," the self, who relates the story of *Sylvie and Bruno,* may slip from one level to another, and the story is told in three concurrent levels. Sometimes the change is made through a word, a recollected movement or odor, or a similarity of appearance—and the shift is automatic and unannounced. These switches in the story come about significantly when the narrator is riding on a train, looking in the fire,[11] contemplating water, or inspecting a shiny substance.

On the first level of conscious, external reality live Lady Muriel Orme, her father the Earl, Dr. Arthur Forester, the hero and Eric Lindon, the villain—as well as the narrator of the story, "I." On the second level of the preconscious and sometimes the dreaming mind of the narrator, are Sylvie and Bruno, their father the Warden, the Vice-Warden and his lady, and their repulsive young son Uggug, the Gardener, the Professor, and the Other Professor. This is the level of Outland. The narrator may function in Outland, and some of the Outlandish characters emerge into Real Life. However, "I," the narrator cannot control when he will become Outlandish and his participation here is unconstant. Finally, the

---

11 Cf. *Faces in the Fire.*

third level, Fairyland, is inhabited by the Warden who has voluntarily retired there, occasionally by Sylvie and Bruno who sometimes visit, and by the Professor who can exist and function there adequately, but the narrator, "I," can slip in only rarely and then in a dream state. The shifts in the levels in the story come about as silently as in Kafka's *Trial* and compared with Rumer Godden's *Take Three Tenses* appear uncontrived and convincing.

The narrator "I" is a professor of mathematics, corresponding inevitably in some degree to Charles Dodgson, the observer of life. Carroll himself stated that Lady Muriel was another version of Sylvie, and it seems that Arthur Forester in a somewhat similar way represents a development of Bruno. The rustic or woodland setting is not so constant in this long work of Carroll's as the garden is in the *Alice* books, but it is implicitly suggested in the names of the characters. Sylvie is, by name, a child of the woodland glade, and Bruno is similarly the playful and mischievous bear. Arthur Forester and Eric Lindon are rivals for Lady Muriel's love (and one cannot help but see the pun that Forester cuts down Lindon in this struggle). Elveston[12] is the home of Lady Muriel and is reached by Fayfield Junction. *Phlizz,* the name of the secret method of the fairy children's attaining invisibility, is a phonetic reversal of Sylvie's name. In contrast to these idyllic suggestions is Uggug, the ugly son of the Vice-Warden, whose repulsiveness is expressed in his name, which sounds like a combination of burp or gulp and the sound of fecal dropping, so similar to many of the neologistic words of Swift. Uggug seems to have some relation to the worst in Bruno and reminds one of the pig baby.

In the background of all this is the mad gardener who sings so entrancingly of all the things he thought he saw, which

[12] *Wonderland* was called *Elfland* in the original version of *Alice's Adventures*. There is also the fact that Elphinston was the home of one of Carroll's ancestors.

amazingly turn out to be quite different. He is, however, much closer to *Wonderland* and the *Snark* than any other character. One feels on reading *Sylvie and Bruno* that its author is trying to explain something to himself and to become aware of some inner dilemmas of his thought and soul, and that this is why he considered it so important. *Wonderland* and the *Snark*, on the other hand, have a quality of spontaneity and unselfconsciousness. He was not trying consciously to learn or to teach in their telling.

It is difficult to summarize the plot of *Sylvie and Bruno*. These two fairy children are always together and in constant interaction. Bruno, a five-year-old boy, is meant to be engagingly mischievous, with baby talk and a lisp which presumably enhanced his interminable cutenesses. He is constantly chaperoned and gently reproved by his sister Sylvie who is perhaps two or three years older. The sweetness of this young pair is associated with so much sentimental stickiness that the average non-Victorian may suffer some revulsion. They flit in and out of the rest of the story like the influence of past memories, and appear sometimes with and sometimes through the other main couple, Lady Muriel Orme and Dr. Arthur Forester, who seems to be not merely a grown-up version but rather the Sylveized adult Bruno. Further, the aggressively bad, but rather charming part of Bruno has joined a similar part from Bruno's (Charles') forefathers to form Eric Lindon, who is rival to Arthur Forester.

There seems little doubt that Bruno represents the mischievous, incompletely tamed child that Charles Dodgson was before five, the part that only continued to live through Carroll. Charles Dodgson's father and grandfathers were Charles Dodgsons also. The father of the author was a relatively merry man, though stern. He and Charles' mother were first cousins, even as Eric Lindon and Lady Muriel were. Eric Lindon had some of the young Charles' grandfather in him, too—for that Charles Dodgson was not a clergyman

195

but a Captain in the Dragoon Guards and died in Ireland under circumstances which were dramatic and would have appealed to the imagination of a growing boy.

Eric Lindon, the army captain, is about to win his suit for the hand of his Cousin Lady Muriel. He is, however, daringly critical of the church and religion, and it is intolerable that he should be victorious. He is finally rejected by the good Lady Muriel in spite of her attraction to him. This permits Dr. Forester to push his suit. The marriage only occurs, however, when it is necessary for Dr. Forester to leave as an emergency calls him into a plague-ridden area where he will almost surely meet death. The marriage is performed but not consummated as the bride and groom separate at the church. (One must recall Charles Dodgson's own obsessive religious doubts at night, and his fear of contamination and especially of contagious disease, which in the case of Arthur Forester is realistically overcome concurrent with marriage.) Lady Muriel is next seen as a widow at the grave of her heroic husband, who, it is suddenly revealed, is not dead at all, and is soon rescued, crippled and shrunken, from the ruins of the plagued country, by none other than the villainous nonbeliever, Eric Lindon, who is now Christianized and will soon leave on a mission to the Heathen (as Charles' youngest and least favored brother Edwin actually did). Now in this broken and scarred, but purified state, Arthur Forester and Lady Muriel are reunited to live together, presumably at the home of her father, the Earl. It is not stated, but one suspects that they lived, however, as brother and sister, not only because of the broken condition of Arthur Forester but because of the general tenor of the end of the story. In the last chapter entitled "Life out of Death," Sylvie returns a precious jewel to her father which she discovers carries the words "All will love Sylvie," which is bestowed again upon her by her father who shows her that the jewel really carries the message "Sylvie will love all—all will love

Sylvie." Thereupon Sylvie becomes an angel and is heard singing in "God's own sky"—"It is love."

Such a pot-pourri of sadomasochistic expiation would be only ludicrous if it did not show the horror of all sexuality, including marriage, of the author. It is the one of Carroll's writings which deals most directly and openly with marriage. In most of his rather oblique references elsewhere, marriage is lampooned as a state of cruel bestiality. One has only to think of the King and Queen of Hearts in *Through the Looking Glass*, or to scrutinize Carroll's verses, to see how unremitting was this impression, as in Tottle's Song in *Sylvie and Bruno* or the Gardener's Song—

> He thought he saw an elephant
> That practiced on a fife
> He looked again and found it was
> A letter from his wife.
> "At length I realize," he said
> "The bitterness of life."

or even more grimly in The Three Voices. In *Sylvie and Bruno* marriage is saved by being nullified.

The name Bruno, so peculiarly un-English, is not wholly explicable. It begins with B, like the names of the crew of the Snark, or like Boy, and he is the only boy of whom Carroll wrote sympathetically. Bruno is certainly the name of a bear and frequently of a dog. The Bear appears variously in *Sylvie and Bruno*, notably in another one of the Gardener's stanzas:—

> He thought he saw a coach-and-four
> That stood beside his bed
> He looked again and found it was
> A Bear without a head
> "Poor thing," he said, "poor silly thing!
> It's waiting to be fed!"

The Warden's Lady—i.e., the mother of Sylvie and Bruno—

in order to disguise herself dresses as a bear upon a lead, which may represent chained brute force and a merry dancing bear. (Here, however, the oral aggressiveness is inherent in claws and teeth. It also brings her and her son into some symbolic identification.)

The Bear is a kind of counterpart figure for the Cat—both are bisexual, but the Bear may be more male and the Cat more female. Both appear in states of decapitation. Dr. Bacon (27) also remarks that the bear is a peculiarly inclusively punning word, having many meanings; besides referring to the animal, it can mean "to labor under a weight" or "to be or make naked," and that it is striking that this portmanteau pun should be put upon the one engaging boy in Carroll's stories. The dog also appears in *Sylvie and Bruno* more consistently than in the *Alice* books. A pug dog guards the house in which time works backward as a result of touching the reversal peg on the Outlandish watch. A mastiff is similarly a guard to the house at the entrance to Dogland, and it is worthy of note that Bruno has no difficulty understanding dog language. This was a land in which human beings belonged to dogs rather than vice versa, and where the King dog actually smiled and forgot his dignity by wagging his tail when Bruno playfully tied his ears under his chin. Then again there is the Charitable Association for Supplying Dogs with Pockets, so that they will not be rendered helpless by having to carry bones in the mouth. It is considered that man's chief advantage over dogs consists in the possession of pockets. In general we note cats are girls' pets and dogs boys' pets. So it is appropriate that dogs should be relatively prominent in this boy story, whereas cats predominate in Alice's lands.

Changes in body size occur but are not frequent in *Sylvie and Bruno*. There is, for example, a megaloscope which reduces an elephant to the appearance of a mouse as in contrast to the microscope which magnifies a flea to the proportions of a horse, which then escapes from the machine and flies, Pegasus fashion, into the sky. Reversals in immediate time and space do occur, but in general both Time and Space are more dependable—except through the shifts in level of consciousness—than in that generally reversed land of *Looking Glass*. Changes in identity also occur, but seem to follow consistent trends and are not as primitive or seemingly as haphazard as in the *Alice* books. The disturbances in time, location and identity are dominated more patently by condensation of past and present. There is almost no dramatic creature or situation of the other Carrollian stories that is not reproduced in some way in *Sylvie and Bruno*, yet the texture of the story is different. *Misch-Masch* though it seems, one detects in it more of longitudinal view of the development of life than is presented elsewhere in Carroll's writing. It does not have the gentle wildness of the *Alice* books.

The pairing of the characters, however, is conspicuous. Looked at in another way, it appears as the splitting of one character into two. Even Sylvie and Bruno have so constant and nearly a symbiotic relationship that the reader is not always quite sure whether they represent one or two identities. Then there is the Warden and the Vice-Warden, the Professor and the Other Professor, the Councillor and the Subcouncillor, etc. It seems that this novel which had an imperative quality to its author, being constructed of insistently remembered fragmentary impressions from a variety of sources and appreciatively considered by him as the best of all his works, was an unconscious attempt to explain his own character development. An inner compulsion drove him to write it.

Two episodes are particularly important. The first occurs when Sylvie, in attempting to educate her distractable little brother, arranged for a spelling lesson, some letters on a board, E-V-I-L. "Bruno looked at it in solemn silence for a minute. 'I know what it *doesn't* spell!' he said at last. 'That's no good,' said Sylvie, 'What does it spell?' Bruno took another look at the mysterious letters 'Why it's LIVE backwards!' he exclaimed." He had discovered this keen interpretation by the device of "twiddling his eyes." He is also on the brink of discovering that both EVIL and LIVE are close to LOVE, though of a peculiarly controlled and orderly sort. At the moment, however, he continues rebellious in the conversation with his sweet sister, and protests against the *Rules* to which Sylvie answers "Yes there ought to be such a lot of Rules, you wicked wicked boy! And how dare you *think* at all about it? And shut up that mouth directly." But since Bruno seems disinclined to shut the wayward mouth, Sylvie shuts it for him—with a kiss. (Sylvie sounds peculiarly like Charles Dodgson's mother, correcting and silencing her darling Charley.) It is interesting to compare this passage of *Sylvie and Bruno* with Carroll's early poem *Brother and Sister* in which the roles are reversed.

> "Sister, sister, go to bed
>   Go rest your weary head!"
> Thus the prudent brother said.
>
> "Do you want a battered hide
>   Or scratches to your face applied?"
> Thus the sister calm replied.
>
> "Sister! do not rouse my wrath
>   I'd make you into mutton broth
> As easily as kill a moth."
>
> The sister raised her beaming eye
> And looked on him indignantly,
> And sternly answered "Only try!" etc.

The verses end with the brother seeking to get a frying pan from the cook in order to make an Irish stew of the sister.[13]

13 In *Useful and Instructive Poetry,* written at twelve to thirteen (28).

The second episode occurs toward the end of the complex wandering story, in a scene undoubtedly cherished by the author as the denouement of the plot. It is a scene in which "I," the narrator, reveals to Lady Muriel his "own double life, and more than that the double life of those dear children" (double here manifestly meaning concealed or hidden, in their slipping from one state of consciousness to another). Lady Muriel speaks then of Sylvie's angelic character and recounts a situation in which, when tempted by Eric Lindon's courtship, she has heard Sylvie singing a strange song —in a voice "as sweet as an infant's first smile, or the first gleam of the white cliffs when one is coming home after weary years." At this point in the conversation, the narrator and Lady Muriel see the two children approach, each with an arm around the other, and the setting sun forming a golden halo around their heads, like the pictures of saints. Now Lady Muriel and the narrator both pass into an "eerie" state in which they see the children but are not seen by them. The song (which Carroll considered his best poem) was the song of Love, in which Sylvie sings with "indescribable sweetness":

> 'Tis a secret, and so let us whisper it low
> And the name of the Secret is Love!

The narrator felt a pang of perfection, and "a sense of awe that was almost terror" as he listened to the refrain of the song,

> For I think it is Love
> For I feel it is Love
> For I'm sure it is nothing but Love!

Bruno was now singing by himself,

> Say whence is the voice that, when anger is burning
> Bids the whirl of the tempest to cease?
> That stirs the vexed soul with an aching—a yearning
> For the brotherly hand-grip of peace?

> Whence the music that fills all our being—that shrills
> Around us, beneath, and above?

and Sylvie's voice came in courageously,

> 'Tis a secret: none knows how it comes, how it goes
> But the name of the secret is Love!

This seems to mark the final conversion of Bruno by Sylvie, and Lady Muriel's capitulation to Arthur Forester rather than to Eric Lindon.

It becomes evident from this story that the search is for a love which will avoid or control all aggressiveness and hostility, and with it all sexuality; a love in which natural human instinctual pressures will be converted into duty, obligation, denial and sanctity; in which the conscience will take the place of instinct, and will sacrifice freedom of thought as well as of action. Sylvie says to Bruno "There ought to be such a lot of Rules, you wicked boy! And how dare you *think* at all about it?" This section of the story, which was written late in Carroll's life, is a lineal descendant of the first poem "My Fairy" in *Useful and Instructive Poetry* written at the age of about twelve, a poem which foretold much of the development of the man,

> I have a fairy by my side
>   Which says I must not sleep,
> When once in pain I loudly cried
>   It said "You must not weep."
>
> If, full of mirth, I smile and grin,
>   It says, "You must not laugh,"
> When once I wished to drink some gin
>   It said "You must not quaff."
>
> When once a meal I wished to taste
>   It said "You must not bite,"
> When to the wars I went in haste
>   It said "You must not fight."

> "What may I do?" At length I cried
> Tired of the painful task,
> The fairy quietly replied
> And said "You must not ask."

The Moral "You mustn't."

At twelve the boy Charles Dodgson, with his wheelbar-rowed train in the Croft Garden, was still struggling for vigor, and his rhymes of this time were among his cleverest. By seventeen the *Rectory Umbrella* showed an eerie confusion of sexes and a kind of subversiveness of humor and ridicule. But by sixty-one, when *Sylvie and Bruno Concluded* was published, he was struggling to resign himself to the personally unlived life in the interest of the deadly ideal of perfection. The boy of twelve, who also wrote, under the title of *Facts,*

> Were I to take an iron gun
> And fire it off toward the sun;
> I grant 'twould reach its mark at last
> But not till many years had passed.
>
> But should that bullet change its force
> And to the planets take its course;
> T'would *never* reach the *nearest* star
> Because it is so very far.

was in many respects wiser than the man of sixty, who accepted the edict of the Fairy that the little boy should not dare to think but should accept more and more rules under the guise of dutiful love. The boy of twelve had written *Rules and Regulations,*

> A short direction
> To avoid dejection;
> By variations
> In occupations
> And prolongation

Of relaxation
And combinations
Of recreations
And disputation
On the state of the nation
In adaptation
To your station
By invitations
To friends and relations
By evitation
Of amputation
By permutation
In conversation
And deep reflection
You'll avoid dejection.

Leave well your grammar
And never stammer,
Write well and neatly,
And sing most sweetly,
Be enterprising,
Love early rising,
Go walks of six miles
Have ready quick smiles.
With lightsome laughter,
Soft-flowing after.
Drink tea, not coffee;
Eat bread with butter.
Once more, don't stutter.
Don't waste your money.
Abstain from honey.
Shut doors behind you,
(Don't slam them, mind you.)
Drink beer not porter,
Don't enter the water,
Till swim you are able.
Sit close to the table.
Take care of a candle.

Shut a door by the handle.
Don't push with your shoulder
Until you are older.
Lose not a button.
Refuse cold mutton.
Starve your canaries
Believe in fairies
If you are able,
Don't have a stable—
With any mangers.
Be rude to strangers.

Moral "Behave"

Carroll said that Lady Muriel was the reincarnation of the fairy Sylvie. It seems evident also that Sylvie is the spiritual representative of the sweet *don't's* of Charles Dodgson's loving mother, repeated through the mouth of the older sister, who shared her name, and who was about as much older than Charles as Sylvie was older than Bruno. Sylvie is more than this, she is the feminizing, emasculating influence in the boy's life, which gradually replaced vigorous emotion with remote idealism. It is further probable that it was not only the mother and this sister whose influence worked to form this fairy part of the boy, but his conquest of his rivalry, fear, resentment and envy of the whole brood of sisters—a conquest by identification with the loved rival. If there was, as we suspect, a seduction in early childhood by an exhibitionistic gardener, this too would very much increase the passive, visually receptive attitude of the child and further increase the feminization. (See pages 227-233.)

Another of Carroll's stories *Novelty and Romancement* (29) deserves consideration here. It is a wail told by a young man of the inglorious name of Leopold Edgar Stubbs, who is *not* the shoemaker Stubbs, nor yet the light comedian Stubbs, but Stubbs who since boyhood had had a passion for poetry, for beauty, for novelty, for romancement. In a specially yearning state Mr. Stubbs happened on a mechanic's shop whose sign actually bore the words "Dealer in Romancement." They discussed at some length the nature of this latter article, e.g., that it pieced things together and made them solider than stone. Returning the next day to collect the long-desired object, Stubbs finds his rosy dream dashed, as he sees that the sign actually reads "Dealer in Roman Cement."

3.

RECONSTRUCTION AND INTERPRETATION OF THE DEVELOPMENT OF CHARLES L. DODGSON AND LEWIS CARROLL

Charles L. Dodgson (Lewis Carroll) came of a family long connected with the history of Cheshire. He was the son of one Charles Dodgson, grandson of another and great-great-grandson of still another. With the exception of his grandfather, this was a line of Church of England clergymen. Thus his identity, in the sense of a strong feeling of place in a constantly well-established family, was even overly prescribed for him by birth. In addition his parents were first cousins and though this may have been a little puzzling to the child, still he consolidated the ancestry and the common background of the parents. The family, too, lived much by itself on a small "farm" on the outskirts of Daresbury without close neighbors. The children were taught mostly at home and Charles seems to have had only one friend from that time, Thomas Vere Bayne,[1] the son of a

---

[1] Thomas Vere Bayne was about three years older than Charles. He later matriculated at Christ Church and took his B.A. in 1852 and his M.A. in 1855. He was a Tutor at Christ Church for twenty years (1852-72), a Senior Censor from 1863-77, and in 1885 became Keeper of the Archives. He seems to have been on continuously friendly terms with Charles Dodg-

schoolmaster clergyman from a few miles away. The Dodgson children all showed the imprint of this communal life, in which the world was the family world, for the boys until they went away to school at twelve or thirteen, and always for the girls. The parents were intelligent people of unusually high cultural and ethical standards, with firm high requirements of achievement and behavior for their children, and seemed to have believed implicitly that the direct and constant development of the Christian ideals of peace, love and charity would answer the needs of the growing children. It was an era in England in which there was the illusion of freedom from devastating wars for the majority of Englishmen, when the Queen was reassuringly good, and English superiority seemed right and safe. The attitude of the enlightened educators was that the child could be molded into the desirable form by untiring direct pressure; and the better schools were emerging from the harsh discipline or adherence only to the form of learning, to a quieter sort of child training which took, however, almost as little account of the individuality of the child as the learning by flogging had done. The Dodgson family's belief in education by the moral precept of love might seem then to be an advanced one indeed.

All of the children bore the stamp of the early family life and training. Only Edwin, the youngest, who was hardly five when the mother died, ever went far from England or

---

son, though the references to him in the Diaries are slight. After his death in 1908, the *Oxford Magazine* published a brief description of his career, indicating that he was not an original scholar; a clergyman who was not a preacher or orator, but devout and regular in all observances of the Church. He shrank from publicity, was stiff where honor or conscience or social amenities were involved, but was one of the kindest, most courteous and companionable of men—fond of a good chat but without gall. An occasional gruffness was the greatest disapproval that his good temper would permit him to express. He was Charles Dodgson's lifelong friend—seemingly a kind of replica of what was soundly good, reserved and kind, but uninspired. He was an admirer of Dean Liddell's, was instrumental in raising a statue to him and assisted in writing his biography.—Extracted from Florence Becker Lennon's account of *Lewis Carroll's Life* (1).

lived for a long time away from the family group. All of the boys, including Edwin, became clergymen, though Charles was ordained only as a deacon and not as a priest; and the only daughter who married selected a clergyman husband, also named Charles. Several, perhaps all of the children had some sort of speech disturbance. Certainly there were some developmental influences which permeated the family. But Charles was to emerge as the uniquely illustrious one of the family of eleven children—and that through his production of nonsense stories and rhymes, so generally un-understandable and yet so appealing in their titillation of the intellect with their kaleidoscopic array of improbable horrors.

It might be expected that in a family in which the parents' marriage was so firmly happy and so prolific, the children would naturally tend to reproduce the pattern set in their own childhood and in turn marry and have large families. This was indeed apparently true in two of the brothers, Wilfred and Skeffington, but among the girls only Mary married. Further, none of the children married until after the death of both parents—a situation which suggests that the freedom to form a new alliance could not be accepted until death had released the bonds of the original one, to which all may have been somewhat too closely bound in the garden society under the loving ruling wisdom of the parents.

In so close and compact a group with eleven children in about eighteen years, there is not generally the time nor the opportunity for the full maternal devotion to each child. The children are pushed off the maternal lap a bit too early, sometimes before they are able to walk well or talk sufficiently to make their wants known. There seems little doubt that Charles was loved dearly by his mother and was her favorite, but he was forced to relinquish his infancy unusually early for the sister Caroline was born the following year, with Mary born when he was three, Skeffington when he was four and Wilfred when he was six. All this may have contributed to his precocity, yet it can hardly have helped but increase his jealousy and resentment of the younger children in a family setting in which rivalry and temper were silenced by maternal kisses and paternal examples of righteousness. Neither Charles Dodgson nor Lewis Carroll ever had many good words to say for babies. "Throw them away." "Tie them in knots and send them into the wilderness." "Roast them and serve them as appetizers for the main meal." These are the sentiments expressed under the guise of humor.

In the content of the *Alice* books, there is no regular order in time or space; animals, humans and flowers have similar characteristics, and similarity in appearance or other attributes is sufficient to furnish the presumption of identity; inanimate objects become animate; there are constant allusions to creatures eating each other up; behavior is inconstantly controlled by threats of extinction, and morals do not exist except as the sing-song maxims of the little girl observer. All this is about as close a portrayal as can be accomplished in language of that realm in childhood's development when the child is emerging from its primitive state of unreason, to the dawning conception of consequences, order and reason. It belongs to that time, generally between fifteen and thirty months, when the language of body activity and response is being supplanted by verbal language. Then utter dependence on the adult's omnipotent power is giving way to awareness of the increased autonomy of walking and talking; then conceptual thought and memory are developing, and past and future gradually become separate from now. In the language of the psychoanalyst this is the period of transition from primary-process to secondary-process domination of the psychic life. Gradually the sensorimotor imagery of that earlier period gives way to the ordered rational goal in thinking which is possible when there can be an anticipation and a memory, an awareness of self and a beginning self-criticism, rather than just the onslaught of immediate sensations and demands. Primary-process thought is supplanted only to appear in ordinary adult life in our dreams, some of our reveries, our madnesses and intoxications.

Charles Dodgson, the ultrarationalist has, as Lewis Carroll, so far reproduced the spirit of this primitive type of "feeling-thought" in *Wonderland* (with perhaps a little less success in *Looking Glass*) with such gentle ease that it awakens in the reader a feeling of fantastic familiarity with an extravaganza of outlandish nonsense. Such an extraordinary gift as the ability to reproduce the spirit of this preverbal era can conceivably come only from some special exigencies in Dodgson's own life from this early period, such that it remained unusually alive and vital to him. Although he had walled it off from conscious awareness with his extreme self-discipline, his dependence on orderliness, his suppression of any exaggeration of feeling, his concern regarding any inaccuracy of statement,[2] yet it remained luxuriantly active until it came forth and demanded expression in his stories for little girls.

That Dodgson was fascinated by little girls and that he fantasied playfully turning into one is written often in his letters and Diaries and demonstrated in his life itself. The stories of the *Alice* books are told from the angle of a little girl of seven and a half who dreams herself into these strange adventures. The garden, entrance into which is sought in both *Alice* books, is, in a general sense, the garden of truly sophisticated knowledge, the secret garden, the innermost, whether of body or of emotion. The whole series of adventures are felt by the child as strange and puzzling to the point of a definite sense of unreality, perplexity, and wonderment. "Am I really myself?" "Do I still know the same things I knew this morning?" the bewildered Alice asks as she falls into the rabbit hole, and believes herself to be dropping through the earth.

[2] In his photography "he had a conscientious horror of touching up his negatives" (2).

This takes us to the question of the young Charles Dodgson's sense of personal identity. Those universal questions of early childhood, "Who am I?" "Why am I I rather than somebody else?" and "How did I come to be?" may have been complicated for him in that until the age of almost five, he was the only boy among four sisters, with two older and two younger. The one nearest in age, Caroline, was only a year younger. It was inevitable that the five little Dodgsons, in the limited quarters of a country rectory should have been nursery tended together, and that the little boy was the strange minority in the sexes of this miniature nursery society. He saw his own body one way and the bodies of the little sisters around him as similar in most respects except for the secret, private, generally hidden and enticing part that was definitely different. It seems likely that during his second year at least he may have been as familiar with even this mysterious area through the little Caroline who came so close after him. He seemed never to settle this difference in his own mind, but to play with the problem in fantasy throughout all his life.

The spirit of both *Alice* books is that of an unplanned sight-seeing trip through a marvelously strange country. The title, *Alice's Adventures in Wonderland* in the one instance, and the entrance through the *Looking Glass* into an extraordinary country in the other, re-emphasize the voyeuristic theme. In the *Snark* the penalty for looking is the disappearance of the spectator. The young Charles Dodgson had so sturdy a curiosity that "Please explain!" was long remembered as a habitual inquiry throughout his little boyhood. Had not the aggressive and sexual drives been too firmly checked in him, it is probable that he would have fulfilled many times over the promise of intellectual genius which was early noted. As his life developed, however, it was only in its less official aspects that these drives broke through and found at least partially sublimated outlets in his writing and in his photography. In the latter, the interest in looking could be given almost full play. He photographed mostly little girls and prominent people. He posed the little girls over and over in various costumes and with infinite patience; and occasionally, it is said, in nature's own costume. Photography had only recently been invented, but young Dodgson became adept and was one of the leading photographers of the day, doing his own developing and printing at a time when this was a tedious and messy job.[3] In it, he showed enormous zeal, care, and skill. One can well imagine that there was a special triumph in seeing the outlines of the picture come to life on the plate; and further through his photography he was able to capture and hold a bit of time and life in unchanging certainty. This was important to him since he was generally so concerned with the fleeting quality of time and the unreliability of body form and size. He kept his photographic plates carefully filed and indexed just as he did his menus and his lists of guests. Aside from his photography and his writing he showed the intensity of his scoptophilic interest only in a reversed or negative form: he was the shyest man but one whom Mark Twain ever had met.

There was not only the boy's close association with his sisters, and especially the one who was nearly a twin to him, to stimulate his curiosity and excite his anxiety. In addition, there was the mother's long series of pregnancies, the occasions of the births themselves, and the quandaries and observations regarding the origins of the succession of Dodgson babies who repetitively displaced him from his mother's lap and breast and pressed on him more and more the role and prerogatives of the elder brother. It is quite probable that he would have preferred less responsibility and more babying himself: "More bread and less taxes"—to reverse one of

[3] Daguerre's photographic process was announced when Charles was seven (1839). It was only in 1851 when Dodgson was nineteen that the collodion "wet plate" was made known, and was patent-free. He worked with it from 1856 to 1880 (3).

Carroll's own chapter slogans (4). Three babies arrived before he was five. That he suffered intensely from very early and organically felt jealousy is attested by the ubiquitousness of expressions of oral aggression in all his writing. The wish to eat up and the fear of being eaten up are written over and over again in his fantasies, and appear on nearly every page of *Wonderland.* There, even the oedipal crime, for which the punishment of death is to be meted out, is given an oral form in the use of the old nursery rhyme of the Jack of Hearts who stole the tarts baked by his mother, the Queen. Dodgson's tendency to identify with the little girl, specifically expressed in his letters to Gertrude Chataway in which he proposes changing identities with her through "drinking her health" on her birthday, was again expressed in oral terms. Even without this bit of evidence, however, one gets the impression of a very early and primitive type of identification in which taking in with the eyes and taking in with the mouth are closely akin. As is true in most cases of so early an involvement of the sense of individual identity, it would seem that Charles came to the oedipal period at five already too burdened.

There appears to be no evidence that Charles Dodgson ever loved any woman in an adult fashion. Some have supposed that he had suffered some hidden and disappointed love relationship with an unknown young woman, and have fortified this assumption by a similar supposition on the part of his nephew-biographer, Collingwood. They point to the poems *Three Sunsets* (1861) and *Stolen Waters* (1862) as indicating such a tragedy. Others have deduced that he was seriously in love with Alice Liddell and wanted to marry her. His love for her was surely deep, constant and serious, but it seems more likely that it was the more possible because he could *not* marry her. There was not only the disparity in years at the beginning, but the facts that the alienation from the Liddells and the separation from Alice occurred so early, that—even if we were to embrace wholeheartedly the theory that the love of a man nearly thirty for a child not yet ten is to be considered an adult type of love—we would still have to realize some peculiar quality in it in that he remained faithful to the child ideal and did not seek to find her again in a grown-up form.

In these two of Carroll's poems as in *Faces in the Fire* he repeats the figure of speech of the loss of the loved one against the background of the setting of the sun, and in *Stolen Waters* and *Faces in the Fire*, he describes his loved one as an old-young woman. The poems seem most likely to be memorial love poems to his dead mother, and significant of his continued oedipal attachment and his uncompleted mourning. The *Three Sunsets*, written when Alice Liddell was six to seven, includes the stanzas,

> So by degrees his spirit bent
> To mock its own despairing cry
> In stern self-torture to invent
> New luxuries of agony,
> And people all the vacant space
> With visions of her perfect face.
>
> Then for a moment she was nigh
> He heard no step, but she was there;
> As if an angel suddenly
> Were bodied from the viewless air
> And all her fine ethereal frame
> Should fade as swiftly as it came.
>
> So half in fancy's sunny trance,
> And half in misery's aching void,
> With set and stony countenance
> His bitter being he enjoyed,
> And thrust for ever from his mind
> The happiness he could not find [5].

The poem ends with the dawn of a new day, but the death of the lover.

His fantasy tales told to the little Liddells about the time of and a little after the writing of this poem seem rather to be unconscious attempts at revival of that early period belonging to the age of two or so, which could never be relived, however, except in combination with life's later complexities. It appears that his oedipal love for his mother was never displaced, except in a typical Carroll fashion—by reversal—in which he insistently fell in love with little girls who were young enough to be his daughters. It is a love, however, which involves too heavy a weight of identification with the loved one. This is tacitly understood by many readers of the *Alice* books who realize, probably without clearly thinking of it, that Alice and the author are one. It is also implicitly confessed by Carroll when he refers to the little Liddells as "Elsie, Lacie, and Tillie,"[4] *Elsie* being a phonetic representation of L-C, as well as a variant of Alice, and *Lacie,* containing also the L.C. and formed from a rearrangement of the letters in *Alice*: again typical Carroll devices. It was understood intuitively by Dodgson's own heartless students who signed their parody "Louisa Caroline," possibly without knowing that these were names of two of his sisters. Charles was the third in his family just as Alice was the third in hers.

This brings us to the realization of the combination of the primitive identification with his sisters and the identification with the mother by reversal of roles, in relation to the unsolved oedipal attachment. In understanding this, it is essential to take into consideration another set of factors. The age of four to five (the phallic-oedipal phase) is a critical time in the lives of most children, being a period of development of special genital awareness due to the influx of heightened sensations in these organs. This is usually accompanied

---

[4] The three little sisters who lived at the bottom of a well, according to the *Wonderland* account.

216

by a sense of generalized activity, energy and expansion. If, however, the possession of individual (including sexual) identity is already confused and considerable energy is bound in resentments which must not be put into action or even revealed, the natural buoyant expansiveness of the period becomes complicated. Especially in boys under strains of this kind, the increased genital sensations accompanying tumescence and detumescence become bewildering and frightening rather than invigorating. The child then enters the oedipal period without ordinary confidence in his infantile sexual dreams. He is undermined from the outset; the heightened attachment may be sharp and persistent but is felt too much in terms of earlier stages of development, with the wish for oral conquest and the fear of an oral retribution.

This, we suspect, was the plight of the little boy Charles. Although he was his mother's first son and probably her favorite, a position which one would expect might have given him, otherwise, a confidence in his attractiveness to the opposite sex, he was never to take the further step and displace or develop his love for her to include that of another grown woman, and never seemingly to have reasonable confidence in himself as a man. He came to have a feeling of aversion almost amounting to terror "of boys and boy nature" (6), but remained affectionately fixated to little girls of eight or so, that time in childhood midway between the two upsurges of sexuality (at the oedipal period and at puberty) when sexual urgency is least strong and even the bodies of boys and girls are most alike.

Alice's Adventures in Wonderland is replete with descriptions of bizarre and unassimilated body feelings, which reproduce—in various body parts as well as in the total body —the phallic form and changes. Alice's body becomes enormously and suddenly elongated or collapses and shrinks sadly. Her *neck* particularly becomes so serpent-like that she is actually mistaken for a serpent hiding in a tree. Her arm and leg, each in turn, seem strange, far away, and hardly part of herself in their grotesquely enlarged form. All of these changes follow eating, or drinking. It seems that in Charles' own development, looking became a substitute for the acquisitiveness of eating. The latter may indeed have been too clearly a sensual indulgence[5] to escape his rigid self-discipline. Looking and its inner reflection of fantasying became his great satisfaction, and undoubtedly contributed early to his intellectual development. In *Through the Looking Glass* this theme of the changing proportion of things, observed in outer objects rather than felt in parts of Alice's own body, is prominent. These extraordinary developments reach riotous lengths in the last scene in which everything shoots upward on the banquet table, candles lengthen to the ceiling, bottles annex wings and flutter about, and general excitement prevails, until the whole collapses again, with the White Queen disappearing into the soup and the Red Queen dwindling to doll size. There are many other examples throughout the story, but this last scene is, naturally, the climax.

Another contributing determinant to Charles Dodgson's concern with body size and changes lay in his repeated observation of his mother's pregnancies, with inevitable notice of her sudden changes from obesity to thinness. Just as the *Alice* books reflect so much the unassimilated phallic problems as well as the recrudescence of the early primary-process type of thought, so his early drawings are striking in their presentation of the fat-thin contrasts. In these, however, there is the combination of presentation and denial of the problem, again through the mechanism of reversal, and the consistent depicting of the man as enormously corpulent

[5] Collingwood quotes Carroll's first letter to the illustrator, Miss E. Gertrude Thomson, as describing himself as "one who for twenty years has found his one amusement in photographing from life—especially in photographing children" (7).

with protruding abdomen and small arms and legs while the woman appears generally thin to the point of emaciation.

Certain other aspects of Dodgson's life and character can be understood in the light of the circumstances of these early formative years and their later consequences—as these appear in the content of his writings and his letters as well as in the relationships and events of his life. It is noteworthy that in Carroll's three major prose works, *Alice's Adventures in Wonderland, Through the Looking Glass,* and *Sylvie and Bruno,* there is no strong, active and well-respected adult male figure. Only in *Sylvie and Bruno* does a male play a central part in the story. There the insufferably cute little Bruno is a major character with Dr. Arthur Forester and Captain Eric Lindon as adult projections of the "good" and "bad" sides of his adult character, which finally become reconciled at the very end. The Earl, Lady Muriel's father, is estimable but hardly more than a part of the backdrop for the rest of the performance. The narrator "I" is male, but is an elderly invalided bachelor, a lecturer in mathematics, and a shadowy figure at best. Neither Arthur Forester nor Eric Lindon comes much to life, and at the end of the tale Arthur Forester starts his marriage in a crippled and depleted state, while Eric Lindon, Christianized, departs to preach to the heathen. In the *Wonderland* and *Looking Glass* world the pallor of the adult males in general is even more sweeping. Mr. W. Rabbit is a scared and fussy little person, wearing white gloves and carrying a fan and a watch which he consults as he worries about whether the Duchess will be cross with him. There follow successively Pat, the cowardly handyman, and ineffective Bill, the lizard; the peremptory but indolent Caterpillar with his oversized hookah; the fish-footman and the frog-footman; the mad March Hare and the equally Mad Hatter; the somnolent Dormouse; the Five, Seven and Two of Spades who are clumsy gardeners and fall on their faces; the timid King of Hearts who wishes to obey his Queen but is sometimes too softhearted; the doubled-up soldiers who serve as arches in the croquet game; the Mock Turtle sighing broken-heartedly; and the Gryphon who knows that nothing exists except in fancy; and finally the forgetful and stupid jurymen. This is the male cast in *Wonderland*. Nor are the males in the *Looking Glass* world more impressive: the White King sulks, is frightened to the tips of his whiskers and makes endless memoranda instead of doing anything; the White Knight who appears first, poorly balanced on a poker and later as an awkward horseman with his foolish inventions dangling from his waist; the ticket taker on the railway carriage; the anonymous passenger dressed in white paper, who resembled Disraeli and advised always getting a return-trip ticket; Tweedledum and Tweedledee, the twins who quarrel about a rattle; Humpty-Dumpty, the conceited and vulnerable; Haigha and Hatta, the Anglo-Saxon messengers who carry hay and ham sandwiches and seem akin to the Hare and the Hatter; the Lion and the Unicorn whose fight is interrupted by the promise of plumcake; and the Red King who spends his time asleep.

In contrast to these are the belligerent and noisy females in both *Alice* books: the Queen of Hearts who threatens general execution by decapitation; the massively Ugly Duchess and her peppery cook; the Red Queen who is the counterpart of the Queen of Hearts; and the sheep shopkeeper who makes customers wait on themselves. Only the untidy White Queen is perpetually muddled and anxious. There are of course the good little girl flowers in the animated garden, though even there the tiger lily was rather nastily vituperative. The females are fewer in number than the males in these strange Alice-lands, and are certainly more deadly than the males.

This may represent a reversal of sexual roles, due to the state of affairs in the rectory garden where Charles maintained his superiority precariously but felt outnumbered and endangered by the sisters. Certainly confusion with a suggestion of ridicule by reversal was one of Charles' major defenses. Still it is somewhat surprising that this reversal of active and passive roles should be represented among the ruling classes too, the Kings and Queens, who occupy the parental positions in society. It is noteworthy that the Queen, especially the Queen of Hearts, is the cruel punisher threatening decapitation endlessly. In the oedipal crime of the boy it is the father who becomes the feared rival who may punish the child by dismemberment. With love focused so strongly on his mother as it seemed to be in the case of the little boy Charles, it might seem then that he would represent the King-father as the awesomely threatening one. It is necessary to realize, however, that Charles' love for his mother was, as already described, too much involved with the wishes of the earliest infantile period rather than having the fullest oedipal quality. It belonged rather to that period when the mother is nearly everything, good and bad, to the children of both sexes; and is the desired one for protection and nurture or the feared one whose anger or withdrawal is devastating. On such a state of emotional development, the father may be somewhat awe-inspiring but is a peripheral and secondary figure at best, not very actively involved in the child's life.

This probably exaggerates but otherwise represents Charles L. Dodgson's relation to his father. He certainly admired this father and wanted to please him. It would have been impossible to question the religious beliefs held by his father: "of course" he followed in his father's footsteps in these matters. Yet he had odd obsessional doubts in the night, which hardly seemed to belong to him by daylight. One is impressed with the respectful affection between the two but not a degree of intimacy which could include disagreements. Thirty years after his father's death, he wrote in a letter of condolence "The greatest blow that has ever fallen on my life was the death nearly thirty years ago of my dear father,

—so in offering my sincere sympathy, I write as a fellow-sufferer. And I rejoice to know that we are not only fellow-sufferers but also fellow believers in the blessed hope of the resurrection of the dead which makes such a parting holy and beautiful instead of being merely blank despair." Touching as this is, the lack of relinquishment of the father after so long a time and the stately, almost impersonal quality of the grief strike a strange note. It may be that he could not accept the death of the father whom he had never fully and intimately accepted in life. Much as he liked little girls, there is no expression of frustrated paternity in him, not even a hint that he would have wanted one of them for a daughter.

The period between six and ten which is so generally a time of extended development of ideals and ambitions of childhood, in which the parent of the same sex as the child is naturally the important model, appeared differently in the case of Charles Dodgson supervising his brothers' and sisters' play in the garden at Daresbury. Already there was something of a motherly or older sisterly quality in his care for and entertainment of the younger children. His activities at this time seemed concerned with the acting out of fantasies probably related to but controlling of the delightfully wild aggressive antics described in Carroll's later tales to his little girl friends. There was a slightly feminine cast to his charming thoughtfulness—his interest in tiny things, his patient arrangements of puppet theatricals, and his protectiveness toward small animals as well as small sisters. It is reported that at Richmond School he could use his fists with the other boys when necessary; but at Rugby he was more unhappy and retreated somewhat into his "liberties with language" and his lengthy letters for the sisters at home. Every child forms basic ideals founded on a combination of and selection from those of both parents, but the dominant ideals follow generally those of the parent of the same sex if that parent is at all acceptable. Charles on the other hand had much in his

nature that suggests the Victorian woman. The exposition
of this appears to be the unconsciously determined meaning
of *Sylvie and Bruno,* the final production of which was so
compellingly important to Carroll. The overly sweet guardian, Sylvie, is clearly related to the protecting guiding
mother, who kisses away all aggressiveness.[6] The good man
becomes the emasculated or crippled Arthur Forester, and
Captain Eric Lindon must atone for his religious doubts by
doing missionary service to the heathen. Nor is this surprising when the nature of the oedipal strivings of the little boy
Charles is recalled.

The observation of patients whose early development has
followed somewhat the lines of young Charles Dodgson's
has led me to believe that in such children the time from six
to ten years is often one of rich fantasy of a peculiarly
varied kind. Then the reanimation of inanimate objects, the
sense of personal communion with Nature, the detailed per-
sonalization of animals, the playing out in games and fantasy
of both sexual roles, or the adoption of an intermediate fairy
identity—all these show how little the child has really finished
with the very first years of his life and how preoccupied with
these early problems he remains. It can be a very rich experience leading to later productiveness; but it is sometimes
one of perilous psychical balance. Then puberty must become a time of reckoning, with its insistence on sexual

6 Collingwood remarks, "Readers of Sylvie and Bruno will remember the
way in which the fairy-children save the drunkard from his evil life, and I
have always felt that Mr. Dodgson meant Sylvie to be something more than
a fairy—a kind of guardian angel." In support of this he then quotes from
a letter written in 1879 by Dodgson to one of his child friends, concerning
some children who had recently lost their mother and who might thereby
be deprived of her guidance: "Many people believe that our friends in the
other world can and do influence us in some way, and perhaps even 'guide'
us and give us light to show us our duty. My own feeling is that it may be
so: but nothing has been revealed about it. That the angels do so is revealed, and we may feel sure of that; and there is a beautiful fancy that
'a mother who has died leaving a child behind her in the world, is allowed
to be a sort of guardian angel to that child'. . ." (8).

decisiveness—in reaction to which the wish to remain a child and deny maturity can get the upper hand. Something of this, we suspect, was what made Rugby so difficult an experience for the adolescent Charles.

Especially do these conditions prevail when there has been too far-reaching and intense a denial or a repression of aggression, until the feelings themselves are avoided as guilty, and with them many of the healthy expanding impulses toward maturity and an active life. That Charles Dodgson's early teaching was such as to make almost any show of hostility a matter of guilt is amply apparent. But how much this extended into forms of aggressiveness which were not hostile is pathetically attested in his poem at twelve *My Fairy* ending with the moral: "You mustn't." There were, however, deeper earlier influences which made aggressiveness problematic and linked it with sexuality; and it was probably the reinforcement of these by the moralistic teaching which made him an unusually gentle and sexually unfulfilled man.

Further, children whose firmness of body identity has been undermined by too constant primitive identifications, especially with children of the opposite sex, will suffer additional bodily uncertainty through any states of sweeping emotion which give feelings of physical distension and explosiveness.[7] Thus anger is less readily borne, not out of any guilt feeling at so early a stage, but out of a sense of imminent general annihilation involving the little one's own body and the outer world as well. It is the sort of annihilation which occurs through overexcitement to the point of confusion in the infantile years; and in loss of contact with outer reality

[7] It may be noted that Bruno (in *Sylvie and Bruno*) suffered from too much excitement, even happy excitement. Bruno explained that in fact he did not *always* wish to be happy: "Sometimes when I am too happy, I wants to be a little miserable. Then I just tell Sylvie about it, oo know, and Sylvie sets me some lessons. Then it is all right" (Chapter on "A Musical Gardener") (9).

of severe rage attacks or actual convulsions later in life. Mr.
Dodgson had a sensitivity to and a preoccupation with convulsions in others as already noted, and such a defense
against shows of aggressiveness in his adulthood, that his
nephew S. D. Collingwood wrote of him,

> Lewis Carroll resembled the stoic philosophers, for no
> outward circumstance could upset the tranquility of
> his mind. He lived . . . the life of calm contentment
> based on the assurance that so long as we are faithful
> to ourselves, no seeming evil can really harm us. But
> in him there was one exception to the rule. During an
> argument he was often excited. The war of words, the
> keen and subtle conflict between trained minds—in
> this his soul took delight, in this he sought and found
> the joy of battle and of victory. Yet he would not
> allow his serenity to be ruffled by any foe whom he
> considered unworthy of his steel; he refused to argue
> with people whom he knew to be hopelessly illogical.
> [The kind of *ruffling* which Collingwood refers to is
> obviously the ruffling of temper rather than of anxiety
> (10).]

Cruelty, anger and tempestuous behavior are dealt with
in the *Alice* books, especially in *Alice's Adventures in Wonderland,* and presented so continuously and in such exaggerated form as to become unbelievable and ridiculous.
Indeed it is all a dream. The present slang phrase "It's a
riot" is expressive of *Wonderland* conditions. The stories
themselves give evidence, however, of the deposit of reactions of this kind in the early experiences in Charles Dodgson's personal history. Furthermore, in such states of generalized explosive excitement some diffuse erotization also
occurs, so that generalized motor and sexual stimulation become more or less fused. Instead of acting in a somewhat
reciprocal fashion as they do in many people, so that repression in the one area increases the tendency to activity in the

225

other, denial of the privilege of one sort of experience pre-
disposes then to (self-) denial of experience of the other
sort. Indeed the explosion of rage has, in its form, a rise to
a pitch or climax followed by sudden deflation, which fits
well with physical erotic climactic patterns. This confluence
of patterns promotes the continued linking of the two drives
even later in life. The sexual, orgastic climax is then feared
as though it were destructive. Such orgastic explosions occur
at the end of both *Alice* books, and Alice awakes.

For Dodgson life must be reasonable, kind and tranquil,
with excitement permitted only in worthy intellectual argu-
ments. Yet he wrote with a deep unconscious knowledge of
exactly the opposite state. It is notable that Dodgson himself
suffered from chronic insomnia. To prevent his thoughts
from wandering in an irrational or illogical way which might
have brought up frightening subjects, he spent many of his
sleepless hours constructing puzzles and mathematical problems, published as *Pillow Problems*. As he explains it, his
motive in publishing these was to show how, by a little determination, the mind

> can be made to concentrate itself on some intellectual
> subject (not necessarily mathematics) and thus banish
> those petty troubles and vexations which most people
> experience, and which—unless the mind be otherwise
> occupied—will persist in invading the hours of the
> night. . . . There are mental troubles much worse than
> mere worry, for which an absorbing object of thought
> may serve as a remedy. There are skeptical thoughts,
> which seem for the moment to uproot the firmest
> faith: there are blasphemous thoughts, which dart,
> unbidden into the most reverent souls; there are un-
> holy thoughts, which torture with their hateful pres-
> ence the fancy that would fain be pure. . . . [11].

But there were other influences too which played their
part in frightening and perhaps fascinating Charles (already

predisposed by his infantile rivalries and resentments), deepening his aversion to the bodily satisfactions and responsibilities of adult life. In consequence, he kept his emotional gaze focused on children at the least sexual period of their young lives.

In the casts of characters of *Alice's Adventures in Wonderland, Through the Looking Glass,* and *Sylvie and Bruno,* there are three off-stage characters whose voices are heard in song and rhyme, but who appear scantily or not at all. All are really memories which come to life in their vividness. All are older men, parodied, foolish inferior characters, but merry and glamorously enchanting in their unexpectedly acrobatic behavior and lilting rhythms. In *Wonderland, Father William* appears in the poetry which Alice recites, on the advice of the Caterpillar in order to test her memory which she fears is failing. In *Looking Glass* world, the *Aged Aged Man* a sitting on a gate is in the White Knight's song which he brings out of *his* memory to comfort Alice, who in turn thinks she can never forget the scene of the foolish Knight sitting swaying in his saddle as he sings. In *Sylvie and Bruno,* the mad, musical gardener comes to life out of the revery of the narrator, "I" as he half sleeps on a railway journey to Elveston, and finds himself automatically conjugating "I thought I saw . . ." as though to test *his* memory. When he reaches "He thought he saw . . . ," this proves to be the switch phrase, which causes a break-through of a stanza of the gardener's song:

> He thought he saw an Elephant
> That practiced on a fife.
> He looked again and saw it was
> A letter from his wife.
> At length, I realize, he said
> The bitterness of Life.

At this point the scene has shifted to a garden enclosure, even as it is in *Wonderland* and *Looking Glass* worlds. It is

227

worth noting that in the *Hunting of the Snark,* a similar but more intense version of the amazing off-stage character exists in the snark itself, who does not actually appear but whose presence is indicated by the sudden vanishing of the Baker. But the Snark has other connections as well.

The rhyme *Father William* is the colloquy between a fat merry old man and a bewildered timid lean one. Father William, in spite of his white hair, insistently stands on his head, balances an eel on the end of his nose, somersaults in the door backward, and defiantly says that he intends "to do it again and again"—all to the consternation of the younger man. He explains that he has always kept his limbs supple with the use of a special ointment which he offers to sell to the young man for a shilling a box; and that since he has reached brainless old age, he no longer fears injuring his brain with his antics as he did in his boyhood. He ends by kicking the anemic youth out.

The character of Father William certainly has some relation to *The Aged, Aged Man a sitting on a gate.*[8] The latter is even older, a beggar who is engaged in senseless pursuits, such as chasing butterflies to bake in mutton pies. He also has *his* ointment, Rowland's Macassar oil which he recommends and offers for sale. The place of the lean young man is taken by the White Knight, who sings the song about the aged man and is himself preoccupied with rejuvenation schemes, e.g., to dye his whiskers green (but hide them behind a fan)[9] and to feed himself on batter, and so go on from day to day getting a little fatter. Father William's acrobatics are toned down and the scene is no longer one of defiance but rather of sad reminiscence which causes the White Knight to weep because it reminds him so

[8] Horace Gregory thinks the Tenniel illustration of Father William's son is Wordsworth's "Idiot Boy." (The Shield of Achilles, p. 100).

[9] Here we seem to get a glimpse of Mr. W. Rabbit in the person of the White Knight.

Of that old man I used to know—
Whose look was mild, whose speech was slow
Whose hair was whiter than the snow
Whose face was very like a crow
With eyes, like cinders, all aglow,
Who seemed distracted with his woe,
Who rocked his body to and fro
And muttered mumblingly and low,
As if his mouth were full of dough,
Who snorted like a buffalo—
That summer evening long ago [12].

The *Gardener,* who is the keeper of the door *out* of the garden in which the fairy children Sylvie and Bruno find themselves from time to time, is again a vigorous though merrily mad soul. He usually appears first as a song heard from some indefinite place, and then later becomes corporeified (a neologism). There is a description of him only on his first appearance, however, when he was clearly "mad, madder and maddest" as he danced his frantic jig and brandished his rake. His feet were large (like those of the elephant of which he sang) and disproportionate to his body, which was rather like a scarecrow that had lost its stuffing. These proportions resemble those of the lean young man who was amazed by Father William, or the White Knight who sang about the aged man whom he had seen years before, and of the aged man himself. The gardener too is the onlooker for he sings repeatedly of the fantastic things which he has seen start out to be one thing and then turn into something extraordinarily and unexpectedly different. His visions and conversation singularly suggest those of the creatures in the garden of *Wonderland* and the *Looking Glass* worlds. Only his exuberant jigging recalls Father William.

That all this is connected with the conception of an older man, a father, but one who may appear either in a degraded form, or as a beneficent lordly King-father, is apparent in the Chapters in *Sylvie and Bruno* which introduce the mad gardener. It is the gardener who is the keeper of the garden door and permits the children to go out to give cake to a miserable beggar who then reveals himself as their father, the Fairy King, who is to teach them about universal—rather than personal love.

The figure appearing sometimes in one guise and sometimes in another, but with its acrobatic, swaying, jigging, snorting rhythm is a typical dream representation of sexual excitement. It is interesting, therefore, to realize that in the very structure of Carroll's stories, these figures all appear as memories which are repeated in dreams. The *Alice* books are presented as dreams, and *Sylvie and Bruno* avowedly represents transitions back and forth between different levels of consciousness, in which the dreaming state plays a prominent part. The gardener's song always comes at the point of a shift from one state to another. The repetitiveness of this excited figure and his constant association with a secret garden, the concern about whether the memory is good in the onlooker and the reciprocal question whether the silly old fellow's brain has been injured—whether his behavior is merrily exciting or a comfort in a state of distress—would lead to the conclusion that there was some actual but repressed memory of the author's which was insistently recurring in hidden forms: that probably in his childhood Charles had been stirred at the sight of an older man, perhaps a gardener, in a state of sexual excitement. Indeed, if one studies the text of *Through the Looking Glass* as it describes Alice's encounter with the White Knight who then sings her the comforting song about the aged, aged man, the fact that this section is a beautiful description of a screen memory becomes apparent.

The very first version of the gardener is, perhaps, the most revealing of all. It appears in Charles' early poems *Useful and Instructive Poetry*, written at about the age of twelve.

Here under the title of *A Tale of a Tail* (13), the boy wrote

> An aged gardener gooseberries picked
>   From off a gooseberry tree
> The thorns they oft his fingers pricked
>   Yet never a word said he.

This presents clearly the stoical ideal, the reaction formation against fear of suffering which Collingwood was to describe as so marked a characteristic of Charles' adult years. The illustration accompanying the poem shows the gardener with witchlike prominence of nose and chin, but a pitifully short ratty tail, presumably the tail to his coat.

> A dog sat by him with a tail
>   Oh *such* a tail! I ween,
> That never such in hill or dale
>   Hath hitherto been seen.

> It was a tail of desperate length
>   A tail of grizly fur
> A tail of muscle bone and strength
>   Unmeet for such a cur.

Obviously the dog is here the awesome creature with a tail possessing virile qualities out of proportion to the degraded character of its owner.

> Yet of this tail the dog seemed proud.
>   And ever and anon,
> He raised his head and barked so loud
> That though the man seemed *somewhat* cowed
>   Yet still his work went on.

> At length in lashing out its tail
>   It twisted it so tight
> Around his legs, 'twas no avail,
>   To pull with all its might.

> The gardener scarce could make a guess
>   What round his legs had got

> Yet he worked on in weariness
> Although his wrath was hot.
>
> "Why, what's the matter?" he did say
> "I can't keep on my feet,
> Yet not a glass I've had this day
> Save one, of brandy neat,
>
> "Two quarts of ale, and one good sup
> Of whiskey sweet and strong,
> And yet I scarce can now stand up,
> I fear that something's wrong."

There is thus a mutual entanglement between cur and gardener, in which one pulls the other and produces or increases a state of intoxication, bewilderment, and confused excitement which reminds us of Charles Dodgson's horror of convulsions, the idiot boy, and alcoholism.

> His work reluctantly he stopped
> The cause of this to view,
> Then quickly seized an axe and chopped
> The guilty tail in two.
>
> When this was done, with mirth he bowed
> Till he was black and blue,
> The dog it barked both long and loud
> *And with good reason too*
>
> Moral—Don't get drunk.

It would seem here that the dog probably represents or is associated with the young boy, as it has seemed to be in the others of Carroll's writings, especially in *Sylvie and Bruno*. It is to be recalled, too, that although he deals with the dog with mercy and respect in this book which also accepts the five-year-old boy as a child of charm in need of taming, he later developed a strong aversion to dogs and was especially

ILLUSTRATION FOR *Tale of a Tail* BY CHARLES L. DODGSON, AGE 13

fearful of being bitten by one. In the entanglement between gardener and cur, subject and object become reciprocally confused, the turmoil ends with—not decapitation—but decaudalization (to coin a word). One suspects further that the obvious pun on *tail*, made manifest in the title *A Tale of a Tail*, indicates further the pressure *to tell* which was created in the boy as he grew to be the man. This is variously expressed in the poem: the tail is "*such* a tail," one "of desperate length"; it is "lashed out" by the cur, who ends up barking "both long and loud and with good reason too." The old gardener bowing with mirth till he is black and blue, reminds one of Father William, the White Knight falling from his horse, the aged aged man whom the White Knight shook "so well from side to side until his face was blue," and of Charles Dodgson himself who felt like rolling on the lawn with horrified laughter after his visit to Bowes where he saw the "mouthing idiot."

The Jabberwock, the Bandersnatch and the Snark are three other offstage creatures, even less clearly described than Father William, the aged man, and the gardener. One sees, however, that they are all mysterious, frightening animals, such as Darwin never wrote about—are interrelated and have some sort of connection with the excited old men. The Jabberwock appears only in a poem, read by Alice in a book at the very entrance to *Looking Glass* world. It is a poem which Carroll had composed as part of a rhyme-writing contest in a family party, and later incorporated into the *Looking Glass* story. In this way it was like the last stanza of the *Snark* which appeared first and then gradually drew the rest of the poem out after it. The business of Jabberwocky occurs at a time when the White King is limp and bewildered after Alice has lifted him from the hearth and dusted him off. He is trying to express his horror and the fact that he will never be able to forget this, whereupon the White Queen tells him that his memory is so bad that he had best make a memorandum of his experience or he will forget even his feelings. Alice, however, interferes with his writing and, guiding the pencil for him, causes him to make, involuntarily, a factual note concerning the behavior of the White Knight. Thus a problem of memory is involved, even as it has been in the instances of the excited old men. (It would seem too that Alice's interference with the White King's memorandum is strikingly like Charles Dodgson's own diary recordings which repress feelings but record facts.)

The *Jabberwocky*, which is possibly the most famous nonsense poem in the English language, contains many arresting words, neologisms, which sound as though we should know their meanings, yet leave us groping, and a little tickled at our own stupidity. To enumerate some of them: brillig, slithy, toves, gyre, gimble, wabe, mimsy, borogoves, mome, raths, outgrabe—occur in the first stanza. Some of the other stanzas are not so loaded, but there is none that does not contain two or three. A few are onomatopoeic—like "whiffling," "galumphing"—but most are built on other principles. These are explained somewhat later in *Through the Looking Glass* when Humpty Dumpty explains to Alice that though he is more than a little slow in mathematics, there are few words he can't explain. It is clear that he, like the adolescent Charles, has much fun taking liberties with language, and indulges in a most unsensible argument of the kind that the adult Dodgson particularly abhorred. Humpty Dumpty explains that he has conquered words and makes them mean whatever he wants them to, but they are troublesome little creatures with tempers of their own and have sometimes to be subjugated.[10] This is accomplished by putting them into portmanteaux, generally two together, subjecting them in this way to extra labor for which they receive extra wages on Saturday night. On Alice's reciting *Jabberwocky*, he ex-

[10] Compare Swift's poems characterizing the temperament of words. Note also the account of the origin of Martin Scriblerus.

plains that *brillig* means "four o'clock in the afternoon when things begin to broil for dinner"; that *slithy* is a portmanteau fusion of "lithe" and "slimy"; *toves* is a portmanteau combination of ideas, containing badgers, lizards and corkscrews and that these little creatures live in the grass at the foot of the sundial and feed on cheese. *Gyre* means to revolve like a gyroscope; the *wabe* is again a portmanteau word for the grass plot *way b*ehind and *way b*efore the sundial; *mimsy* is "*mi*serable" combined with "*flimsy*." In *mome* the adhesiveness is a little different: it is probably composed of fro*m* h*ome*. Thus the animated words can be made to combine in various ways. In the Preface to the *Hunting of the Snark,* Carroll quotes Humpty Dumpty's portmanteau theory with approval and, stating that *frumious* is derived from "fuming" and "furious," explains that the two words might come into collision in the mind and articulation of the speaker, whereupon the person with the perfectly balanced mind said "frumious." It is certainly a just solution, and perhaps avoids stammering. (We would suspect that *frustrated* was also somewhere in the portmanteau, however.)

The story of the *Jabberwocky* is that of the little boy who, though warned by his father to beware the Jabberwock, the Jubjub bird, and the Bandersnatch, ventures out into the forest, sword in hand, on a summer afternoon and actually encounters the fabulous Jabberwock, who with eyes aflame comes whiffling and burbling through the wood. He succeeds in beheading this monstrous creature and is given a hero's welcome by his father on his return. The scene then sinks again into the hot afternoon, in which the slithy toves gyre and gimble around the sundial just as they had at the opening of the poem. The illustration by Tenniel shows a small boy with girlishly long hair manfully striking with a small sword at a gigantic creature which looms over him and is many times his size. This is the Jabberwock which resembles a particularly ugly gryphon but has a long serpentine neck, an ugly face with bared teeth, a tail like a prehistoric animal, eagle-like claws and oversize rear hoofs. Its wings are spread like a huge bat. The first impression of the Tenniel illustration is of a monstrous octopus, since neck and tail add to the effect of multiple attacking, and encircling members. It seems probable that the whole poem presents the drowsy fantasy of a small child in a garden on a summer afternoon, and that the Jabberwock is an enormous enlargement and fusion of the little animals—lizards, worms and other small creatures condensed as toves, which are first seen at the foot of the sundial.[11] It is a kind of small boy's dream of glory, of slaying the dragon and bringing his trophy home victoriously. But it has other meanings too.

The encounter with the *Jabberwock* is certainly related to the *Hunting of the Snark* in which a whole crew participate. The Baker's uncle calls him a "beamish" nephew just as the father has congratulated his "beamish" son in *Jabberwock*. The latter looks "uffish" before the appearance of the Jabberwock and the Bellman has the same "uffish" expression when he hears of the terrors of the Boojum snark. When the Butcher and the Beaver, who had become comrades through anxiety, hear "a scream shrill and high" and know danger is at hand, they think it is the voice of the Jubjub and begin

[11] One sees another version of this experience in the description of Miss Enid Stevens (later Mrs. Shane) of her visits to Mr. Dodgson in his rooms at Oxford. The tiles around the fireplace bore pictures of the animals, small and large, which have become famous through Mr. Carroll's stories and which were surely derived from the slimy little ones—frogs, toads, etc., the belligerent but civilized earthworms, and the host of other garden dwellers at Daresbury and Croft.

"As I sat on Mr. Dodgson's knee before the fire," writes Miss Stevens, "he used to make the creatures have long and very amusing conversations between themselves. The little creatures on the intervening tiles used to 'squirm' in at intervals. I think they suggested 'The Little Birds are feeding' etc. in *Sylvie and Bruno*."

Mr. Dodgson's other explanation—e.g., the bird which ran its beak through a fish and the dragon hissing defiance over its left shoulder—was that they were representations of the various ways in which he was accustomed to receive his guests (14).

to count the shrieks. Then the Beaver is so disconcerted that he "outgribes"[12] in despair just as the "momeraths" "outgrabe" in *Jabberwock*. The Butcher then gives a kind of illicit and not entirely proper lesson in natural history to the Beaver (until recently his enemy) and explains that the Jubjub is a desperate bird as it lives in a state of perpetual passion; and is so very upright and incorruptible that it collects—but does not contribute at all charitable meetings. It is obviously a bird from which one keeps a safe distance. The grateful Beaver feels he has learned more from the Butcher in ten minutes than he could have learned in seventy years of formal study from books. This bond of their mutual experience with the Jubjub bird cements their friendship forever.

Once again it is seen that the land of the Snark is close to that of Jabberwock, for the Banker in the Snark hunting finds himself grabbed at by a fear-inspiring Bandersnatch with frumiously snapping jaws and an extensible neck like the Jabberwock's. The poor Banker faints, recovering only after the others have expelled the Bandersnatch; but then he can only stammer in his fright:

To the horror of all who were present that day
He uprose in full evening dress
And with senseless grimaces endeavored to say
What his tongue could no longer express.

Down he sank in a chair—ran his hands through his hair
And chanted in mimsiest tones
Words whose utter inanity proved his insanity
While he rattled a couple of bones.

It is the Baker however who, though seemingly so inefficient, becomes the hero of the expedition, which is at least in part a would-be bridal journey as indicated in the following:

[12] To "outgribe" as explained by Humpty Dumpty was to utter a sound between bellowing and whistling with a kind of sneeze in the middle. To hear it once made one quite content—not to hear it again. A "Rath" was a kind of little green pig.

> He came as a Baker, but owned when too late
> And it drove the poor Bellman half mad
> He could only bake Bride-cake—for which I may state
> No materials were to be had.

It is the Baker too who finally sees the Snark and suffers the fate of all those who encounter a Boojum Snark.

While any direct explanation of the nature of the Boojum is evaded by Carroll, some hints are given indirectly. *Boo* seems from the poem itself to be derived in part from "boo," the frightening syllable which is also the first syllable of "boohoo," a word Carroll used sometimes in jests with his little girl friends. "Jum" is related to jam, which is suggested in the Baker's tale in which jam and judicious advice are offered to the Baker to nerve him from his faint at the mere mention of the Boojum. Jam is then the antidote to jum. "Jam" comes around to an opposite again in the pun on the word jam in *Sylvie and Bruno* where the word Boojum is explained as a kind of elision of sounds for Bootjack or Bootjam, the jack removing the jammed boot. In the same story, is the chapter "Jabbering and Jam" in which jabber clearly means chattery talk, and jam like wine is the senseless subject talked about with fine distinctions as to degrees of sensual enjoyment. Jabber in Jabberwock may have this hidden meaning but is more manifestly the little boy who goes on a walk and jabs with his sword. Thus object and subject of Jabberwocky are somehow the same.

The Baker, in revealing his terror of the special Boojum sort of Snark, tells the assembled crew,

> I engage with the Snark—every night after dark—
> In a dreamy delirious fight:
> I serve it with greens in those shadowy scenes
> And I use it for striking a light.[13]

but that he knows very well that if he ever encounters a Boojum Snark he will vanish away, and this thought has

---

[13] Here, the combination of eating and looking is very clear.

caused him to faint at the very word *Boo*. The end of the
Hunting of the Snark portrays the Baker's fate exactly as he
has fearfully predicted.

> They gazed in delight, while the Butcher exclaimed
>   "He was always a desperate wag!"
> They beheld him—their Baker—their hero unnamed—
>   On the top of a neighboring crag,
>
> Erect and sublime, for one moment of time,
>   In the next, that wild figure they saw
> (As if stung by a spasm) plunge into a chasm
>   While they waited and listened in awe.[14]

[14] In the *Rectory Umbrella* was a poem *The Storm* which is clearly a forerunner of *The Aged Aged Man* and this part of the *Snark*. Charles Dodgson was preoccupied (or as Bruno corrupted the word to describe Uggug—"porcupined") by these themes from boyhood. Only the specially significant stanzas which show the resemblance to these two later poems are here quoted:

> An old man sat anent a clough
> A grizzled old man and weird
> Deep were the wrinks in his age and brow,
> An' hoar his snowy beard,
> All tremmed before his glance, I trow
> Sae savagely he leared.

It is an interesting question whether the misspelling of "leer" to "lear" is a hidden reference to the work of Edward Lear, then popular.
There follows then a description of the old man watching a vessel at sea while the storm gathers:

> Above the thunder-cloud frowns black,
> The dark waves howl below,
> Scarce can she hold along her track,
> Fast rocking to and 'fro.
> And oft the billow drives her back
> And oft her straining timbers crack,
> Yet onward doth she go.
>
> — — — — — — —
>
> The old man gazed without a wink,
> An' with a deadly grin:
> "I laid a wager she would sink
> Strong hopes had I to win.
> 'Twas ten to one, but now I think
> That Bob will sack the tin."
> Then from the precipice's brink
> He plunged head foremost in.

From Introductory Chapter I, of *Diaries* (15).

"It's a Snark!" was the sound that first came to their ears
And seemed almost too good to be true.
Then followed a torrent of laughter and cheers:
Then the ominous word "It's a Boo—"

Then silence. Some fancied they heard in the air
A weary and wandering sigh
That sounded like "jum!" but the others declare
It was only a breeze that went by.

And the concluding stanza is:

In the midst of the word he was trying to say,
In the midst of his laughter and glee,
He had softly and suddenly vanished away—
For the Snark *was* a Boojum, you see.

Thus it is apparent that the disappearance caused by merely meeting a Boojum Snark is equated with fainting, taking leave of one's senses, losing one's head, having a fit or convulsion, being struck dumb or caused to stammer, and finally being frightened or awed in the extreme. Indeed one ramification or another of this theme is almost omnipresent in Carroll's writing.

Many children have some fabled ogre, often in animal form, or some "secret," with which they scare each other and themselves. This is the antithesis of the imaginary companion whose presence is comforting, strengthening or relieving. Psychoanalysis reveals that it is generally some representation of the primal scene, in which the sexual images of the parents are fused into a frightening or awe-inspiring single figure. This is probably the significance of the *Snark*, in which the last "fit" is an acting out of the primal scene with the Baker first standing "erect and sublime" and then plunging into the chasm between the crags. The *Jabberwock* too seems but another variation of the Snark, but in the hunting of the latter, a whole crew of children participate—i.e., they tell this secret to each other, under the leadership of the Baker, who is rather clearly identified as Charles, and think of this as a frightening exploration. The part of the poem in which the Butcher gives the docile Beaver a lesson in natural history is probably but a thinly disguised picture of a consultation among the little Dodgsons regarding the mysterious life of their awesome parents. It is only the Baker, however, who really knows and suffers.

The screams—which are counted—seem quite possibly to be the clue to that recurrent mystery of the Dodgson household—the births of eight babies after Charles, just as there are eight fits in this poem of agony. This, it appears, is the deepest underlying cause of Charles Dodgson's concern about pain and whether he can bear to see the sufferer and be helpless to offer relief.

One other connection of this whole picture of the awful fascination and terror of the sexual life of the adults and the stirring effect of even fantasying about it, is brought out again in *Sylvie and Bruno* where there is an extraordinary description of an attack of rage, so severe as to have almost a convulsive quality. This is suffered by "Prince" Uggug, the loathsome boy, who is described as prickly and porcupinish, but obviously gets beyond this stage of irritability (16).

> All along the gallery that led to the Prince's apartment an excited crowd was surging to and fro, and the Babel of voices was deafening: against the door of the room three strong men were leaning vainly trying to shut it—for some great animal inside was constantly bursting it half open, and we had a glimpse . . . of the heat of a furious wild beast, with great fiery eyes and gnashing teeth. Its voice was a kind of mixture— there was the roaring of a lion, and the bellowing of a bull, and now and then the scream of a gigantic parrot. "There is no judging by the voice!" the Professor cried in great excitement. "What is it?" he shouted to the

241

men at the door. And a general chorus of voices answered him "Porcupine! Prince Uggug has turned into a Porcupine."

It is then arranged to entice and trap the animalish Uggug into a kind of tunnel made by blankets and into a cage like an oversize mousetrap. When the door to this contraption was about to be opened, "the fearful monster threw the door open for itself, and with a yell like the whistle of a steam-engine, rushed into the cage." (Again one sees the probable outline of the primal scene.) Bruno watches this odd scene and moralizes complacently that he can never become so porcupinish since he has always been filled with love—for Sylvie. It is only a little later on that the Professor explains to Bruno that a Boojum is a Bootjack—but remembers vaguely that *Boojum* had once referred to a creature in a fable, but he has forgotten all about that now. It is possible that this picture of the animal, after a terrible struggle, bursting forth amidst blankets, uttering a yell and then subsiding into a cage, is also a disguised representative of the birth of a baby —disguised by the need to keep it away from too clear a recognition. But it is also a picture—much closer to conscious awareness—of rage; and of the state of massive overstimulation which results in bursting, exploding devastating feelings. It is probable that within the cage of extreme reasonableness, intense self-criticism, control to the point of pedantic accuracy, and infinite patience of the Christ Church lecturer on mathematics, the adult Charles Dodgson, there were old mad memories, like prehistoric monsters, Boojums, which he, like the Professor in *Sylvie and Bruno*, thought he had forgotten. It appears that the little boy Charles lived too full and exciting a life and was confronted with life's greatest mysteries too emphatically before he could assimilate them. Love and maternal kisses may have quieted and healed, but they did not explain. "Please explain" became Charles' repetitive request.

The Boojums finally broke through the restraining bars surrounding them, and repeated themselves endlessly in hidden fantasy forms in the games of Charles and the others in the quiet rectory garden, and in the stories of the famous Lewis Carroll.

Even Sylvie, angel that she was, had not quite eradicated her temper, for on one occasion (17) this same bad boy, Uggug, emptied some butter on her dress pretending to give her a present. "Sylvie coloured crimson as she shook off the butter from her frock; but she kept her lips tight shut, and walked away to the window where she stood looking out and trying to recover her temper." Very soon Bruno returns and restores her with a birthday present—of a kiss. Birthdays abound in the Carroll stories—as well as the suggestion of un-birthdays and un-birthday presents. Indeed, there was a baker's dozen of birthdays in the immediate Dodgson family.

There is one other important aspect of the Carroll stories from a psychological angle: the nature of punishment. This is of two kinds, decapitation and vanishing. In *Sylvie and Bruno*, Prince Uggug, the Repulsive does get boxed on the ear, and this is a chastisement which Carroll wrote about early as "The First Ear-ring" in the *Rectory Umbrella* (18), but in general a more sweeping decapitation is prescribed. When Carroll first met the children of George Macdonald, he tried to prove to the six-year-old Greville that he had better have his head changed to a marble one in order to avoid the pain of being combed. In *Alice's Adventures in Wonderland,* the Queen of Hearts pushes the order "Off with his head!" so far that is becomes ridiculous. The Cheshire cat turns the tables by outwitting such a threat and, with its provokingly persistent smile, lives in a state of detachability of its head from its body. The head gardener sings of seeing a bear without a head, but nonetheless waiting to be fed. With her neck elongated, Alice's head gets so far away from her body that she wonders whether they will ever get together again. Tweedledum threatens that if the King were to wake up every one would go out like a candle, since everyone exists only in his head and dreams. The Baker simply vanishes when he encounters the Boojum Snark. Otherwise animals eat each other up or threaten to do so and there are plenty of fights between contemporaries, as between Tweedledum and Tweedledee or the Lion and the Unicorn. Sometimes the play is so disrupted by fighting as in the croquet game that one can well sympathize with Alice's remark "Take care of the sense and the sounds will take care of themselves."

It is impressive that in Carroll's stories there are no blind creatures, no threats of loss of arm, leg or nose (although tails did suffer); no specialized tortures; no shutting up in dungeons, no floggings, such as exist in many fairy tales. There *is* concern about beauty and ugliness, about fatness and thinness, about intelligence or stupidity, but the most constant punitive threat is of extinction, either by disappearance of the whole body or by decapitation. The absence of more usual kinds of castration threats is therefore striking. It appears that in Carroll's fantasy world, such fear of body injury is displaced to the head (19), rarely to the tail, or envelopes the entire body. It is the mother, the Queen of Hearts, the Red Queen, who is dreaded and feared as the potential punisher, quite contrary to the actual nature of Charles' own mother. But this is not so inexplicable or strange as it might first seem when we consider what has already been deciphered regarding the character of the little boy's oedipal longings toward his mother. Further, they were overburdened with orally felt jealousies of the younger children, and with so great a sensitivity to excitement that it must have seemed that he, quite like the porcupinish Uggug, would blow up and burst. It was the mother who could practically *annihilate* him by turning her attention elsewhere.

As he grew up, he established an extraordinary self-discipline and iron control. He obviously had a horror of little boys and would have preferred to be a little girl. The sadistic impression of sex and of birth which—in the days of home deliveries—confronted him four times by the time he was six and as many times again between six and fifteen, left a paralyzing impression. Masturbation, sexual union, birth—such glimpses as he had of them—left a terrified fascination in their wake, and caused a retreat from an ideal of sexual love, to one of brotherly-sisterly universal love, as is so clearly expressed in *Sylvie and Bruno,* a love that would mean equanimity, peace and serenity. He seems to have almost abolished any sexual wishes in himself and to have attempted to live in his mind alone—by reason, learning, imagination, and looking.

The mind (in which vision played so important a part) then became his important vital source both of pleasure and acquisitiveness. And it was injury to the mind that he feared most, by loss of consciousness, of memory or of reality sense. He made mnemonic devices for himself, catalogued and recorded endlessly, built up in fact extensive projections of his disciplined mind in the order and thoroughness of his records. But he was unnerved by seeing fainting, convulsions and idiocy, which seemed to provoke fear of similar reactions in himself. He may even have feared the loss of control inherent in sleep.

His sensitivity to excitement from whatever stimulations increased his fears and may have given him in childhood those very sensations which alarmed him most—feelings of alienation from himself, of "losing the head," of being beside himself. Even pleasurable excitement may be intolerably intense to a sensitive child, as Bruno well knew (20) and explained to the Other Professor: that when he was too happy he was uncomfortable and needed to be a little miserable, and so would set himself straight again by getting Sylvie to give him lessons.

That the adult Charles Dodgson could not entirely deny

his sexual nature and responded with some stirring after being with his little friends is strongly indicated in his letters to Agnes and Amy Hughes (21). Here after writing of the kisses he was sending to Agnes and her two sisters, his mind went by alliterative association to the three troublesome kit-cats that had visited him, unbidden. He had first been angry and attacked them, but they were persistent and rang his bells with increasing vehemence, so he put them to bed be-tween sheets of blotting paper and attempted to sleep him-self, in spite of their endless ringing. In the morning he fed them and drove them out, only to have them return per-sistently. Finally they spilled sticky gum between the sheets of his books, quite ruining some of them. Ultimately he quieted them by making them drink ink! This delightful fantasy is nonetheless a fairly clear unconscious confession of his sexual arousal—probably in response to the three little Hughes girls (the little cats of Finborough Road), his strug-gle with his own feelings, and his attempts to divert or sublimate them in his writing.

PART THREE

CERTAIN COMPARISONS BETWEEN SWIFT AND CARROLL

CERTAIN COMPARISONS
BETWEEN SWIFT AND
CARROLL

In the lives of most children there is a time between the two great epochs of developmental pressures, the oedipal period and puberty—a midway point in which the expansion of growth is fairly even. No great conquests of the body functions are being undertaken. Locomotion and speech are well established and further elaborated in intricate usages for fun as well as for utility. No dramatic change of body contour or proportions is under way. Reasonable body controls have become relatively firm, both in the discharge of body functions and of emotional tensions. The child has emerged from the almost exclusive society of the family into the society of the school. It is a time in many children when sexual problems are not so pressing and much of the aggression is invested in learning and exploring. At eight to nine, too, the bodies of boys and girls are more alike in size, weight and contour than they have been before or will be again, once the pubertal changes have definitely begun. This is a period which seemingly had great significance in the inner development of both Jonathan Swift and Lewis Carroll.

Both men showed deep attachments to little girls of eight to nine. Stella was this age when Swift first met her. Alice was younger at the time of the first meeting with Carroll, but she was almost eight at the time of the river excursion with her sisters and the two young Oxford dons. It was this age which Carroll immortalized in *Alice's Adventures in Wonderland* and in his repetitive choices of little girl friends for some time afterward.[1] No matter that he was not always absolutely precise in his adherence to the model of this age period, and later in life allowed his fancy to wander a bit in the direction of the little girls of eleven or so whose slight curves gave a promise of incipient womanhood, or that in his early manhood he was able to feel some attractiveness in charming little boys. Still it is amply clear that the age of eight or nine was the most winning to him, and that too decisively feminine a form was as disturbing to him as the frankly masculine one.

The value of this age as nonsexual in pressure and intermediately sexual in form seems apparent in the case of Swift. Soon after meeting the eight-year-old Stella and beginning her tutoring, he had returned to Ireland where he embarked on the earnest courtship of Varina which, as it developed, came to show such disastrous ambivalence. From this he turned to the little girl Stella again, finally in her young womanhood, some time after the disruption of the courtship of Varina—taking her with the "nurse" Dingley to live near him in Ireland and to continue his teaching of her, always with the expressed goal of making her as much the young boy as possible. Thus he attempted to avoid the dangerous pitfalls of attractions to one of the feminine gender. That he was not able to shield himself completely from normally directed passions was apparent in his long and tragic relationship with Vanessa. Again the terrible ambivalence came

[1] Swift, however, allowed his little girl to grow up—i.e., he continued his relationship with her, strange though it was, through many years until she died; keeping her always in a kind of little girl position. He showed, however, his capacity to be attracted to grown women but not to fulfill his promises. He seems also to have had a greater relationship with the actual individual woman, narcissistic though it was, than was true with Carroll, for whom there was such a succession of little girls that one is forced to conclude that the symbol, little girl of eight, played a greater role.

into play with a force which may have done much to undermine all three—himself, Vanessa, and Stella. For some years he was in an emotional balance of varying security between Stella and Vanessa, with Charles Ford serving as an importantly fortifying buffer.

In contrast to this, Carroll seemed never to have even this much passionate attachment to a grown woman. While some think that he really wanted to marry Alice, there is no direct evidence of this, and at most one must assume that such an inspired love occurred, if at all, when she was still a child and he a young man of thirty or so; and that it was largely the child image which fascinated him. My own belief that the child Alice was in some measure a reversed-in-age image of his mother was given further support by some as yet unpublished photographs taken by Carroll. These are in the possession of Mr. Helmut Gernsheim, who kindly showed them to me. Each of these shows a little girl, dressed only in a nightgown, reclining on a couch or chaise longue, in a strikingly unchildlike position. In all the gown is drawn down so that the chest is more or less bared and in one it is also drawn up well above the knees. The hands are generally clasped at the waist and the appearance is one of sleep or unconsciousness. The pictures strongly suggested to me an inhibited erotic interest involving both breasts and genitals, *and* the posture that of a sleeping or dead woman. In view of the rest of Carroll's story revealed in his writings and the bare facts of his life, it seems that these pictures may represent a fusion of the mother, peaceful after the birth of a child, the nursing mother, and the dead mother. All this is then guarded against or nullified in the little model's being a child before the age of puberty,[2] possibly founded on his younger sisters.

[2] The following verses at the beginning of the *Nursery "Alice"* tell the story rather clearly:

> A mother's breast:
> Safe refuge from her childish fears,

251

Swift and Carroll shared other inner defenses against unacceptable instinctual demands. Especially noteworthy is the compulsiveness of both men: certain rigidities of self-regulation, and the overly strong aversion to dirt. As is nearly always the case, such vigorous defenses can have only limited effectiveness and the instinctual demands break through and begin to invest the defensive measures themselves or to disrupt them, often quite unexpectedly. Thus Swift showed with dramatic clarity that his intense hatred of dirt was an effort to check his strong interest in it, and he ended by keeping the interest in dirtiness and his vociferous hatred of it mostly quite separate, existing side by side, without seemingly being aware of the paradoxical behavior involved. That his interest in dirt and its derivatives was closely bound with aggressive (chiefly hostile) feelings is also apparent in his life story. The indulgence in dirt was further linked with his writing which was clearly more skatological than his speech. His inner feeling about this interest—the ambivalence of his indulgence—may well have been an important factor in stimulating him to anonymity or to temporary concealments behind pseudonyms. To be sure both these literary devices were more generally accepted and used in Swift's day than in Carroll's, or at the present time. But Swift was particularly

---

From childish troubles, childish tears,
Mists that enshroud her dawning years!
See how in sleep she seems to sing
A voiceless psalm—an offering
Raises, to the glory of the King
    In Love: for Love is Rest.

    A Darling's kiss:
Dearest of all the signs that fleet
From lips that lovingly repeat
Again, again their message sweet!
Full to the brim with girlish glee,
A child, a very child is she
Whose dream of Heaven is still to be
At Home: for Home is Bliss [1].

facile in the adoption of them. The tendency to polarization of attitudes and interests, so characteristic of him, lent itself admirably to his satirical writing. He could sympathize so wholeheartedly that he could make an identity of the apparent author whose views he also ridiculed. One suspects that in certain instances he was attempting to bring together the disparities of his nature or at least to discharge the tensions created by his warring urges.

The various significances of his literary masks, the varying degrees of dissociations in his character, and the interplay between intracharacter images is the subject of a recent careful literary study by Ewald (2), *The Masks of Jonathan Swift*. There are also the critical literary studies of Davis (3) and the biography by Quintana (4). These are largely, however, from a literary rather than a psychological point of view.

In Swift's school days in which his compulsive cleanliness included efforts to restrain his thoughts (even as they might be betrayed in his writing) from being involved in unclean hostilities, these rigid restrictions interfered with his education and possibly with his learning, so that he seemed somewhat dulled if not downright stupid. He must have had a deep inner realization of his abilities, for we see nowhere a real self-doubt regarding his intellect, only an anger that it was not recognized when he himself could not demonstrate it. It was only when the dirty aggression broke through and was given place along with his overcivilized cleanliness that his full intellectual powers began to be apparent. It is also to be seen quite clearly and dramatically that the female genitals were felt by him to be dirty and that some prejudiced aversion based on an old inner infantile confusion of female organs and lower bowels came quickly into play when he approached any love relationship which might have gone on to a full genital consummation. Then he withdrew, felt besmirched and angry and fought out his conflict largely in

253

terms of dirtiness and cleanliness until he had managed to permit these two traits equal but separate places with him again, and often diverted his anger into righteous channels.

Carroll's compulsiveness was both symptomatically and structurally more complex, widespread and massive. The enormous number of ritualized activities, suggesting both an effort to keep things under total and reasonable control and a reliance on irrational magic in the doing, have already been described. These rituals were like an extensive web of steel filaments which looked like gossamer threads but bound him firmly. That it was not so much the hostile aggressions of the anal period and the stress of too strong or too early toilet training belonging to the mastery of the bowel functioning, but a more primitive oral cannibalistic aggression which was feared, is obvious in the *Alice* books. More than this even he seemed to fear a general muscular explosiveness which might bring total destruction to himself and all others. Against this he wove endless intertwining defenses in which he had himself so encased that there were few peepholes of relief and release. There is indication that he may have had some infantile struggles of urinary control which left a symptomatic imprint in his fantasy life, but there is no indication of the channeling of his expressions of anger by coprophiliac interests to an extent comparable to that of Swift. It is possible that the infant Charles Dodgson suffered early and severe rages of a shattering nature, which were followed by so perfect a control as to permit him no overt expressions of hostility. This we cannot know as a certainty. It is clear, however, that whether or not such explosive feelings within himself ever culminated in recognizable temper outbursts, he did very early react strongly to muscular aggression, sensed as dangerously near convulsive death in others. What general hostility he inevitably felt, was early grounded in fantasy and the very control of muscle aggression became a shield of muscular tension and physical rigidity. Even the fantasies must have been sensed as extremely dangerous, for he made an idol of reasonableness and factuality, and had difficulty in sleeping, probably out of fear of relaxing conscious control of his thinking. Only when his irrational fantasy escaped in his humorous stories to little girls and won great recognition for him could he find the way to an acceptance of unreason. In *Sylvie and Bruno,* published only a few years before his death, he could legitimatize his interest in dreams and varying levels of consciousness. Earlier his main outlets, such as they were, were in kissing and in looking. The kissing, it seems, was a peculiarly appropriate counteraction to the overwhelming oral jealousy and devouring tensions which beset the little boy with the endless succession of new babies coming between himself and his mother. It was also a permitted indulgence between himself and his mother and later became the form of love-making with his little girl companions. The extent of his preoccupation with this subject is apparent in its ubiquitousness in his letters, and especially the peculiar perseveration expressed in such letters as the one written to Isa Bowman[3] in 1890. The Bowman children had written him a greeting bearing "millions of hugs and kisses." He then computed that *millions* must mean at least two millions, that as each kiss took at least three seconds, he would have to spend twelve hours a day for twenty-three weeks in kissing in order to receive their message. He replied then by sending Isa a homeopathic two-millionth of a kiss (5). It will be remembered that as his mother had sent him no less than a trillion kisses, he may have spent a lifetime or more in receiving them. The gratification of looking which is such

---

[3] Isa Bowman was a child actress who was one of his later little girl friends. It seems that he made some effort to supplant the older image of Alice with the younger Isa who, with her sisters Nellie and Emsie, became his favorites, just as the three little Liddells had been twenty-five years earlier. She played the part of Alice in *Alice's Adventures in Wonderland* on the stage, and his acrostic poem to her at the beginning of *Sylvie and Bruno* is reminiscent of a somewhat longer one at the beginning of *Through the Looking Glass.*

a peculiarly dexterous combination of activity and passivity, and so close to fantasy, was his other big sensory gratification, and was made official through his photography.

Neither Swift nor Carroll is known to have had an overt perversion though both suffered distortions of emotional development leading in this direction, and both sacrificed mature genital gratification in their struggles. This sacrifice itself may have been the negative of perversion. Swift's disturbance, however, was closer to the neurotic. He *almost* achieved a genital functioning, but excessively vulnerable, slipped by regression mostly to the anal-sadistic expression of his conflicts and urges, and the strengthening of special concomitant defenses and character traits. His sense of reality was in general good, such impairments as it suffered coming rather from the complications of identity and identification of his early life. He was a man whose dominant character remained strong throughout his life and though he could put forward temporarily one aspect of himself or another in the service of a literary tour-de-force, he did not lose himself in any fundamental sense in these subterfuges. He shared much with the actor in his skill of impersonation. In the content of his writing his changing identities were more frequently those which are common neurotic confusions: reversal of sexes, reversal of generations, identification of total body with phallus and vice versa.

Carroll's defenses, on the other hand, controlled a disturbance, so basic and primitive as to be closer to the psychotic. His outer life seems to have been impoverished in emotional attachments and in achievements, and his reality sense cramped and invaded by the prohibitions invoked against his hostile fantasies which terrified him, until they became masked in humor. He then, even in official life, became more and more two men, Lewis Carroll and Charles Dodgson, sometimes with an imperative need to keep them apart. In the content of his writing his confusions of identity were manifold, bizarre and almost kaleidoscopic, involving not only individuals but time, space, and inanimate objects. That one man could have held in check so vast a Hitlerian fantasy as is expressed in the *Alice* books and that he should finally have expressed this in a form which touches and bemuses people in the psychotic part of Everyman's soul which is generally disclaimed, is not only a colossal personal achievement but represents the birth of a unique form of literary art which has not been equalled.

This, I believe, is the basis of the peculiar cultish attitude of the admirers of the *Alice* books. Just as the mystic union with the breast, dating from the earliest weeks of infancy, is the basis of the oceanic religious feeling of union with God and the Universe, so the terrible cannibalistic rage which sometimes follows this is held in check by inner defensive maneuvers which, when externalized and organized in religious rituals, involve the turning of the oral rage into a nondestructive re-incorporation and assimilation of the inner and outer worlds, symbolized in the Christian religion by the communion service. In those individuals in whom these early months and years are particularly tormented ones, the vulnerability is greater and the work of restraint more intense. But some nucleus of this primitive infantile struggle persists in everyone. It is Carroll's supreme art that he furnishes an unconscious outlet through humor for exactly these primary destructive pressures without a provocation to action. Readers are charmed and comforted rather than stimulated by the fantastic adventures which he conjures up. It is a mistake, however, to consider that *Alice's Adventures in Wonderland* appeals equally positively to all children. There are many children who recoil from or are frightened by the story, probably because they are themselves in a stage of development in which such primitive urges have—for one reason or another—been rearoused and only barely mastered again. They can ill-afford the danger of another arousal. Such children will turn away from the story as silly, boring, or cruel. But in general, the sadism of the *Adventures* is so outspoken and so grotesque a caricature that it protects rather than stimulates. There is a quaint Victorian expression of this in Carroll's preface to the *Nursery Alice,* in which he states that it is his ambition to have this book, in the nursery form, read by children aged from naught to five, and adds, "Nay, not so. Say rather to be thumbed, to be cooed over, to be dog-eared, to be rumpled, to be kissed by the illiterate, ungrammatical, dimpled Darlings. . . ." He proceeds then to the anecdote of the child so admonished against greediness and told never to expect more than *one* of anything, that on awakening from sleep she was puzzled at possessing two feet. It seems that Carroll would like the illiterate darling of naught to five to eat up the book, and that kissing, like the communion service, may have been a personal way of counteracting the destructive devouring urges.

In 1936, Dr. Paul Schilder presented a paper entitled "Psychoanalytic Remarks on 'Alice in Wonderland' and Lewis Carroll" to an audience made up of psychoanalysts (6). This paper stressed the great anxiety portrayed in Alice —anxiety to the point of bewilderment and a state of dissociation. No detailed study of Carroll's life was offered, but Schilder suspected that Carroll's preoccupation with little girls had come about through the deflection of the author's oedipal problem from the mother onto a younger sister. He also emphasized a relation between extreme sadism and spatial disturbances and suspected further an intrinsic connection between primitive aggression and the production of nonsense. He opened and closed his paper, however, with questions regarding the appropriateness of the *Alice* books for children's reading, but cited no direct observations regarding either their harmfulness or their beneficent qualities. His paper, though to a scientific group, was reported in the daily press and became the target for sharp comments from the outraged protectors of *Alice*. One newspaper editorial suggested that anyone who sought to understand symbolism or hidden meanings should be kicked downstairs in the manner of the inquisitive young man and Father William; another made "a declaration of war" and warned psychiatrists "to take their hands off our Alice," an attitude which was also proclaimed by Alexander Woollcott in a preface to Carroll's *Complete Works*, which was presently issued (7). Some commentators professed to think Dr. Schilder's article a practical joke. Several turned the tables and accused him of being a sadist.[4] Others were simply frumious (frustrated and furious). While the implications that the *Alice* books may be harmful to children is unsubstantiated by Schilder and is a dubious premise, the reaction of stormy touchiness seemed to indicate an almost religious protectiveness, especially since the main counterassertion was that the writings should not be examined or investigated at all.

In 1945, Mrs. Florence Becker Lennon published her full-length biography of Carroll, *Victoria through the Looking Glass*, in which she combined a psychological study of the author's personality as shown in his writings with a detailed survey of the special influences of the Victorian era which formed the setting for and possibly promoted these developments. Again there was a storm of protest, much of which focused on her hardiness in daring to look into Carroll's private feelings at all. There was, however, some acclaim. Certainly many people prefer, like Woollcott, to believe that children live in a state of "simple love for all living things" and are angered at the idea that primitive aggressive instincts are strong in the child as well as in the adult. In 1947, John Skinner and Dr. Martin Grotjahn published (8) complementary articles on *"Lewis Carroll's Adventures in Wonderland"* and *"About the Symbolization of*

---

[4] Dr. Lauretta Bender has kindly permitted me to see the collection of clippings which contain the journalistic comments on Dr. Schilder's paper.

Alice's Adventures in Wonderland," in which Alice's adventures are presented as really those of Carroll himself; especial emphasis is put on his evasion of sexuality and of adulthood in his identification with the child Alice; and it is indicated that the author had some fantasy of the phallus as a girl, "to be admired but not used." Grotjahn further stresses the adventures as portraying a fantasy of return into the mother's body. This seems doubtless true and may have been stimulated by the little boy's being very frequently made aware of the birth of siblings. It seems, however, that this is only one of a number of determinants to the terrain of the story. In accordance with his interpretation of the destructive entrance into the womb of the earth, he sees the awakening as a rebirth.

Empson in his book *Some Versions of Pastoral* (9) emphasizes that in the *Alice* books, the *child-as-judge* assimilates the tradition of the pastoral which characterizes Victorian and Romantic literature. Alice is the little girl version of the swain. Indeed we would say that she is both a pleasantly feminine and yet essentially neutral figure, a just and questioning, as well as stoical observer of the turmoils of life, appropriately guileless, to wear the cloak of judgment. It is our belief that a peculiar condensation of stresses in Dodgson's own life created this figure in unusually pure form (which we have attempted to show in the study of *Sylvie and Bruno*), which fit then so extraordinarily as a collective symbolic figure of the time. The books in their entirety contain, however, so much that is true in general, regardless of era and place, that the appeal is as universal as that of fairy tales of obscure origin.

Swift has had no such strong defenders as Carroll. Neither has he been subjected to much psychological investigation. Evelyn Hardy (10) has written a biography, in which the psychological interest is paramount and sound. Hanns Sachs is said to have written a psychoanalytic study of Swift which was never published.[5] But it is doubtful whether any study of Swift could arouse such fierce protectiveness as is readily at hand for Carroll and Alice. Swift wrote to produce the direct shock; Carroll wrote with gentle gruesomeness, but always under the umbrella of nonsense.

[5] This is mentioned in Ferenczi's article on "Gulliver Fantasies" (11).

PART FOUR

NOTES ON NONSENSE

NOTES ON NONSENSE

Satire, parody, caricature, and nonsense —all of these appear in the works of both Carroll and Swift, but in different combinations and proportions. Swift's great strength was in his roughly vivid satire. Carroll's greatest charm appeared in his extraordinarily beguiling nonsense. Many feel revulsion from Swift's open carnality, his coprophilia and his obvious pleasure in offending. Some few, both children and adults, withdraw a bit benumbed from Wonderland's fierce sadism, gently expressed though it is. Satire, parody and caricature are thinly veiled but clear forms of attack, whether on single individuals or social organizations, an attack by distorting exaggeration, disproportion and ridicule. The effect is of distorting mirrors held up as though to say "This is how you look! See your image, so grotesque and misshapen, yet clearly you. It is all reflected here for anyone to see." In their exaggerations, they are loaded or charged forms of expression. The derivation of the words caricature and satire in themselves indicates this quality: satire from the Latin *satira* or *satura* from which *sated* and *saturate* also come; while caricature is from the Italian *caricare*, to charge, overload or exaggerate.[1] *Parody* from the Greek *para* and *oide* would mean a song which parallels, closely resembles or imitates another. Thus in parody, the written expression, the likeness to the original, is emphasized in the form and the exaggeration or distortion

[1] As noted by Kris (1).

is in the content. The principle of emphasizing weaknesses through magnifying distortions and incongruities against a background of repetition of basic form similarities appears then in the written form of parody, in the pictorial communication of caricature, in the mimicking impersonations of the comic actor. The media are different but the essential principles are the same. Satire is somewhat more complex in form, dealing as it does generally with social organizations and institutions rather than focusing on individuals, but its methods are basically similar: to reproduce recognizable, generally accepted likenesses upon which frailties or inconsistencies are "played up." The effect is to "take off" the subject—i.e., to reduce by ridicule. Satire, appearing as it does in a literary rather than a graphic form, adds some to the dimensions in time and space, encompassing more details and complexities, but often loses somewhat the sharpness of impact on the reader which is so characteristic of caricature, which is generally starkly simplified.

There are parodies of two sorts from the angle of the aim of the writing—those which copy with some apparent admiration and those which attack with clear ridicule. There have been periods when in the teaching of school boys and in the fashionable habit of the day, it was the approved custom to write in the way of the classical authors. Here the aim was not so much, if at all, to attack the original as to furnish an approved cloak for the amateur or the pretender. But the more frequent use of parody is to ridicule the original author, by using his form, which ideally is striking and easily recognized, to enclose ridiculous content which, however, also has some points of resemblance to the original. Both Swift and Carroll were prolific writers of parody. Swift, even when not directly ridiculing, wrote frequently in classical or other forms in a way which gave an extra pressure or humorous outline to what he wrote. Thus, *Gulliver's Travels* was written after the fashion of the accounts of returned ex-

plorers—and while it thus somewhat spoofed these picturesque heroes, it contained political satire as well, but its
specific fantasies were largely determined by the unconscious need for an expression of his own lifelong conflicts.
Carroll's parodies were certainly rarely aimed mainly at
ridiculing the original author, either in form or content,
though those written in his adolescence had more of this
quality than the later ones. He, too, took the popular or
well-known form and used it for his own content which often
had very little to do with the original. His parodies seemed
indeed to assume a kind of organic life of their own, for they
sometimes went through a series of changes, in whole or in
part, and grew as they progressed. This could not have taken
place if they had been primarily chained to ridiculing the
original; but was rather the externalization with increasing
refinement of the long-standing inner fantasies of Carroll
himself—fantasies which had been rearoused by even relatively slight similarities to the original poem. The emergence
of the *Aged Aged Man* is a striking example. The effect is of
the parody writer having then borrowed his neighbor's horse
on which to gallop off on his own errands—sometimes even
changing horses in the course of his journey.

But in parody usually the two-sidedness or ambivalence
of the comic is especially apparent: the combination of admiration and derogation, of respect and attack, which is so
characteristic of jealousy or envy. In satire and caricature,
and generally in parody, there are at least two images co-
existent—the usual one and the exaggerated one. Each has its
own realistic claim. But the second is the one which has
previously been denied, hidden or considered forbidden. The
effect of the caricature may depend in some measure on the
sharp revelation and the relief of being permitted the more
than frank exposure of that which has been partially denied.
There is, too, the effect of the surprising reversal—that which
has been concealed or only partially revealed is brought out

in brazen proportions, and the generally accepted facsimilar image recedes. For the full effect of caricature, the individual attacked must be known to the spectator and the irregularities of his nature at least slightly suspected. The caricature delivers up the hidden and overannounces it, sometimes thus organizing and legitimatizing the earlier vaguer observations of the spectator. Without this implicit preparation for the caricature the latter "falls flat" (i.e., does not seem vital) or it appears only as grotesque, strange or eerie and not as sharply comical. Further, pictorial caricature depends much on the fact that inner emotional attitudes influence, are reflected in, and modify many bodily attitudes and details of appearance—e.g., postures, mannerisms, wrinkles. Caricature takes liberties not only by exaggerating these but by making body appearance, form and proportions carry the burden of presenting the inner man, often in an overly simplified way and sometimes according to quite primitive concepts of representation. This is conspicuously true in matters of size—large size representing strength or the expectation of strength, and puniness or smallness appearing for weakness or dependence. Such distortions of size may involve the entire body or different body parts. This is well illustrated and discussed by Wolfenstein (2).

E. Kris's presentations (3) of the *"Psychology of Caricature,"* the *"Principles of Caricature"* and *"Ego Development and the Comic"* are of great value here. Continuing from Freud's *Wit and Its Relation to the Unconscious* (4), he emphasizes that the similarity between dreams and caricature is due to the operation of the primary process. This we have seen in profusion in the *Alice* books (where Carroll himself recognized that he was talking in the language of dreams); and it is true in much of *Gulliver* also. Primary-process imagery is almost the only literature language of Carroll, and is certainly the strongest language of Swift. Kris stresses the economy in portrait caricature, its having a special "punch" when it utilizes few lines and resembles the "scrawlings of children."[2] The effect then is like that of an extremely terse joke. The ability to produce this—tersely simple—effect possibly depends on the caricature's having the capacity to catch the similarity of expression or form of his victim with that of less valued objects and to convey this through a portrait which combines both. For example, the caricatures of Theodore Roosevelt, which emphasized with a few rudimentary lines the prominence of his teeth, suggested at once their resemblance to those of the ferocious game which he hunted. The ease in seeing such basic similarities is a lively function of the child in whom identity differentiations, taken for granted by the adult, are not yet firmly grounded.

Little Red Riding Hood saying to the Wolf disguised as grandmother, "But grandmother what big teeth you have" is not quite so improbable an observation as it would sound to the adult. Children do make such observations, e.g., that grandmother has "dogs' teeth" more readily than most adults. This is probably due not only to the child's perceptiveness being unobstructed by the more complicated values and interpretations which adults have experienced and learned since childhood; but it may be that it is also influenced by the child's being in a relatively closer relation to its own body sensations than the adult, with a resultant sharpening of the awareness of the body of the other. Indeed the image of the latter may sometimes even be distorted by the body tensions of the young observer. Thus the child in a state of aroused visual curiosity is quick to notice, comment on, and draw in his pictures the eyes of those around him.

That caricature is a combination of regression and aggression is underlined by Kris, who points out further that its use demands a considerable degree of security and mastery, i.e., of control as a background. Otherwise the drop to regression does not entail pleasure. One must not be really

2 Hogarth, *The Bench* (London, 1758), quoted by Kris (5).

endangered by the regression to enjoy it. Children's particularly funny and sharp observations are often not meant to be funny by them, but are funny to the adults, who have the advantage of distance and mastery. "The controlled use of the primary process is the essence of the caricaturist's power" (Kris).

What is true in this way concerning the appreciator of the caricature is also true in a degree of its maker. But here the story is more complex. The child shows pleasure in making fun of another's awkwardness or failure only when he himself has mastered this same movement or activity;[3] and we would add, if his mastery is relatively recent. His mastery gives him a feeling of superiority which is reaffirmed in his amusement—and made doubly strong if he further permits himself to mimic or caricature the less favored one. Thus it would seem mastery must have been achieved, but not to such a degree as to be completely taken for granted. Kris states succinctly that "most comic phenomena seem to be bound up with past conflicts of the ego—that they help it to repeat the victory and in doing so once more to overcome half-assimilated fear" (6).

In a brief but important clinical article (7), Annie Reich has presented the case of a young woman peculiarly talented in the art of caricaturing, mimicking or impersonating others; and has shown that one of the important drives entering into this was the need to project onto others the disturbances regarding her own body image and especially her comparison of herself with her mother and sisters. This little acting-out play could then be endlessly repeated in a sublimated form in her witty mimicry of other women. It may be suspected that something of this kind occurs in varying degrees in the making of caricatures and cartoons, whether in the pictorial or written form. It is possible that the tendency to caricature others is essentially a form of acting out, in which

[3] Emphasized by Wolfenstein.

270

the repetitive abreacting of old hurts is disguised by the displacement in content and the sublimated form of the goal.

The effect of sheer nonsense contains other elements. It leaps the barriers of apparent similarities and exists seemingly in its own incomparable realm and independent right, denying even relationship by contrast and comparison, which are implicit in exaggeration and simile. Nonsense is not only the lack of reason or loss of expected order, but it is the defiance of reason which men value most, and it is achieved by apparent isolation, inconsequence and generally heedless disconnection. There is a quality of (generally quiet) explosive destructiveness about sheer nonsense—an unannounced nihilism—which is never absolutely achieved to be sure, but is felt in its subtle implications.

But one aim of the present study is to scrutinize these forms of wit in the writings of the two men, Swift and Carroll, and to uncover if possible the nature of the strong compelling drives back of these particular richnesses in their writing. While caricature is a graphic art which uses the body as its subject, satire is not always so corporeally based. In Swift's satires, however, the holding up of his subjects to ridicule is frequently dependent on his presenting his people as physically bizarre, loathsome or ill-formed, or by so focusing on some body part that it appears out of proportion. Some find insistent outlines of satire in Carroll's nonsense and impute to him a doubly sly attack—first in the satire and then in the hiding of it until it is only just discernible. Whatever the satirical intentions of this author may have been, it is his nonsense which is most appealing. And throughout, it is embellished with a kaleidoscope of changing body distortions, and of nonsensical songs and rhymes. In these also there is generally an outline of parody, though the content usually is just too removed from the original to furnish any sharp attack on the model from which it is derived. The parodies are unlike other parodies in this respect. In some,

271

Carroll utilized the organization of another's work for some form on which to start and then went quietly woolgathering by himself, the borrowed form furnishing at least some minimal structure for his writing. Thus his parodies combine parody and nonsense. The effect may be to imply that he can write better nonsense than the original author has done, but the implication if present is so well concealed that again it appears as the merest teasing attack rather than an outright one. His early drawings and original verses, most of which were produced during his adolescence and early manhood, have a sharper cartoon or satirical bite than is felt from the nonsense of his maturity, openly sadistic though the latter is.

For the appreciation of caricature or cartoon, the time and situation must be peculiarly ripe and the sharpest effect is attained when the portrayal is concise. The rise of portrait caricature after the sixteenth century may have been influenced by the invention of the printing press permitting the wide circulation of pictorial written attacks before the special situation which provoked them had passed.[4] The timing of certain caricatures and jokes is as important as the timing of a psychoanalytic interpretation which has its greatest effect when it "just fits" and the analysand is somewhat prepared for it but has been unable to come to it himself. In our present era, when other means of communication have outstripped circulation even of the newsprint, the caricature and cartoon as political weapons have become less popular, and the caricaturing tendency has lent itself to more complicated and perhaps more sophisticated forms. The cartoons of today are less numerous and depend less on primitive ridicule through body distortions, but consist more of the portrayal of situation in a graphic form. In that sense, they are closer to satirical writing than were the early caricature cartoons. They consequently do not attack a specific person

[4] For a fuller discussion of the rise of portrait caricature, see Kris (8).

or an acute situation but a prolonged situation or a tendency of the times. Even in these, it is interesting to see how often the faces or figures of the cartoons, such as appear in the *New Yorker*, reflect something of the actual appearance of the artist author. On examination, the lines of the face of the habitual cartoon people of individual artists may also be seen to be very similar to the lines of the artist's signature. Indeed the tendency of present cartoon drawing has been described as calligraphic. (Here the serpent bites its tail, for writing was originally derived from picture writing.) Even in these sophisticated cartoons there is some revelation of the artist's self-image. The use of the word *Profile* to describe portrayals (usually humorously appreciative) of the work and personalities of well-known people again indicates how much there is a basic body concept underlying descriptions which do not literally deal much with physical attributes.

The psychological techniques based on projective examination methods, the Rorschach, the drawing tests, and the examination of children's drawings—e.g., the work of K. Machover and associates (9)—all indicate the extent to which the body tensions representing inner pressures and conflicting attitudes, either due to the exigencies of uneven maturation processes or the impact of sharp conflicts, are decipherable in the writings and drawings of individuals even when the latter do not intend to reveal themselves in this way or may actually be unaware of the full nature of their preoccupations. What is true in a simple way of the reflection of the caricaturist's own state—or at least its alerting him to allied states in others—may be true in a more complex way regarding the projection of the fantasies of the satirist to combine with or be expressed through the conditions which he satirically portrays in word pictures.

In Swift many of his body tensions, based on the early anal fixation and its impairing effect on his genitality, were dealt with by their representation in his superego which attempted to control or prohibit their direct personal satisfaction and to channel them rather to ambitious and idealistic aspirations of achievement in the outer world. In this, often volatile and sometimes unstable equilibrium, his drive to satirize played a double-edged and balancing or possibly restoring function. Over and over again when he had been personally hurt and disappointed by others or had himself become involved in inevitable personal cruelties toward others, he retired in rage or depression from which he relieved himself by venting his anger in pursuit of a socially accepted and righteous goal. But in the satires arising under such circumstances, the underlying body imagery generally asserted itself. A *Tale of a Tub* and the Fourth Voyage of *Gulliver* are especially conspicuous examples.

In Carroll's writing, the body tensions are less openly admitted and the projected distortions are more grotesque and extreme than is true in Swift's tales and poems. The origin of these, in sensations of genital and total body tumescence, arising from certain definite experiences of childhood, was compulsively and unconsciously presented by the writer at different periods of his life. The memories themselves were undoubtedly not consciously recalled, but were wrapped in many sheaths of denial. I have attempted to show this in the presentation of the various forms of *The Aged Aged Man*, as it arose at different epochs in the writer's life. Parody and caricature accomplished partial denials; but nonsense was the most effective of all.

With Carroll, the rise of nonsense as a form of expression, however, far outstripped parody, satire or caricature, although all were present in minor degrees. The controlling and encasing functions of his superego were paramount and in themselves unbelievably aggressive—toward him. They seem to have been derived from the extreme intensity of his pregenital aggressions; from the way in which these engulfed and carried with them the normal phallic urges; and from the enforced precocity of the conscience development which prohibited so widely and so devastatingly. His nonsense, detached and meaningless as it consciously appeared to him and as he intended it to be for others, nonetheless contained his innermost secrets, the primal-scene excitations, the oral-anal-phallic urges bringing their complementary fear of punishing destruction. All this was concealed and expressed in the body sensory imagery of the primary process—which, reproduced by an adult, uses words always with double orientations, that of the adult and that of the very young child, who mouths the word, feels it, plays with it and brings many sensations to and from it. The word becomes the focus of condensation of polymorphous-perverse drives. But the need to produce nonsense—somehow to assert himself—could only be given full sway when and after he had abrogated any genital claims and identified himself as a little girl. He was then not in so great a danger and could let loose to the extent of spinning his amusing nonsense. But little boys who reminded him of what he might have been, became increasingly intolerable to him.

The *Alice* books especially, but all of Carroll's writings abound with references to castration fears. But the self-castration of identification with the prepuberty girl was probably necessary as a kind of neutralization before he could unconsciously reveal the full depth and intensity of his overwhelming primitive aggressive impulses. This leads to another significance of nonsense: it appears to represent the defiant acceptance of this struggle against an aggression so great that it endangers the very reason—in body terms, the head itself. One cannot say that it results only from the displacement to the head of the genital castration fears. It is that; but it represents too the triumph over the fear of headlessness (losing the head, losing the mind, being beside oneself) which is implicit in rage. In this sense, its strongest root may precede genital castration fears and be based rather on fear of loss of contact and consciousness through anger. In fact, the extreme rage is very close to a convulsion.[5] The preponderance of oral elements in the rage expressed in the *Alice* books may also have been an important determinant in the allocation of the castration to the head. This in turn is reinforced by the very addiction to daydreaming (an essentially psychic function) in those who are fearful of their own muscular and verbal aggressiveness. There is probably no more succinct symbol possible for the triumph of nonsense in its gently devastating isolation than that of the Cheshire cat, sitting with an invisible body aloft in a tree, only its head appearing. Even as the head fades, the grin remains. This is a grin, occasionally described by patients who are appalled to find themselves smiling in situations of great conflict or even of outer chaos.

Swift too knew a good deal about nonsense. Murry, in discussing this writes: "*A Tale of a Tub* . . . is an outpouring of the comic spirit which, when it is in its full career recognizes no tabus and makes a joke of everything. Perhaps the greatest masters of this comic spirit are Aristophanes and Rabelais. A German critic has described Aristophanes as inspired by the *Weltvernichtungsidee*: the idea of world annihilation. For the comic spirit, any cosmos is an illusion to be shattered; but—this is the point—to be shattered gaily, not desperately, with an exuberance of high spirits, and almost with the suggestion that the same force of genius which destroys the existing cosmos might easily create another and a better. . . . In a real sense this comic spirit is orgiastic" (10). In the serio-comic conclusion to *A Tale of a Tub*, Swift describes his own writing of nonsense: "I am trying an experiment very frequent among authors; which is to write upon nothing;

[5] It is interesting that the other great master of nonsense in the English language was Edward Lear, an epileptic who is reported never to have had any genital sexual interest in a woman.

when the subject is exhausted, to let the pen move on; by some called the ghost of wit, delighting to walk after the death of the body" (11).[6]

[6] Also quoted by Murry.

REFERENCES AND NOTES

INTRODUCTION

1. Greenacre, Phyllis, Certain Relationships between Fetishism and Faulty Development of the Body Image. *The Psychoanalytic Study of the Child*, Vol. VIII, pp. 79-98. New York: International Universities Press, 1953. This deals with the fetish as a bisexual object, necessary to complete and to stabilize the body image which has been impaired early in development. The fetish then permits possible genital functioning.

PART I—JONATHAN SWIFT

Chapter 1: The Life of Jonathan Swift

1. Scott, Sir Walter, Life of Swift, *The Life and Works of Jonathan Swift*, Vol. I, pp. 161-162. London: Bricker & Son, 2nd ed., 1883.
2. Hardy, Evelyn, *The Conjured Spirit, Swift*. London: Hogarth Press, 1949, p. 27. This description of himself appears in a letter of Swift's to the Reverend Kendall, February 11, 1691. In this he states quite clearly that when alone his tendency to brood and speculate demanded an outlet in speech, more completely in writing.
3. Craik, Henry, *The Life of Jonathan Swift*. London: John Murray, 1882, p. 20, footnote.
4. Murry, John Middleton, *Jonathan Swift*. London: Jonathan Cape, 1954, p. 15.
5. Johnston, Denis, The Mysterious Origin of Dean Swift. *Dublin Historical Record*, Vol. III, No. 4. Old Dublin Society, June-August, 1941, pp. 81-98.
6. Craik, op. cit., p. 8; and Johnston, op. cit.
7. Stephen, Sir Leslie, Swift, in *English Men of Letters Series*, ed. John Morley. London: Macmillan, 1882, p. 2.
8. Craik, op. cit., p. 20; and Johnston, op. cit.
9. Davis, Herbert, *Stella*. New York: Macmillan, 1942, pp. 1-10.
10. Pilkington, Letitia, *Memoirs*, ed. J. Isaacs (originally published Dublin, 1748). London: George Routledge & Sons, 1928, pp. 57-

58. Letitia Pilkington was the wife of a Dublin clergyman; and was a writer of somewhat shallow and pretentious quality. She was something of a protege of Swift's and undoubtedly knew him well. Her accounts, however, vivid and anecdotal, cannot be entirely relied upon.

11. Swift, Dean, *Essay Upon the Life, Writings and Character of Dr. Swift* (publisher's name not given) 1755, pp. 22-24.

12. Craik, op. cit., p. 15.

13. Stephen, op. cit., p. 7.

14. Ball, J. Elrington, ed., *The Correspondence of Jonathan Swift*, Vol. IV, pp. 76-77. London: G. Bell & Sons, 1914.

15. Rossi, Mario and Hone, Joseph, *Swift, or the Egoist*. London: Victor Gollancz, 1934, p. 58.

16. Letter to Reverend Kendall, in Ball, op. cit., Vol. I, pp. 3-6.

17. Ehrenpreis, Irvin, Swift and Mr. John Temple. *Modern Language Notes,* March, 1947, pp. 145-154.

18. Murry, op. cit., pp. 25-41.

19. Wilde, W. R., *Closing Years of Dean Swift's Life.* Dublin: Hodges & Smith, 1849, pp. 6-49.

20. Williams, Harold, ed., *Jonathan Swift's Journal to Stella.* Oxford: Clarendon Press, 1948, p. 403.

21. Freeman, A. Martin, *Vanessa and Her Correspondence With Jonathan Swift.* London: Selwyn & Blount, Ltd., 1921, p. 125.

22. Williams, Harold, ed., Ode to Sir William Temple, *Swift's Poems.* Oxford: Clarendon Press, 1937, p. 32.

23. Ball, op. cit., Vol. I, p. 34, footnote.

24. Atkinson, Edward D., *An Ulster Parish.* Dublin: Hodges, Figgis & Co., Ltd., 1898, p. 105.

25. Swanzy, Henry Biddall, *Biographical Succession Lists of the Diocese of Dromore,* ed. Canon J. B. Leslie. Belfast: R. Carswell and Son, Ltd., 1933, p. 43.

26. Stephen, op. cit., p. 31.

27. Murry, op. cit., p. 101.

28. Hardy, op. cit., p. 74.

29. Craik, op. cit., Appendix XI: The Character of Mrs. Johnson, p. 549.

30. Williams, *Swift's Journal to Stella,* pp. li-lix.

31. Freeman, op. cit., pp. 128-133.

32. Ibid., pp. 178-179.

33. Scott, op. cit., Vol. I, p. 240.

34. Hardy, op. cit., p. 175.

35. Craik, op. cit., p. 529.

36. Quintana, Ricardo, *The Mind and Art of Jonathan Swift.* London: Methuen & Co., Ltd., 1936 (reprinted 1953), p. 233.

37. Williams, *Swift's Poems,* Vol. II, p. 721.

38. Freeman, op. cit., pp. 147-177.
39. Smith, David Nichol, ed., *The Letters of Jonathan Swift to Charles Ford*. Oxford: Clarendon Press, 1935, p. vii.
40. Williams, *Swift's Journal to Stella*, Vol. I, p. 210.
41. Smith, op. cit., p. xxi.
42. Quintana, op. cit., p. 239.
43. Craik, op. cit., p. 324, footnote.
44. Ball, op. cit., Vol. III, p. 173.
45. Rossi and Hone, op. cit., p. 311.
46. Sheridan, Thomas, *The Life of Reverend Dr. Jonathan Swift*. London: Bathhurst, Strahan, Collins, Revington, 1784, p. 472.

Chapter 2: Gulliver and Swift

1. Smith, David Nichol, ed., *Letters of Jonathan Swift to Charles Ford*, p. 92.
2. Ibid, p. 100.
3. Ibid, p. 122.
4. Fenichel, Otto, Die symbolische Gleichung Mädchen-Phallus. *Internationale Zeitschrift für Psychoanalyse*, Vol. XXII, 1936, pp. 299-314.
5. Eddy, William A., ed., *Satires and Personal Writings of Jonathan Swift*. London: Oxford University Press, 1951, p. 102.

Chapter 3: The Clinical Picture

1. Hardy, op. cit., p. 238.

Chapter 4: An Interpretation

1. Eddy, op. cit., pp. 101, 141.
2. Williams, *Swift's Poems*, Vol. II, pp. 541-550.
3. Smith, *The Letters of Jonathan Swift to Charles Ford*, p. 105.
4. Williams, *Swift's Poems*, Vol. II, pp. 407, 524, 580, 584.
5. Eddy, op. cit., p. 249.
6. Grant-Duff, I. F., A Onesided Sketch of Jonathan Swift. *Psychoanalytic Quarterly*, Vol. VI, 1937, pp. 238-259.
7. Eddy, op. cit., p. 129.
8. Nicolson, Marjorie, The Microscope and English Imagination. *Smith College Studies in Modern Language*, Vol. XVI, No. 4, July, 1935, pp. 3, 50-57, 87.
9. Williams, Another (Riddle), *Swift's Poems*, Vol. III, p. 930. Compare this with Carroll's animation of words, p. 234.
10. Williams, *Swift's Journal to Stella*, Vol. 1, pp. 210, 261.
11. Ehrenpreis, Irvin, Swift's "Little Language" in the *Journal to Stella*. *Studies in Philology*, Vol. XLV, No. I, January, 1948, pp. 80-88.

12. Freud, Sigmund, Family Romances (1909), *Collected Papers,* Vol. V, pp. 74-79. London: Hogarth Press, 1950.
13. Quoted by John M. Bullitt, *Jonathan Swift and the Anatomy to Satire.* Cambridge: Harvard University Press, 1953, p. 4.
14. Ibid., p. x.
15. Swift, Jonathan, *A Tale of a Tub.* New York: Random House, Modern Library, 1950, pp. 458-480.
16. Greenacre, Phyllis, op. cit., pp. 79-98.
17. Ferenczi, Sandor, Gulliver Fantasies. *International Journal of Psycho-Analysis.* Vol. IX, 1928, pp. 283-301.

PART II—LEWIS CARROLL

Chapter 1: The Life of Charles L. Dodgson

1. Hatch, Evelyn M., ed., *Letters of Lewis Carroll to His Child Friends,* Letter LXIII. London: Macmillan, 1933, pp. 97-98.
2. Hudson, Derek, *Lewis Carroll.* London: Constable, 1954, p. 35.
3. Collingwood, S. D., *Life and Letters of Lewis Carroll.* London: T. Fisher Unwin, 1898, pp. 2, 54.
4. Ibid., p. 13.
5. Hudson, op. cit., p. 26.
6. Collingwood, op. cit., pp. 11, 13.
7. Hudson, op. cit., p. 26.
8. Green, Roger L., ed., *The Diaries of Lewis Carroll,* Vol I. London: Cassell & Co., Ltd., 1953, p. 153.
9. Carroll, Lewis, *Alice's Adventures Underground.* New York: Macmillan, 1932, p. 40.
10. Collingwood, op. cit., p. 50.
11. Ibid., p. 25.
12. Hudson, op. cit., pp. 23-24.
13. Collingwood, op. cit., p. 28. See also Green, op. cit., Vol. I, pp. 13-19.
14. Carroll, Lewis, Sylvie and Bruno, *The Complete Works of Lewis Carroll.* New York: Random House, Modern Library, 1933, pp. 498-499.
15. Ibid., p. 498.
16. Hudson, op. cit., p. 48.
17. Collingwood, op. cit., pp. 34, 63. The first of these pictures shows an emaciated family taking a homeopathic meal. The second is a caricature of studies from the English poets, Milton's Lucidas: An enormously stout man tears out his hair, while a skeletal young woman bows in front of him.
18. Collingwood, S. D., *The Lewis Carroll Picture Book.* London: T. Fisher Unwin, 1899, p. 2.
19. Hudson, op. cit., p. 54, footnote.

20. Lennon, Florence Becker, *Victoria Through the Looking Glass.* New York: Simon and Schuster, 1945, p. 208.
21. Collingwood, *The Lewis Carroll Picture Book,* pp. 2, 16-17.
22. Lennon, op. cit., p. 41.
23. Green, op. cit., Vol. I, p. 19.
24. Carroll, *Complete Works,* p. 962. In the poem *Stolen Waters,* the face of the loved one is described as "withered, old and gray"— the same phrase that is used of the tree, which is broken by the Headstrong Man in *Useful and Instructive Poetry.*
25. Lennon, op. cit., pp. 189-250.
26. Green, op. cit., Vol. II, p. 385.
27. Carroll, *Complete Works,* p. 975.
28. Taylor, Alexander L., *The White Knight, A Study of C. L. Dodgson.* London: Oliver & Boyd, 1952.
29. Liddon, Henry Parry, *Life of Edward Bouverie Pusey.* London: Longmans Greene, 1893, pp. 2-30.
30. Tuckwell, William, *Reminiscences of Oxford.* London: Smith, Elder & Co., 1900, pp. 160-163.
31. Carroll, Lewis, *Useful and Instructive Poetry.* London: Geoffrey Bless Ltd., 1954, pp. 15, 16, 19, 21, 28.
32. Collingwood, *Life and Letters of Lewis Carroll,* p. 57.
33. Hatch, op. cit., pp. 100-102.
34. Carroll, *Complete Works,* pp. 100-102.
35. Ibid, pp. 1129-1139.
36. Lennon, op. cit., p. 41.
37. Tuckwell, op. cit., pp. 161-162.
38. Elton, Oliver, *Frederick York Powell, A Life and Selection from His Letters and Occasional Writings,* Vol. II, pp. 365-366. Oxford: Clarendon Press, 1906.
39. Green, op. cit., p. 78.
40. Carroll, *Complete Works,* pp. 753-779.
41. Hudson, op. cit., pp. 191-199, footnote.
42. Green, op. cit., Vol. II, p. 385.
43. Gernsheim, Helmut, *Lewis Carroll, Photographer.* New York: Chanticleer Press, Inc., 1949.
44. Collingwood, *Life and Letters of Lewis Carroll,* p. 193.
45. Green, op. cit., Vol. I, pp. 130-131.
46. Carroll, Lewis, *The Russian Journal,* ed. John F. McDermott. New York: E. P. Dutton & Co., 1935.
47. Collingwood, *Life and Letters of Lewis Carroll,* p. 65.
48. Hudson, op. cit., pp. 37-39, footnote.
49. Green, op. cit., Vol. I, p. 178.
50. Hudson, op. cit., p. 130.
51. Green, op. cit., Vol. I, p. 188.
52. Hudson, op. cit., pp. 203-206, 217-218.

53. Ibid., pp. 202-207.
54. Green, op. cit., Vol. II, p. 316.
55. Green, op. cit., Vol. I, pp. 255, 257; Vol. II, pp. 280, 289, 329. These and other entries indicate Carroll's friendship with the Heaphy's, from about 1867 well into the '80's. Thomas Heaphy was a painter of ectoplasmic phenomena which he claimed to have seen.
56. de Sausmerez, Fred B., Early Theatricals at Oxford. *Nineteenth Century,* February, 1932, pp. 235-238.
57. Green, op. cit., Vol I, pp. 90-91.
58. Hudson, op. cit., pp. 90-91.
59. Green, op. cit., Vol I, p. 133.
60. Green, op. cit., Vol. II, p. 316.
61. Kris, E., *Psychoanalytic Explorations in Art.* Chapter 7: Principles of Caricature. New York: International Universities Press, 1952.
62. Taylor, op. cit., p. 38.
63. Bacon, Deborah, The Meaning of Nonsense, A Psychoanalytic Approach to Lewis Carroll. Doctor's Thesis, Columbia University, New York, 1950.
64. Weaver, Warren, Alice's Adventures in Wonderland: Its Origin and Its Author. *Princeton University Library Chronicle,* Vol. XIII, No. 1, Autumn, 1951.
65. Collingwood, op. cit., pp. 286-288.
66. Green, op. cit., Vol. II, p. 457.
67. Ibid., p. 501.
68. Ibid., pp. 527-528.
69. Ibid., pp. 541-542.
70. Weaver, op. cit.

Chapter 2: The Character of Dodgson as Revealed in the Writings of Carroll

1. Weaver, op. cit.
2. Green, op. cit., Vol II, p. 382.
3. Collingwood, *Life and Letters of Lewis Carroll,* pp. 388-394.
4. Weaver, Warren, personal communication.
5. Collingwood, op. cit., p. 407.
6. Green, op. cit., Vol. II, p. 474.
7. Furniss H., *Confessions of a Caricaturist.* London: Bradbury, Agnew & Co., 1902, Vol. I, p. 106; and idem, *Some Victorian Men.* London: John Lane, 1924, pp. 74-80.
8. Green, Roger L., *The Story of Lewis Carroll.* London: Methuen & Co., Ltd., 1949, p. 152.
9. Carroll, Lewis, Phantasmagoria, *Complete Works,* pp. 880-884.
10. Collingwood, *Life and Letters of Lewis Carroll,* p. 34.
11. Ibid., p. 33.

12. Carroll, *Useful and Instructive Poetry*, pp. 28-29.
13. Collingwood, *The Lewis Carroll Picture Book*, pp. 18-24.
14. Carroll, *Complete Works*, p. 805.
15. Collingwood, *Life and Letters of Lewis Carroll*, p. 379.
16. Ibid., p. 391.
17. Arnold, Ethel, Reminiscences of Lewis Carroll. *Atlantic Monthly*, June, 1929, pp. 782-789.
18. Brewer, E. Cobham, *Dictionary of Phrase and Fable*. Philadelphia: J. B. Lippincott, 1894, p. 224.
19. Williams, Sidney Herbert and Falconer, Madan (*Handbook of the Literature of C. L. Dodgson*) quote a letter from Mr. Perkins in the *London Times*, July 7th, 1931.
20. Hatch, op. cit., pp. 64-68.
21. Ibid., pp. 64-68.
22. Collingwood, *Life and Letters of Lewis Carroll*, p. 173.
23. Lennon, op. cit., p. 89.
24. Ruhl, Arthur, Finding of the Snark. *Saturday Review of Literature*, March 18, 1933, pp. 490-491.
25. Green, op. cit., Vol. II, p. 329.
26. Collingwood, *Life and Letters of Lewis Carroll*, p. 383.
27. Bacon, op. cit.
28. Carroll, *Useful and Instructive Poetry*, p. 28.
29. Carroll, *Complete Works*, p. 1079.

Chapter 3: Reconstruction and Interpretation of the Development of Charles L. Dodgson and Lewis Carroll

1. Lennon, op. cit., pp. 76-77.
2. Collingwood, *Life and Letters of Lewis Carroll*, p. 102.
3. Gernsheim, op. cit., p. 221.
4. Carroll, Sylvie and Bruno, *Complete Works*, Preface, Chapter I, p. 287.
5. Carroll, Three Sunsets, *Complete Works*, p. 946.
6. Collingwood, *Life and Letters of Lewis Carroll*, p. 226.
7. Ibid., p. 197.
8. Ibid., p. 208.
9. Carroll, *Complete Works*, pp. 369-377.
10. Collingwood, *Life and Letters of Lewis Carroll*, pp. 272-273.
11. Ibid., pp. 320-322.
12. Carroll, *Complete Works*, p. 245.
13. Carroll, *Useful and Instructive Poetry*, pp. 23-24.
14. Collingwood, *The Lewis Carroll Picture Book*, p. 371.
15. Green, op. cit., Chapter I, pp. 23-24.
16. Carroll, Sylvie and Bruno, *Complete Works*, pp. 737-739.
17. Ibid., p. 306.
18. Collingwood, *Life and Letters of Lewis Carroll*, p. 35.

19. Ibid., p. 83. About 1860, Charles Dodgson met the two children of George MacDonald and seemed to take a fancy to six-year-old Greville, a beautiful boy. Mr. Dodgson fancifully told the boy that he should have his head changed for a marble one, so that his hair would not need combing (or cutting?).
20. Carroll, Sylvie and Bruno, *Complete Works*, p. 370.
21. Hatch, op. cit., pp. 65-68.

PART III—CERTAIN COMPARISONS BETWEEN SWIFT AND CARROLL

1. Carroll, Lewis, *The Nursery "Alice."* London: Macmillan, 1889.
2. Ewald, William Bragg, *The Masks of Jonathan Swift.* Cambridge: Harvard University Press, 1954.
3. Davis, Herbert, *Stella.* New York: Macmillan, 1942; idem, *The Satire of Jonathan Swift.* New York: Macmillan, 1947.
4. Quintana, op. cit.
5. Bowman, Isa, *Lewis Carroll.* New York: E. P. Dutton & Co., 1900, pp. 23-30.
6. Schilder, Paul, Psychoanalytic Remarks on "Alice in Wonderland" and Lewis Carroll. *Journal of Nervous and Mental Diseases*, Vol. 87, 1938, pp. 159-168.
7. Carroll, *Complete Works.* Introduction by Alexander Woollcott. New York: Random House, Modern Library, 1937, pp. 1-9.
8. Skinner, John and Grotjahn, Martin, Lewis Carroll's Adventures in Wonderland, and about the Symbolization of Alice's Adventures in Wonderland. *American Imago*, Vol. IV, No. 4, 1947, pp. 3-31, 32-41.
9. Empson, William, *Some Versions of Pastoral.* London: Chatto and Windus, 1935.
10. Hardy, op. cit.
11. Ferenczi, Sandor, Gulliver Fantasies, op. cit.

PART IV—NOTES ON NONSENSE

1. Kris, Ernst, *Psychoanalytic Explorations In Art.* Chapter 6: The Psychology of Caricature. New York: International Universities Press, 1952, pp. 174-189.
2. Wolfenstein, Martha, *Children's Humor.* Glencoe, Ill.: The Free Press, 1954, pp. 11-218.
3. Kris, op. cit., Chapters 6, 7, 8, pp. 173-216.
4. Freud, Sigmund, *Wit and Its Relation to the Unconscious* (1905). London: Kegan Paul, Trench, Trubner, 1922.
5. Kris, op. cit., p. 192.
6. Kris, op. cit., Chapter 8: Ego Development and the Comic, p. 215.
7. Reich, Annie, The Structure of the Grotesque-Comic Sublimation. *Bulletin of the Menninger Clinic*, Vol. XIII, 1949, pp. 160-171.

8. Kris, op. cit. See also Gombrich, Ernst H. and Kris, Ernst, *Caricature*. London: The King Penguin Books, 1940.
9. Machover, Karen, *Personality Projection in the Drawing of the Human Figure*. Springfield, Ill.: Charles C. Thomas, 1949.
10. Murry, John Middleton, *Jonathan Swift*, op. cit., p. 81. See also Entire chapter: The Troglodyte Philosopher, pp. 86-103.
11. Swift, *A Tale of a Tub*, op. cit.

BIBLIOGRAPHY

ACWORTH, BERNARD: Swift. London: Eyre & Spottiswoode, 1947.

ARNOLD, ETHEL: Reminiscences of Lewis Carroll. *Atlantic Monthly*, June, 1929, pp. 782-789.

ATKINSON, EDWARD D.: *An Ulster Parish*. Dublin: Hodges, Figgis & Co., Ltd., 1898.

BACON, DEBORAH: The Meaning of Nonsense, A Psychoanalytic Approach to Lewis Carroll. Doctor's Thesis, Columbia University, New York, 1950.

BALL, J. ELRINGTON; ed.: *The Correspondence of Jonathan Swift*. London: G. Bell & Sons, Ltd., 1914.

BOWMAN, ISA: *Lewis Carrol*. New York: E. P. Dutton & Co., 1900.

BREWER, E. COBHAM: *Dictionary of Phrase and Fable*. Philadelphia: Lippincott Co., 1894.

BULLITT, JOHN M.: *Jonathan Swift and the Anatomy of Satire*. Cambridge: Harvard University Press, 1953.

CARROLL, LEWIS: *The Nursery "Alice."* London: Macmillan, 1889.

——: *Alice's Adventures Underground*. New York: The Macmillan Co., 1932.

——: *The Complete Works of Lewis Carroll*. New York: Modern Library, 1933.

——: *The Russian Journal*, ed. by John F. McDermott. New York: E. P. Dutton & Co., 1935.

——: *Useful and Instructive Poetry*. London: Geoffrey Bless, Ltd., 1954.

——: see Green, R. L.; Hatch, E. M.

COLLINGWOOD, S. D.: *Life and Letters of Lewis Carroll*. London: T. Fisher Unwin, 1898.

——: *The Lewis Carroll Picture Book*. London: T. Fisher Unwin, 1899.

CRAIK, HENRY: *The Life of Jonathan Swift*. London: John Murray, 1882.

DAVIS, HERBERT: *Stella*. New York: The Macmillan Co., 1942.

——: *The Satire of Jonathan Swift*. New York: The Macmillan Co., 1947.

DE SAUSMEREZ, FRED B.: Early Theatricals at Oxford. *Nineteenth Century*, February, 1932, pp. 235-238.

BIBLIOGRAPHY

EDDY, WILLIAM A., ed.: *Satires and Personal Writings of Jonathan Swift.* London: Oxford University Press, 1951.

EHRENPREIS, IRVIN: Swift's "Little Language" in the *Journal to Stella. Studies in Philology,* 45:80-88, 1948.

——: Swift and Mr. John Temple. *Modern Language Notes,* March, 1947, pp. 145-154.

ELTON, OLIVER: *Frederick York Powell, A Life and Selection from His Letters and Occasional Writings.* Oxford: Clarendon Press, 1906.

EMPSON, WILLIAM: *Some Versions of Pastoral.* London: Chatto & Windus, 1935.

EWALD, WILLIAM BRAGG: *The Masks of Jonathan Swift.* Cambridge: Harvard University Press, 1954.

FENICHEL, OTTO: Die symbolische Gleichung Mädchen-Phallus. *Internationale Zeitschrift für Psychoanalyse,* 22:299-314, 1936.

FERENCZI, SANDOR: Gulliver Fantasies. *International Journal of Psycho-Analysis,* 9:283-301, 1928.

FORSTER, JOHN: *The Life of Jonathan Swift.* New York: The Macmillan Co., 1942.

FREEMAN, A. MARTIN: *Vanessa and Her Correspondence With Jonathan Swift.* London: Selwyn & Blount, Ltd., 1921.

FREUD, SIGMUND: *Wit and Its Relation to the Unconscious* (1905). London: Kegan, Paul, Trench, Trubner, 1922.

——: Family Romances (1909). *Collected Papers,* 5:74-79. London: Hogarth Press, 1950.

FURNISS, H.: *Confessions of a Caricaturist.* London: Bradbury, Agnew & Co., 1902.

——: *Some Victorian Men.* London: John Lane, 1924.

GERNSHEIM, HELMUT: *Lewis Carroll, Photographer.* New York: Chanticleer Press, 1949.

GOMBRICH, ERNST, H. and KRIS, ERNST: *Caricature.* London: The King Penguin Books, 1940.

GRANT-DUFF, I. F.: A Onesided Sketch of Jonathan Swift. *Psychoanalytic Quarterly,* 6:238-259, 1937.

GREEN, ROGER L.: *The Story of Lewis Carroll.* London: Methuen & Co., 1949.

——, ed.: *The Diaries of Lewis Carroll.* London: Cassell & Co., Ltd., 1953.

GREENACRE, PHYLLIS: Certain Relationships between Fetishism and Faulty Development of the Body Image. *The Psychoanalytic Study of the Child,* 8:79-98. New York: International Universities Press, 1953.

GROTJAHN, MARTIN: About the Symbolization of Alice's Adventures in Wonderland. *American Imago,* 4:32-41, 1947.

HARDY, EVELYN: *The Conjured Spirit, Swift.* London: Hogarth Press, 1949.

HATCH, EVELYN M., ed.: *Letters of Lewis Carroll to His Child Friends.* London: Macmillan, 1933.

HEILMAN, ROBERT B.: Introduction to the Modern Library Edition of *Gulliver's Travels.* New York: Modern Library, 1950.

HONE, JOSEPH: See Rossi, M.

HUDSON, DEREK: *Lewis Carroll.* London: Constable, 1954.

JOHNSON, SAMUEL: *The Poetical Works of Dr. Jonathan Swift, With the Life of the Author.* Edinburgh: Apollo Press, 1778.

JOHNSTON, DENIS: The Mysterious Origin of Dean Swift. *Dublin Historical Record,* 3:81-98, 1941.

KRIS, ERNST: *Psychoanalytic Explorations in Art.* New York: International Universities Press, 1952.

———: see Gombrich, E. H.

LANE-POOLE, STANLEY, ed.: *Swift's Letters and Journals.* London: Kegan, Paul, Trench & Co., 1885.

LENNON, FLORENCE BECKER: *Victoria Through the Looking Glass.* New York: Simon and Schuster, 1945.

LIDDON, HENRY PARRY: *Life of Edward Bouverie Pusey.* London: Longmans Greene, 1893.

MACHOVER, KAREN: *Personality Projection in the Drawing of the Human Figure.* Springfield, Ill.: Charles C. Thomas, 1949.

MADAN, FALCONER: see Williams, S. H.

MURRY, JOHN MIDDLETON: *Jonathan Swift.* London: Jonathan Cape, 1954.

NICOLSON, MARJORIE: The Microscope and English Imagination. *Smith College Studies in Modern Language,* 1935.

ORRERY, JOHN, EARL OF ORRERY: *Remarks on the Life and Writings of Dr. Jonathan Swift.* Dublin: George Faulkner, 1752.

PILKINGTON, LETITIA: *Memoirs* (1784), ed. by J. Isaacs. London: Routledge & Sons, 1928.

QUINTANA, RICARDO: *The Mind and Art of Jonathan Swift* (1936). London: Methuen & Co., Reprinted 1953.

REICH, ANNIE: The Structure of the Grotesque-Comic Sublimation. *Bulletin of the Menninger Clinic,* 13:160-171, 1949.

ROSSI, MARIO and HONE, JOSEPH: *Swift, or the Egoist.* London: Victor Gollancz, 1934.

RUHL, ARTHUR: Finding of the Snark. *Saturday Review of Literature,* 1933, pp. 490-491.

SCHILDER, PAUL: Psychoanalytic Remarks on "Alice in Wonderland" and Lewis Carroll. *Journal of Nervous and Mental Diseases,* 87:159-168, 1938.

SCOTT, SIR WALTER: Life of Swift. *The Life and Works of Jonathan Swift.* London: Bricker & Son, 1883.

SHERIDAN, THOMAS: *The Life of Reverend Dr. Jonathan Swift.* London: Bathhurst, Strahan, Collins, Revington & Co., 1784.

SKINNER, JOHN: Lewis Carroll's Adventures in Wonderland. *American Imago*, 4:3-31, 1947.

SMITH, DAVID NICHOL, ed.: *The Letters of Jonathan Swift to Charles Ford.* Oxford: Clarendon Press, 1935.

STEPHEN, SIR LESLIE: Swift. *English Men of Letters Series,* ed. by John Morley. London: Macmillan, 1882.

SWANZY, HENRY BIDDALL: *Biographical Succession Lists of the Diocese of Dromore,* ed. by Canon J. B. Leslie. Belfast: Carswell & Son, Ltd., 1933.

SWIFT, DEAN: *Essay Upon the Life, Writings and Character of Dr. Swift.* London, 1755.

SWIFT, JONATHAN: *Directions to Servents and Other Pieces in Prose and Verse.* Dublin: George Faulkner, 1752.

——: *Gulliver's Travels, A Tale of a Tub, The Battle of the Books.* New York: Random House, 1950.

——: See Ball, J. E.; Eddy, W. A.; Johnson, S.; Lane-Poole, S.; Smith, D. N.; Williams, H.

TAYLOR, ALEXANDER L.: *The White Knight, A Study of C. L. Dodgson.* London: Oliver & Boyd, 1952.

TUCKWELL, WILLIAM: *Reminiscences of Oxford.* London: Smith, Elder & Co., 1900.

VAN DOREN, CARL: *Swift.* New York: Viking Press, 1930.

WEAVER, WARREN: *Alice's Adventures in Wonderland*: Its Origin and Its Author. *Princeton University Library Chronicle,* Vol. XIII, 1951.

WILDE, W. R.: *The Closing Years of Dean Swift's Life.* Second edition. Dublin: Hodges & Smith, 1849.

WILLIAMS, HAROLD, ed.: *The Poems of Jonathan Swift.* Oxford: Clarendon Press, 1937.

——: *Jonathan Swift's Journal to Stella.* Oxford: Clarendon, 1948.

WILLIAMS, SIDNEY HERBERT and MADAN, FALCONER: *Handbook of the Literature of C. L. Dodgson.* London: Oxford University Press, 1931.

WILSON, C. H.: *Swiftiana,* 2 vols. London: Richard Phillips, 1804.

WOLFENSTEIN, MARTHA: *Children's Humor.* Glencoe, Ill.: The Free Press, 1954.

ACKNOWLEDGMENTS

The writing of a book is an exciting project for its author, no matter how much disappointment, frustration and tedious labor may be involved. To those friends who, not in the vortex, are yet drawn into the activity—the next of kin as it were—the evolution of a book must be a trying, and sometimes a downright irritating, experience. It is to these good friends that I would first of all express my gratitude for the various kinds of practical help and support they have given me. Specifically would I further acknowledge indebtedness to Dr. Lauretta Bender, Mr. and Mrs. Christopher Brunner, Dr. Heinz Hartmann, Dr. Mary O'Neil Hawkins, Dr. Edith Jacobson, Dr. Ernst Kris, and Dr. Edward Kronold for their helpful contribution of books and articles; to Mr. Helmut Gernsheim, for graciously showing me his collection of Carroll's photographs and permitting me to reproduce one in this volume; to Mr. Denis Johnston for his discussion of Sir John Temple as well as for his help in the explorations of Laracor; to Mrs. Florence Becker Lennon for her generosity in putting at my disposal her collection of letters, articles, and other documents concerning Lewis Carroll; to the Reverend Canon W. L. M. Protheroe for his help in determining the christening dates of the Dodgson family; to Dr. Bettina Warburg for a photostatic copy of a letter from Swift to Sir William Temple; to Dr. Deborah Bacon for permission to quote from her thesis *The Meaning of Nonsense;* and to Mr. Warren Weaver for sending me specific information concerning Carroll.

Further grateful acknowledgment is due to the various publishers and agents who have granted permission to quote as follows:

from the *Story of Lewis Carroll* by Roger Green, published by Abelard-Schuman, Inc., New York;

from the *Correspondence of Jonathan Swift,* edited by J. Elrington Ball, published by G. Bell & Sons, Ltd., London;

from *Jonathan Swift* by J. Middleton Murry, published by Jonathan Cape Ltd., London;

from *Lewis Carroll* by Derek Hudson, published by Constable & Co., London;

from *The Conjured Spirit* by Evelyn Hardy, published by the Hogarth Press, London;

from *An Ulster Parish* by Edward D. Atkinson, published by Hodges Figgis & Co. Ltd., Dublin;

from *Useful and Instructive Poetry* by Lewis Carroll, published by Macmillan Co., New York;

from *Lewis Carroll's Letters to his Child Friends,* edited by Evelyn M. Hatch, published by Macmillan Co. Ltd., London;

from *The Mind and Art of Jonathan Swift* by Ricardo Quintana, published by Methuen & Co. Ltd., London;

from *The Diaries of Lewis Carroll,* published by the Oxford University Press;

from *Victoria Through the Looking Glass,* by Florence Becker Lennon, published by Simon & Schuster, New York;

from *Life and Letters of Lewis Carroll* and *Lewis Carroll Picture Book* by S. D. Collingwood, through the service of A. P. Watt & Son, representing the Dodgson estate.

Finally to those who have given essential aid in secretarial, editorial, and library research work, I am most thankful: Miss Faith Waterman, Mrs. Sophie Meyer, Miss Selma Gordon, Miss Betty Lord, and Miss Nancy Starrels; and Miss Lottie Maury of the International Universities Press, whose skill in handling both author and product lessened many difficulties.

Phyllis Greenacre

INDEX

Acworth, Bernard, 287
Addison, Joseph, 53, 54
Aged, Aged Man, The, 227, 228, 239
   ff., 267, 274
Aggression
   and dirt, 252
   and learning, 253
   in childhood, 259
   see also Anger, Cannibalistic at-
      titudes, Cruelty, Decapitation,
      Explosiveness, Rage, *and* Sadism
Air
   and smelling, 181
   interest in, 174-175
   see also Eating and breathing
Alexander the Great, 77
"Alice," 9, 10, 12, 115, 174, 181-187,
   211, 216, 218, 227, 231, 243,
   249, 250, 255 ff., 257, 258, 260
Ambivalence
   compared in Swift and Carroll,
      252-253
America, 77
Anality, 101-102, 104, 107
Anger, 201
   and sibling rivalry, 200, 210
   see also Aggression
Animation of inanimate objects, 120
   ff., 182, 186, 210, 223
Arbuthnot, John, 82, 108
Arnold, Ethel, 287
"Arthur Forester," 193, 194, 219,
   223
Artist, revealing inner life, 11
Artistic production
   and dream, 64
   nature of appeal to others, 11-12
Atkinson, Edward D., 33, 287
Attachment to young girls, com-
   pared in Swift and Carroll, 250-
   251
Aunt Judy's Magazine, 192

Babies, *see* Dodgson, Charles Lutwidge *and* Swift, Jonathan:
   babies, attitude toward

Bacon, Deborah, 287
"Baker," 187, 188, 189, 236, 237,
   238, 239, 240
   as Dodgson, 243, 244
Ball, J. Elrington, 32, 287, 290
Balnibarbi, 76
"Bandersnatch," 228, 235, 237
"Banker," 187, 237, 238
"Barrister," 187
Battle of the Books, The, 30
Bayne, Thomas Vere, 207
Bear, 197, 198
   as related to cat, 198
*Beautiful Young Nymph Going to
   Bed, A,* 93 ff.
"Beaver," 187, 236, 237, 240, 241
"Bellman," 187, 188, 238
   see also Hughes, Agnes
Bender, Lauretta, 259 ff.
Berkeley, Lady, 37
Berkeley, Lord Charles, 19
Bewilderment, and anxiety, 258
"Bill," 219
"Billiardmarker," 187
Biography and pathography, 12-13
Bisexuality, 101
   and latency period, 223
   in caricatures, 130
   in Jabberwocky, 235
   in poem to Gertrude Chataway,
      191
   see also Dodgson, Charles Lut-
      widge *and* Swift, Jonathan:
      sexuality, attitudes toward
Body image, 10-11
   and fetishism, 114
   and pregnancy, 218
   and tumescence, 217-218, 274
   disturbances of, 64-74, 96, 109-
      115, 129, 145, 146, 172-174,
      181-182, 198, 243, 265, 266,
      271
Body imagery, 109-111
   and satire, 110
Body-phallus, 109, 256

293

Blefuscu, 67, 69
Bok, Edward, 164
Bolingbroke, Lord Henry, 25, 61
"Bonnetmaker," 187
Boohoo, 176
"Boojum," 159, 160, 236, 238, 240
"Boojum Snark," 187, 188, 189, 242-243
see also "Snark"
"Boots," 187
Bowman children, 176, 255 ff.
Bowman, Isa, 255, 287
Breast, reactions to, 70, 94, 112-114
Brent, Mrs., 47
Brobdingnag, 69-75
"Broker," 187
Brother and Sister, 173, 200
Brewer, E. Cobham, 287
"Bruno," 123, 193, 194, 195
as Dodgson, 195, 198, 199, 201, 202, 219, 224 ff., 242, 243, 245
Bruno's Revenge, 154, 192
Buffalo, 147
Bullitt, John M., 110, 287
"Butcher," 187, 236, 237, 241
Busch, Wilhelm, 13

Cadenus and Venessa, 43, 52, 56
Caesar, 77
California, 77
Cambridge, 63
Cannibalistic attitudes, 70, 82, 112, 200, 210
and sibling rivalry, 173
rage and oral jealousy, 257
Caricature, 124, 129, 131, 145, 166, 172, 174, 182, 265, 268
and aggression, 269
and body imagery, 270
and cartoon, 273
and dreams, 268
Carroll, Lewis
book reviews, aversion to, 153 ff.
comparison with Jonathan Swift, 9-14, 115
cultist attitude toward, 10
Diaries, 124, 132 ff., 134 ff., 136 ff., 138, 142 ff., 143, 144, 145, 147, 148, 150, 151, 155, 156, 157, 158, 160, 161, 163, 164, 166, 171, 190, 211, 239 ff.

humor and horror, 158
parodies, 172, 173, 265, 266, 267
see also Dodgson, Charles Lutwidge
Castration complex
fears, 70, 89, 98
identification with girl, 275
threats, 244
see also Decapitation, and Extinction
Cat, 122, 123, 171, 173, 177, 178-181, 184, 186, 198
see also "Cheshire cat," Dinah, Dodgson, Charles Lutwidge, and Hughes, Agnes
Caterpillar, 219, 227
Character defenses, compared in Swift and Dodgson, 256
Chataway, Gertrude, 140 ff., 175, 176, 191, 214
"Cheshire cat," 177 ff., 182, 186, 243
Clogher, Bishop of, 48
College Rhymes, 190
Collingwood, Charles, brother-in-law of Charles L. Dodgson, 154, 164
Collingwood, Mrs. Charles, see Dodgson, Mary Charlotte, sister of Charles L. Dodgson
Collingwood, Stuart D., nephew of Charles L. Dodgson, 128, 131, 143 ff., 145, 147, 155, 162, 166, 189, 214, 218 ff., 223 ff., 287
Color, 76
Comic Times, 139
Compulsiveness, compared in Swift and Dodgson, 252-254
Conduct of the Allies, The, 45
Convulsions, 130 ff., 142, 156, 157, 169, 183, 187, 225, 232-233, 240, 276
Craik, Henry, 19, 48, 278, 287
Croft Rectory—findings, 149
Cruelty
in "Alice" books, 138, 182
in fantasy, 178
see also Aggression, Anger, Rage, and Sadism
Cult of Alice, 257, 259
Cybernetics, 77

Darwin, Charles, 158, 233

Davis, Herbert, 21, 253, 287
Decapitation, 183, 185, 197, 220,
   221, 243
   and nonsense, 275-276
   see also Castration complex
Defoe, Daniel, 61
Delaney, Patrick, 47
Denial
   in caricature, 274
   mechanism of, 52, 60
Depersonalization, 121, 183
de Sausmerez, Fred B., 287
Diaries of Lewis Carroll, see Carroll,
   Diaries
*Difficulty of Knowing One's Self,
   The,* 57
Digressions, 36
"Dinah," 173-177
Dingley, Rebecca, 39-40, 47-49, 58,
   61, 90, 103, 250
Directions to Nurses, 93
Discovery, The, 38
Disraeli, 220
Dodgson, Charles Lutwidge
   adolescence, 224, *see also* Rich-
      mond School, *and* Rugby
   aggression, absence of direct, 10;
      oral, and compulsiveness, 254;
      repressed, 224
   anatomy and physiology, interest
      in, 155, 156, 158
   anger, 125
   animals, interest in, 123, 127, 146,
      171, 177-181, 236, *see also*
      Dodgson, Charles Lutwidge,
      vivisection
   argumentation, 225
   as teacher, 161, 242
   babies, attitude toward, 138, 155,
      156 ff., 169, 174, 182, 190, 194,
      210, 213-214
   birth and family, 119-122, 195,
      207
   boys, attitude towards little, 123,
      148, 154, 169, 179, 195, 217,
      219, 232, 244, 245, 250, 275
   breathing, interest in, 171-176
   cannibalistic trends, 173, 176, 217
   caricature, 124, 129, 131, 145, 166,
      167, 172, 174
   character revealed; in *Sylvie and*

Bruno, 223; in writings of Lewis
   Carroll, 165-206, 219
childhood, 119-131, 207-209
colors, attitude toward, 166
compulsiveness, 168-169
Croft, 119, 203
cruelty revealed; and the ridiculous, 225; in fantasies, 182; in
   writings, 225
Daresbury, 207, 222
deafness, 132 ff., 166
death, attitude toward, 193
death of, 164
depersonalization, 121, 211
dreams, interest in, 150, 153 ff.,
   192, 193, 194, 230
eating and breathing, attitude toward, 171-176
eccentricities, 165-169
excitement, attitude toward, 224
   ff., 226
explosiveness, fear of, 254
fairies, 193
fantasies, acted out, 222; aggressive, in control of temper, 254;
   and games, 243; and inventive-
   ness, 166; animals, 177, 178-
   182; cruelty, shown in, 182; of
   changing identity, 176; of injury, 244; stories, 216
father, relationship to, 127, 138,
   139, 154, 155, 208, 221-222
fears, about health, 10; of convulsions 130 ff., 142, 156, 157, 169,
   225, 232-233; of fainting, 245;
   of infection, 175, 176, 196
femininity, in appearance, 166; in
   attitude toward children, 222
ghosts, interest in, 155, 159
girls, attitude towards little, 138,
   144, 148, 161, 165 ff., 169, 172,
   175-176, 178, 191, 211, 212,
   216, 217, 245, 249, 255, 258,
   275
guilt and aggression, 224
hair, interest in, 131 ff., 228
Holy Orders, 137, 143, 151
identity problems; fantasy change
   of identity with girl, 211, 214;
   identification with wheelbarrow,

Dodgson, Charles Lutwidge (*cont'd*)
120-121 ff.; in relation to sisters, 212
idiocy, attitude toward, 156, 232-233, 240, 245
insomnia, 166, 255; and doubting, 221; and obsessional thinking, 226
jealousy, and cannibalistic trends, 214; and orality, 255
kissing, 122, 132, 134, 135, 145, 163-164, 178, 191, 200, 210, 223, 242, 243, 246, 252 ff., 255, 258
knots and cords, interest in, 169
latency period, 222
laughter and horror, 157
Lewis Carroll, attitude toward, 120, 121 ff., 164, 170
looking and eating associated, 218
love, attitudes toward, 196-197, 200, 201-202, 214, 245; as Christian doctrine of duty, 120-121, 208; as moral precept, 208
magic, in defenses, 254; interest in, 159
male adults, attitude toward, 219
manual dexterity, 124, 128, 165
marionettes, interest in, 124, 159 ff., 122
marriage, attitude toward, 155, 188, 196
mathematical interests, ability, 126, 160; articles, 140, 160 ff., 165 ff.; general interests, 126, 141, 160-161; lecturer, 10
memory, concern about, 147, 165, 227, 228-234
migraine, 162
mother, relationship to, 132-134, 136-138, 205, 208, 209, 215, 217, 221, 244, 251-252, 255; *see also* Dodgson, Charles Lutwidge, oedipal problems
mumps, 132 ff.
New Year's resolutions, 160 ff.
nudity, interest in, 145, 163
obsessional doubting, 221
oedipal problems, 214-215; reversal, 216, 217, 221, 223, 244, 251-252; *see also* Dodgson,

Charles Lutwidge, father, relationship to; mother, relationship to
Oxford, 140, 172
pain, attitude toward, 158, 190, 191, 231, 241, *see also* Dodgson, Charles Lutwidge, stoicism
parents, first cousins, 121, 195, 207
parodies, in drawings and early writing, 130 ff.
physical appearance, 166
photography, 144, 145, 161, 218 ff., 211 ff., 213, *see also* Gernsheim, Helmut
pseudonym, "BB," 190; "Lewis Carroll," 139, 164, 166
puzzles, 124, 140, 165, 226
rage in infancy, 254
religion, attitude toward, 147, 151, 160, 162, 163, 192, 196, 223, 226; *see also* "Sunday afternoon," *and* Holy Orders
reversal as defense, 221
reversal of sexes in sketches, 218-219; *see also* Bisexuality
respiratory illnesses, 162, 164
Richmond School, 126, 222
Rugby, 126, 128, 129, 131, 132, 172, 222, 224
sadism, in drawings, 145, 172
sado-masochism, evident in writings, 197, 200
scoptophilia, 213, 255; and photography, 255-256
screen memory, 151, 230
self discipline, 211, 218, 244
sexuality, attitudes toward, 197, 212, 214, 227, 245-246, 251, 260; sublimation of sexual and aggressive drives, 212
sketching, 145, 163, 172, 218
small things, interest in, 222
space, interest in, 173, 182, 199; *see also* Body image, disturbances
stammer, 123, 125, 159 ff., 166, 190
stoicism, 255
"Sunday afternoon," 128
temperature, interest in, 174

Dodgson, Charles Lutwidge (*cont'd*)
  theatre, interest in, 143, 155, 161,
    162, 163, 222
  time, interest in, 168, 173, 174,
    182, 199
  travels, 146
  unconscious, interest in the, 193
  urinary problems indicated, 254
  vivisection, 123, 159; *see also*
    Dodgson, Charles Lutwidge,
    animals
  walking, interest in, 10, 167
  whooping cough, 132 ff.
Dodgson family
  Dodgson, Caroline Hume (sister
    of Charles L.), 119 ff., 209,
    212, 216
  Dodgson, Charles, Archdeacon
    (father of Charles L.), 119 ff.,
    121, 127; death of, 154, 155,
    221; *see also* Dodgson, Charles
    Lutwidge, father, relationship to
    Dodgson, Charles Lutwidge,
    and Carroll, Lewis
  Dodgson, Edith (niece of Charles
    L.), 159
  Dodgson, Edwin (brother of
    Charles L.), 119 ff., 132, 174,
    190, 209
  Dodgson, Elizabeth Lucy (sister of
    Charles L.), 119 ff., 150, 155
  Dodgson, Frances Jane Lutwidge
    (mother of Charles L.), 119 ff.,
    122, 132, 143 ff., 205, 208; *see
    also* Dodgson, Charles Lut-
    widge, mother, relationship to
  Dodgson, Frances Jane (sister of
    Charles L.), 119 ff., 150, 205
  Dodgson, F. Menella (niece of
    Charles L.), 143 ff.
  Dodgson, Henrietta Harington
    (sister of Charles L.), 119 ff.
  Dodgson, Louisa Fletcher (sister
    of Charles L.), 119 ff., 216
  Dodgson, Margaret Anna Ashley
    (sister of Charles L.), 119 ff.
  Dodgson, Mary Charlotte (Mrs.
    Charles Collingwood, sister of
    Charles L.), 119 ff., 154, 155,
    159, 163, 190, 209

Dodgson, Skeffington Hume
  (brother of Charles L.), 119
  ff., 125-126, 154, 209
Dodgson, Wilfred Longley (broth-
  er of Charles L.), 119 ff., 155,
  159, 190, 209
Dodgson, Mrs. Wilfred Longley,
  154, 159, *see also* Donkin,
  Alice
Dog, 177, 198, 231; as King, 198;
  as boy, 198
Donkin, Alice (Mrs. Wilfred Dodg-
  son, sister-in-law of Charles L.),
  154
"Dormouse," 219
Drapier, M. B., 19, 53
Drapier, Letters, The, 19, 53
Dryden, Elizabeth, 19, 30
Dublin, 23, 27, 38, 42, 45, 46, 48,
  49, 54, 55, 58-59, 66, 90
"Duchess, the Ugly," 219, 220
Duckworth, Canon, 149

"Earl, The," father of Lady Muriel,
  219
Eastbourne, 147
Eating and being eaten, 182, 189,
  244
  and looking, 238 ff.
  body changes and tumescence,
    218
  see also Cannibalistic attitudes
Eating and breathing, 172-177
Eddy, William A., 82, 288, 290
Ego, early organization of, 104
Ehrenpreis, Irvin, 28, 103, 287
Elephant, 197, 198, 227
Elphinston, Elfland, and Elveston,
  194
Elton, Oliver, 287
Empson, William, 260, 287
England, 17, 27, 39, 40, 42, 43, 45,
  52, 55, 56, 57, 58, 63, 73, 74,
  76, 77, 78, 83-84, 95, 96, 101-
  102
"Eric Lindon," 193, 195
  as C. L. Dodgson, 195, 196, 202,
    219, 223
Ewald, William B., 253, 287
Excrements, 76, 80, 85, 92-94, 96,
  107

Excrements (cont'd)
  see also Anality, Swift, interest in
    cleanliness, and Toilet training
Excitement, fear of, 245, see also
    Anger, Explosiveness, and Rage
Exhibitionism, 94-96
Explosiveness, 218, 224, 226-227
  see also Excitement, Orgasm, and
    Rage
Extinction, threats of decapitation in,
    174, 175, 183, 187, 188, 190,
    210, 244
  see also Castration complex

Faces in the Fire, 193 ff.
Facts, 203
Fairy as conscience, 202
Fairyland, 193
  Fayfield junction, 194
Family romance, 88-90, 97, 101,
    103-105
  and anal problems, 104
Fantasy animals and primal scene,
    240
  and intellectual development, 218
  and latency period, 223
  and mathematics
  of sexual life of parents, 241
"Father William," 227, 228, 229,
    259
Fenichel, Otto, 288
Fenton (brother-in-law of Jonathan
    Swift), 35, 40
Ferenczi, Sandor, 261, 288
Fetishism, 10-11, 109-110, 114
  see also Body image, disturbances
First Earring, 243
Fish, in Swift's screen memory, 25,
    25 ff.
Fits, 183, 187, 240
  and primal scene, 240
  see also Convulsions
Flea and flying horse, 199
Ford, Charles, 54-55, 58, 60-61, 93,
    101, 251
Forster, John, 288
France, 45, 61
Freeman, A. Martin, 288
Freud, S., 104, 268, 288
Furniss, Harry, 170, 288

Garden, 146, 147, 177, 181, 182,
    184, 187, 229-230
Gay, John, 82
Gernsheim, Helmut, 145, 251, 288
Giffard, Lady, 24, 28, 38
Gombrich, Ernst H., 288, 289
Grant-Duff, I. F., 944 ff., 288
Green, Roger L., 132 ff., 171, 287,
    288
Greenacre, Phyllis, 11, 278, 288
Gregory, Horace, 228 ff.
Grotjahn, Martin, 259, 288
"Gryphon," 220
Guildford, 155, 164
Guilt, 64, 65, 96-97; and punish-
    ment, 183, 184
"Gulliver, Lemuel," see Gulliver's
    Travels
Gulliver and Swift, 60-82
Gulliver's Travels, 9, 11, 12, 22, 26,
    53, 56, 60, 82, 87, 93, 95, 102,
    109,
  animals, small, 70
  Balnibarbi, 62, 76, 100
  "Bates, James," 62, 99
  Blefuscu, 67-69
  body image, disturbances, 64-74,
    96, 109-115
  breast, attitude toward, 70, 94,
    112-114
  Brobdingnag, 61, 62, 69-74, 111
  cannibalistic trends, 65, 70, 82,
    112, 200, 210
  clitoris, identification of Gulliver
    with, 71
  decapitation, 71
  education, Lilliput, 68
  exhibitionism, 64, 66, 70, 71
  fantasy, abstract, 75; and reality,
    77; of fellatio, 72; of rebirth, 74
  ghosts, 77
  giants, 69-75
  Glubbdubdrib, 62, 77, 102
  Hopewell, 75
  horses, 25 ff., 26, 61, 66 ff., 81
  Houyhnhnms, 61, 62, 79-81, 93,
    94, 103
  kidnappings, 72, 73-74
  Lagado, 176
  Laputa, 62, 75-77, 100

Gulliver's Travels (*cont'd*)
 Lilliputians, 25, 62, 64-68, 70, 73, 74
 Luggnagg, 77-78, 102
 magicians, 77
 Munodi, 76
 nurse, 39, 70, 71, 72, 83, 84, 107
 nursing period, 65
 reality testing, absence of, 75
 rebirth fantasy, 74
 ropes, chains, interest in, 67-68
 scientific exhibits, 76
 scoptophilia, 71
 screen memory, 68 ff.
 sexes, attitude toward, 69, 71
 Struldbruggs, 78, 92, 97
 "Swallow," 62, 82
 toilet problems, 64-65
 unreality, feelings of, 74
 urination, 65, 67, 71
 voyages, first, 25, 62-69, 96, 111; second, 62, 69-74, 93, 96, 97; third, 61, 62, 75-77, 92, 96, 99; fourth, 26, 60-63, 77-81, 85
 Yahoos, 26, 56, 61, 79-81, 85, 93-95, 103

Haigha and Hatta, 220
Hannibal, 77
Hardy, Evelyn, 19, 38, 48, 84, 260, 278, 288
Hare, Thomas, 168
Hargreaves, Caryl, 162
Hargreaves, Mrs. Reginald, 162, *see also* Liddell, Alice
Hatch, Evelyn M., 287, 289
Heaphy, Thomas, 159
Heilman, Robert B., 289
Ho Chien, 10
Hogarth, 269 ff.
Holiday, Henry, 160, 170
Homosexuality, 97
 see also Bisexuality
Hone, Joseph, 289
Horses, 25 ff., 26, 66 ff., 81
 see also Houyhnhnms
Houyhnhnms, 79-81
Hudson, Derek, 10, 127, 129, 130, 142 ff., 143, 151, 156
Hughes, Agnes, 178-181, 246
Hughes, Amy, 180, 246

Hughes, Emily, 180
Hume, 99 ff.
Humor and hostility, 9, 87, 256-257
"Humpty Dumpty," 220, 234, 235, 237 ff.
Hunting of the Snark, 140 ff., 142, 149 ff., 155, 159, 160, 175, 181, 187-192, 195, 212, 227, 236, 239
Hypochondriasis, 29
 see also Dodgson, Charles Lutwidge, fears, *and* Swift, Jonathan, fears

"I," Charles L. Dodgson as, 195, 227
Identification, 41, 88, 106, 109
 of Carroll with "Alice," 211
 primary, 92
 through looking and eating, 214
 with loved one, 216
Identity, problems of, 88
 changing, 191, 199
 confused, 183
 confused, compared in Swift and Dodgson, 257
Impotence, 94
Ireland, 17-19, 24, 27, 29, 34, 39, 42, 43, 52-53, 55, 56, 57, 58, 63, 74, 83, 95
Isle of Wight, 147, 191

"Jabberwock," 233, 236, 237
 and primal scene, 240
Jabberwocky, 234, 235
James II, 27
Japan, 62, 75, 78
Jealousy and orality, 244
Jenkins, Rev. John Howe, 152
Johnson, Esther (Hester), *see* Stella
Johnson, Mrs. (mother of Esther), 31, 42
Johnson, Samuel, 289, 290
Johnston, Denis, 20, 21, 49, 278, 289
Joke, 36-37, 54, 87
 see also Swift, Jonathan, joking
Jones, Betty, 27, 33
Journal to Stella, 30 ff., 41, 42, 47, 54, 69, 102, 105
"Jubjub bird," 235, 236, 237

Kafka, Franz, 154
Kendall, Rev., 278
Kilkenny, School, 24
Kilroot, 32
"King of Hearts," 185, 197, 219
Kissing, see Dodgson, Charles Lutwidge, kissing
Klang associations, 102
"Knave of Hearts," 173, 183, 214
Kris, Ernst, 265, 268, 270, 272 ff., 288, 289

Lady of the Ladle, 173, 190
"Lady Muriel Orme," 193, 194, 201, 202
    as Sylvie, 205
Lady's Dressing Room, The, 93
Lagado, 76
Lane, Poole Stanley, 289, 296
Language and speech
    aggression, verbal, 225
    and nursing, 70, 102
    animation of words, 102, 108
        compared in Swift and Dodgson, 234 ff.
    baby talk, 123, 195
    Boojum, explained, 242
    disturbances among Dodgsons, 209
    klang associations, 102
    language, role of, in Swift, 90-91, 102-108
    Lisp, Bruno's 195
    "Little Language" of Swift and Stella, 41, 43, 69, 84, 103, 105
    neologisms, compared in Swift and Carroll, 194
    play with language and words, 124, 125, 126, 139, 140, 222, 234
    Portmanteau words, 160, 235
    running, 125, 139, 140, 142, 182, 192, 198, 199-200, 233
    stammering, 123, 124, 125, 159 ff., 166, 190, 240
    words as foci of the polymorphous perverse, 275
Laputa, 75, 76
Laracor, 39, 54
Latency period
    aggression during, 249

compared in Swift and Dodgson, 249
    growth during, 249
Lear, Edward, 13, 130, ff., 239 ff., 276 ff.
Lennon, Florence Becker, 132, 134 ff., 141 ff., 189, 207 ff., 259, 289
Leslie, J. B., 290
Leyden, 62-63
Liddell family
    alienation from Dodgson, Charles Lutwidge, 151
Liddell, Alice, 134, 135, 148, 150, 151, 152, 153, 214, 215, 251, 255 ff.
Liddell, Dean, 139, 151, 164
Liddell, Edith, 148, 150
Liddell, Harry, 148
Liddell, Lorina, 148, 150
Liddell, Mrs., 152
Liddon, Dean Henry, 143, 146, 290
Life and Character of Dr. Swift, 92
Lilliputia, 64-69, 73
"Lion and Unicorn," 185, 220, 244
Lobotomy, 77
London, 42, 54, 55, 58, 62, 63
Long, Anne, 42
Love
    as conscience, 201
    as doctrine of duty, 121
    see also Dodgson, Charles Lutwidge, love and Swift, Jonathan, love
Lucretius, 98
Luggnagg, 77-78, 102

MacDonald, George, 153
Machover, Karen, 273, 289
Macmillan Company, 169
"Mad Gardener," 193, 194-195, 227, 229, 243
"Mad Hatter," 219, 220
Madan, Falconer, 289, 290
Maper, Dorothy, 54
"March Hare," 219, 220
Masturbation, 98-100, 115, 245
McDermott, John F., 287
Meditations upon a Broomstick, 37
Memoirs of the Life of Scriblerus, 82, 90-91, 99

Memory
concern about, 245
see also Dodgson, Charles Lut-
widge, screen memory, and
Swift, Jonathan, screen memory
Ménière's disease, 29, 92
Millard, Magdalen, 120-121 ff.
Misch-masch, 131
"Mock Turtle," 220
Modest Proposal for Preventing Chil-
dren of Poor People being a
Burden to their Parents, A, 58,
65 ff., 112
Moor Park, 29, 40
see also Temple, Sir William
Moore, Thomas, 186
Morley, John, 290
Murry, John Middleton, 20, 29, 30-
31, 276, 278, 289
My Fairy, 202, 224

Narcissism, 99
Negativism, 104
Newman, Cardinal, 136
Newry, Lord, 152
Nicolson, Marjorie, 100, 289
Nightmare, 183, see also Dreams
Nonsense, 9-10, 103, 127, 130, ff.,
141, 182, 187, 189, 209, 234,
261, 265-277
and castration, 275
and "Cheshire cat," 276
and explosive aggression, 271, 274,
275
Nose, 94
Noveltry and Romancement, 205
Nursery Alice, 258
Nursing, 65, 70-72, 78, 112-113

Oedipus complex
crime and interest in eating, 214
period of, 88-89, 96-97, 101-102,
104, 214-215, 251-252
see also Dodgson, Charles Lutwidge, oedipal problems and
Swift, Jonathan, oedipal problems
Omnipotence, 96
infantile, 96
Orality, 101, 112-113

jealousy and Communion Service,
257
Orgastic excitement
aged, aged man, 229
awakens Alice, 226
mad gardener, 230
Orrery, John, 289
"Other Professor," 193, 194, 245
Outland, 193
Oxford, 9, 30, 82

Paget, Sir James, 142
Pall Mall Gazette, 159
Parnell, 82
Parody, 265, 266
compared in Swift and Carroll,
266
nature of, 267, 271-272
see also Carroll, Lewis, parodies
Pastoral Dialogue, 93 ff.
Pairing and splitting of characters
in "Alice" Books, see individual
characters: "Haigha and Hatha,"
"Lion and Unicorn," "Red
King," "Red Queen," "White
King," "White Knight," "White
Queen," "Tweedledee and
Tweedledum,"
in Swift's birthday poem to Stella,
50
in Sylvie and Bruno, 199-201
Pathographic method, 12-14, 63-64
ff.
Penis, 70, 94, 113-115
Perkins, Michael, 178
Perverse trends, compared in Swift
and Carroll, 256
Phantasmogaroia, 155, 171 ff.
Photography, 44
see also Gernsheim, Helmut
Physical Research Society, 159
Pigs, 182, 194
Pilkington, Letitia, 289
Pillow Problems, 226
Pinafore, HMS, 104
Pompey, 77
Pope, Alexander, 82, 95
Portmanteau animals, 187
Powell, Frederick York, 141
Pregnancy, 70, 74, 78, 90, 91, 115,
213, 218

Price, Bartholomew, 160 ff.
Primary process
  and caricature, 268
  in "Alice" books, 210-211
Primal scene, 240, 242
Prince and the Pauper, The, 104
Problem, The, 38
"Professor," 193, 241
Protheroe, Rev. Canon W.L.M., 120
  ff.
Psychotic states, 76
  trends, 256
Puberty, determination of sexual
  role, 223
Punning, 62 ff., 102
  see also Language
Pusey, Canon, 136

"Queen of Hearts," 183, 185, 197,
  214, 219, 220, 243, 244
Quintana, Ricardo, 48, 253, 289

Rage, 183
  and birth, 241
  and convulsions, 276
  and loss of reality contact, 255
  and nonsense, 276
  see also Aggression
Raikes, Alice, 150
Rationalization, 94-95
Reaction formation, 93
Reality sense compared in Swift and
  Carroll, 256
Rectory Umbrella, 129, 130, 131,
  172, 203, 239, 243
"Red King," 185, 244
"Red Queen," 185, 186, 244
Reich, Annie, 270, 289
Repression, 52, 60
Resolutions When I Come to be Old,
  35
Reynolds, Sir Joshua, 172
Ribaldry, 10
Rorschach test, 273
Rossie, Mario, 289
Rugby, see Dodgson, Charles Lut-
  widge, Rugby
Ruhl, Arthur, 189, 289
Rules and Regulations, 203
Ruskin, John, 142, 160
Russian Journal, 147

Sadism
  and spatial disturbances, 258
  impressions of sex and birth, 245
  in Alice's Adventures in Wonder-
    land, 258
  see also Aggression
Satire, 17, 31, 87, 189, 267
  and body imagery, 110
  and nonsense, 271
  and sublimation of aggression, 274
  compared in Swift and Carroll,
    265
  see also Nonsense, 265-277
Schilder, Paul, 258, 259, 289
Science fiction, 62
Scoptophilia, 95, 245
  and orality, 218
  see also Gulliver's Travels, scopto-
    philia, and Voyeurism
Scott, Sir Walter, 18, 46, 278, 289
Screen memory, 25, 151, 230
  see also Dodgson, Charles Lut-
    widge, screen memory, and
    Swift, Jonathan, screen mem-
    ory
Scriblerus Club, 82
"Scriblerus, Martin," 82, 90-91, 98-
  99, 112
Secession of Martin Scriblerus, 82
Secondary process, development of,
  210
Secrets of childhood and primal
  scene, 240-241
Semantics, 77
Senses, substitution of one for an-
  other, 76
Sexes
  confusion of, 36-37, 68-69, 71, 84-
    87, 94-109
  denial of differences, 68-69, 109
  reversal of, 71, 109
Sexual development compared in
  Swift and Dodgson, 256
Shakespeare, revised for girls, 165
  ff., 192
Sheridan, Thomas, friend of Swift,
  47, 55, 57, 58
Sheridan, Thomas, biographer of
  Swift, 33, 289
Shute, Mrs. Alice, 163
Sitting on a Gate, A, 157

Skinner, John, 259, 289
Sleep, 52, 60
    see also Dodgson, Charles Lut-
    widge, insomnia
Smith, David Nichol, 290
Smith, H.J.S., 161
"Snark," 187, 188, 227, 233, 237,
    240, 244
    see also "Boojum Snark"
Space
    problems of, in "Alice" books, 184
    see also Dodgson, Charles Lut-
    widge, space
Speech
    as body discharge, 76-77
    see also Language
Splitting of characters, see Pair-
    ing of characters
Stella, 24, 31, 33, 35 ff., 37-44, 46-
    52, 54-58, 61, 63, 74, 84-86, 94-
    95, 106, 108, 114, 250, 250 ff.,
    251
    see also Johnson, Hester
Stephen, Sir Leslie, 21, 25, 35, 47,
    290
Stevens, Enid (Mrs. Shane), 236
Stolen Waters, 214
St. Patrick's Cathedral, 18
St. Patrick's Hospital, 59
Storm, The, 239 ff.
Strephon and Chloe, 93
"Struldbruggs," 78
Stuttering, 108, see also Dodgson,
    Charles Lutwidge, stammer
Swanzy, Henry B., 33, 290
Swift family
    Swift, Abigail Erick (mother of
    Jonathan), 20-23, 27, 40-41, 63,
    78 ff., 83, 88, 91, 97, 101
    Swift, Godwin (uncle of Jona-
    than), 19, 21, 23, 26, 83, 88, 97
    Swift, Jane (sister, Mrs. Fenton),
    20, 21, 23-24, 28, 35, 40, 42,
    49, 63, 85, 92, 97, 101, 105-106
    Swift, Jonathan (father), 19-21,
    23, 49, 77, 83, 97, 104-105
    Swift, Thomas (grandfather), 19,
    96, 105
    Swift, Thomas (cousin), 24, 26,
    28, 97

Swift, Willoughby (cousin), 24,
    26, 97
Swift, Jonathan,
    anality, 35, 36, see also Swift,
    Jonathan, cleanliness, dirt, skato-
    logical interests, toilet training
    and Gulliver, 60-82, 85, 93-97,
    111-114
    and horses, 26, 66, 79, 94, see
    also Houyhnhnms
    and "Yahoos," 79-80
    anger, 84, see also Swift, Jonathan,
    irascibility, rage
    babies, attitude toward, 9, 58, see
    also Resolutions When I Come
    to be Old
    birth of, 19-20, 48, 55, 65 ff., 78,
    83, 88-89, 98, 101; fantasies, 90-
    91, see also Swift, Jonathan,
    family romance
    bisexuality, 101
    body preoccupations, 83-84, 93-
    95, 100, 108-109, 110
    cannibalistic trends, 112 see also
    Modest Proposal
    Castration problems, 89, 92, 98
    character, 17, see also Swift,
    Jonathan, self-estimate
    childhood of, 19-26, 68, 83-85,
    88-89, 91, 108
    children, attitude toward, 35, 57-
    58, 65-81, see also Swift, Jona-
    than, babies
    cleanliness, emphasized, 34-35, 49,
    65, 79, 85, 94, 109
    deafness, 92
    death of, 58-59, 88
    dirt and excreta, interest in, 85
    discretion emphasized, 45, 49
    educational interests, 17, 37, 42,
    68, 79, 94, see also Battle of
    Books, Tale of Tub
    excretions and writing, 108
    family romance, 90, 97, 104
    father, relationship to, 31, 83, 87,
    96, 97 ff., 104
        death of father, 19, 78, 83,
        88, 96-97
        to Sir William Temple, as
        father, 90

Swift, Jonathan (*cont'd*)
　see also Swift, Jonathan, oedipal
　　problems, *and* Swift, Jona-
　　than, elder
fetishism, 109
fish, in screen memory, 25, 68
fixation, 101, 102, 107
flirtation, first, 27, *see also* Jones,
　　Betty
food, special enjoyment of, 9, 85,
　　92, 95
friendships, *see* Ford, Charles
gastro-intestinal symptoms, 92, 93
genital functioning, impaired, 101,
　　106
girl, attachment to young, 32, 85,
　　249; Yahoo maiden, 80-81
guilt feelings, 92
headache, 92
health, 89
　　preoccupation concerning, 10,
　　　29-30, 52, 57, 63, 84, 89, 91-
　　　93
　　see also Swift, Jonathan, illnesses
hypochondriacal tendencies, 41, 92
　　see also Swift, Jonathan, infec-
　　　tion fears
identity and identification, prob-
　　lems, 88
　　with fantasy sister, 105
　　with nurse, 108
illnesses of, 29, 89, 91-93, 113
　　fears, 84
infancy, 83
infection, fears of, 84
　　see also sub health, preoccupa-
　　　tion concerning
insanity, fears of, 92
irascibility of, 9, 53-54, 58, 84, 97
Irish Rights, championed, 17-19,
　　46, 52-53
jealousy, 84, 112
joking, 18, 23, 37, 53, 87
kidnapping, 21, 39 ff., 65, 73, 74,
　　83-84, 88, 91, 95, 112-113
Kilkenny, School, 24-26, 80, 83,
　　108
Kilroot at, 32
Laracor at, 38-39
life of, 17-59

letters, 17, 23, 33, 41-44, 47-55,
　　60-61
love, attitude toward, 27, 33, 37,
　　56, 86, exchanged for fame and
　　power, 86
manners, interest in, 17, 49, 67, 79
marriage, attitude toward, 33, 35-
　　36, 37, 38-39, 47, 49, to Stella,
　　47-48, 89
masturbation fantasies, 98, 99
memory, early, 25, 68
mother, relationship to, 20-24, 27,
　　41, 78, 83, 89, 104, 105; *see
　　also*, Swift, Jonathan, oedipal
　　problems, *and* Swift, Abigail
　　Erick
nurse, relationship to, 21-22, 83-
　　84, 93-95, 101, 107-108, 111-
　　112; *see also*, Swift, Jonathan,
　　identification with nurse; kid-
　　napping, *and* Gulliver's Travels,
　　kidnapping, nurse
oedipal problems, 89, 96, 97, 101,
　　102, 105, *see also* Swift, Jona-
　　than, father, mother
oral fixation, 101, *see also* Swift,
　　Jonathan, food, *and* Gulliver's
　　Travels, breast, breast-phallus,
　　fellatio
Oxford, master's degree, 30
political interests, 9, 17, 40, 43,
　　45, 52-53, 63
posthumous birth, 84
precocity, 84
pseudonyms, 17-18, 52-53, 55
punning, 62 ff., 102
rage, 97
rebelliousness, 25-26, 30, 97
religion, attitude toward, 17, 18,
　　30, 31, 32, 38, 47, 63
reticence, about own life, 13, 17,
　　50-51, *see also* Swift, Jonathan,
　　discretion emphasized
revengefulness, 10, 54
satire of, 17-19, 53, 85, 87, 94;
　　roots of, 31
school years, 24-26, 83-85, 91, *see
　　also* Swift, Jonathan, Kilkenny,
　　Trinity
screen memory, 25
Scriblerus, 98, 99

Swift, Jonathan (*cont'd*)
  self estimate, 19
  sexuality of, 36-37, 40, 57, 84-87, 94-103, 106, 114, 253; aggression and, 86; reversal of sexes, 40; *see also,* Swift Jonathan, bisexuality, education, genital function, masturbation fantasies, women
  sister, relation to, 23-24, 32, 101, *see also* Swift, Jane
  Skatological interests, 10, 36, 85, 92-93, 95, 252, *see* also Swift, Jonathan, anality
  St. Patrick's Cathedral, 18, 25, 29, 45-46
  Stella, relationship to, 31-32, *see also* Stella
  Temple, Sir William, relationship to, 27-39, *see also* Temple, Sir William
  toilet training, 93, 107
  travel, planned, 9, 63
  Trinity College, 25-26, 33, 63, 80, 85, 105
  tutor, as, 38-39
  voyeurism, 95, *see also Gulliver's Travels,* scoptophilia
  walking, interest in, 10, 29-30, 52, 79, 91
  Whitehaven, 21-22, 74, 96
  women, relationship to, 9, 27, 32-37, 101; body of woman, 86-87, 93, 108-110, *see also* Betty Jones, Stella, Vanessa, *and* Varina
"Sylvie," 193, 194, 195, 199, 201, 202, 223, 243, 245
Sylvie and Bruno, 123, 128, 138, 154, 162, 170, 180, 181, 192-207, 219, 223, 224 ff., 227, 230, 232, 238, 241, 242, 245, 255 ff., 260
Sylvie and Bruno Concluded, 153, 154, 192, 203
Symbolic realization, 77

Tait, Dr. A. C., headmaster at Rugby, 128
Tale of a Tail, A, 231

Tale of the Tub, A, 30-31, 36, 274, 276
Tangled Tale, A, 169
Tate, Mr., headmaster at Richmond, 126
Taylor, Alexander, 159, 290
Temple, Lady Dorothy (wife of Sir William), 28, 36
Temple, Sir John (father of Sir William), 21, 49, 90
Temple, John (son of Sir William), 28
Temple, Sir William, 21, 24, 27-32, 34-39, 40, 48, 49, 63, 66, 87, 89-90, 97, 105-106, 113
Tenniel, Sir John, 153, 170, 228 ff., 235, 236
Tennyson, Alfred Lord, 142
Terry, Ellen, 143
Thomson, E. Gertrude, 145, 218
Three Sunsets, 214
Three Voices, The, 197
Through the Looking Glass, 121, 125, 149, 150, 151, 155, 157, 174, 175, 181, 184-187, 189, 197, 211, 212, 217, 219, 220, 227
Thurber, James, 13
Time, considered
  and eating, 173
  in "Alice" books, 184
Toilet training, 64-65, 93-94, 107
Tories, 43, 45
The Train, 139
Transvestitism, 71, 109
Tuckwell, Rev. William, 137, 141, 290
Twain, Mark, 166, 213
"Tweedledum and Tweedledee," 185, 220, 244
Two Brothers, The, 173

"Uggug," 193, 194, 241-242, 243, 244
Unicorn, *see* "Lion and Unicorn"
Upon a Lonely Moor, 158
Urination, 68, 71
Useful and Instructive Poetry, 129, 131, 200 ff., 202, 230

Van Doren, Carl, 290

Vanessa, (Esther, or Hester van Homrigh), 30, 33, 38, 42-47, 50-58, 60, 61, 66, 69, 74, 78 ff., 85-86, 94, 106, 108

Van Homrigh, Esther or Hester, *see* Vanessa

Van Homrigh, Mary ("Mollkin"), 30, 46, 51

Varina, 32, 33-37, 63, 85, 105-106, 114

"Vice Warden," 193, 194

Voyeurism, 95-96; *see also* Scoptophilia

"Warden," 193

Waring family

Waring, Jane, *see* Varina

Waring, Richard, 33

Waring, Rev. Roger, Archdeacon of Dromore (father of Jane), 32

Waring, Westenra, 32

Waring, William, 32

Weaver, Warren, 161 ff., 164, 165, 168 ff., 290

Weierstrass, Karl, 141 ff.

Whigs, 38

Whitby Gazette, 139

Whitehaven, 22, 74

"White King," 123, 174, 185, 220, 233

"White Knight," 123, 164, 185, 186, 220, 227, 228, 229, 230

"White Queen," 174, 185, 186, 218, 220

"White Rabbit," 149 ff., 173, 184, 219, 228 ff.

Whiteway, Mrs. (Nurse to Swift), 47

Wilberforce, Samuel, Bishop of Oxford, 143, 147, 149

Wilde, Dr. W. R., 29

Wilhelm von Schmulz, 190

William, King of England, 27, 30, 66

Williams, Harold, 290

Williams, Sidney Herbert, 289, 290

Wilson, C. H., 290

Wolfenstein, Martha, 270, 290

Woollcott, Alexander, 259

Wordsworth, William, 157, 186, 228 ff.

Yahoos, 26, 79, 80